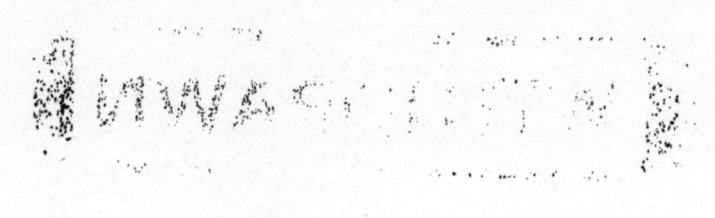

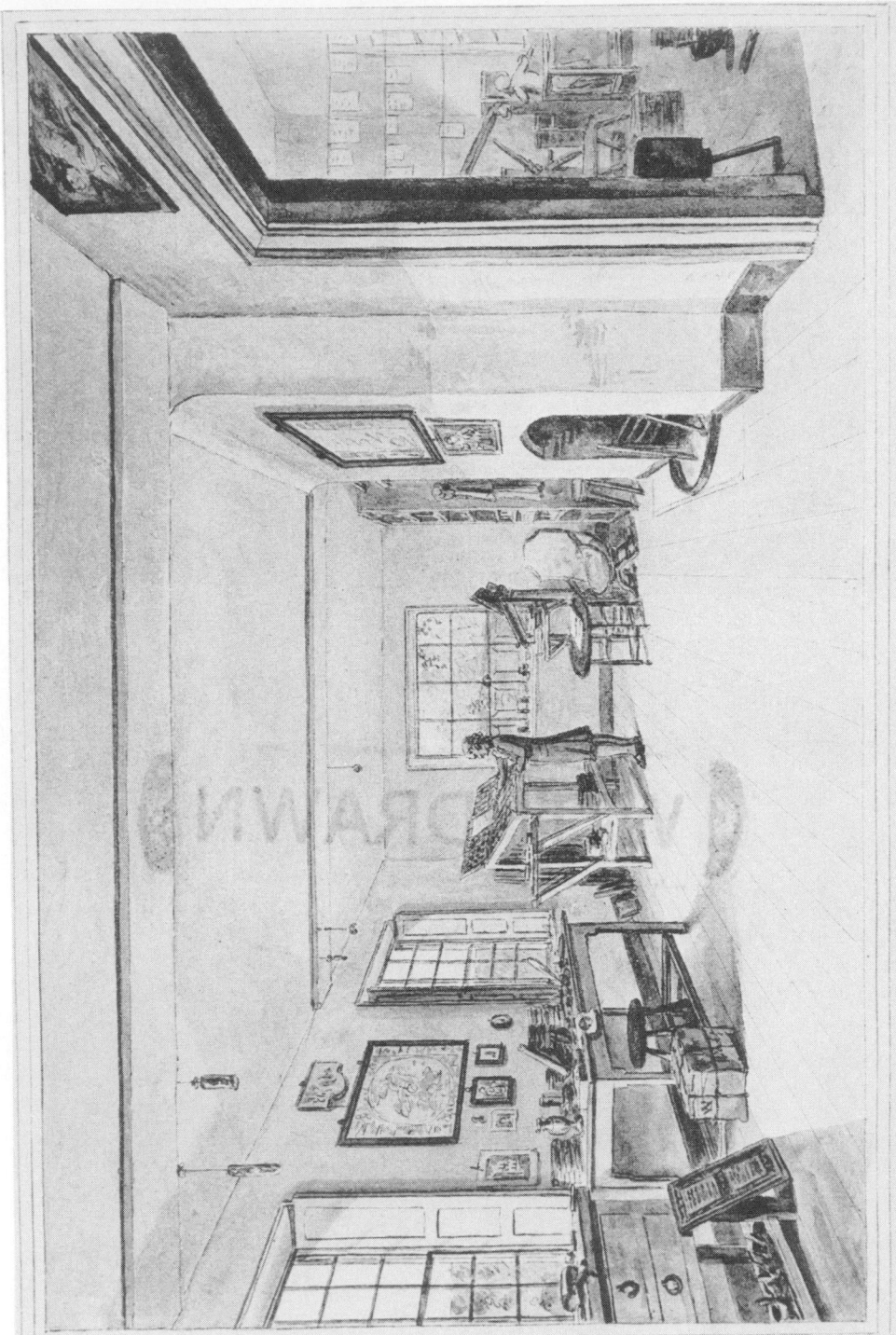

Inside of the PRINTING-HOUSE at Strawberry hill.

A
BIBLIOGRAPHY
OF THE
Strawberry Hill Press

WITH A RECORD OF THE PRICES AT
WHICH COPIES HAVE BEEN SOLD
INCLUDING A NEW SUPPLEMENT

BY

A. T. HAZEN

TOGETHER WITH A BIBLIOGRAPHY
AND CENSUS OF THE DETACHED PIECES

BY

A. T. HAZEN AND J. P. KIRBY

BARNES & NOBLE
BOOKS
10 East 53d St., New York 10022
(a division of Harper & Row Publishers, Inc.)

and
DAWSONS OF PALL MALL
Folkestone, England
1973

First Published 1942
New edition by permission of Yale University Press 1973

Dawsons of Pall Mall
Cannon House
Folkestone, Kent, England

Distributed in the U.S.A. 1973 by
Harper & Row Publishers, Inc.
Barnes & Noble Import Division

ISBN: 06 492761 X

Printed in Great Britain
by Photolithography
Unwin Brothers Limited
Old Woking, Surrey

INTRODUCTORY NOTE

To accompany the photographic reprint of the original *Bibliography*, 1942, this Supplement has been prepared so that both purchasers of the reprint and present owners of the original edition may have a record of the significant corrections and additions that have been identified or acquired during thirty years. They are arranged in the order of the original *Bibliography* by entry numbers, so that any user can examine an entry in the *Bibliography* and then determine at a glance whether any new information of interest to him is here recorded.

Important revisions of the *Bibliography* up to 1948 were noted in the introduction to my *Bibliography of Horace Walpole*, pp. 12–13: the recovery of Walpole's own collection of Detached Pieces, and his portfolio of Etchings by Amateurs with titles printed at his press (Detached Pieces No. 87, rejected by me in 1942). Details of these matters are incorporated under the Detached Pieces below.

The Supplement includes additional copies of the various books now at Farmington: these are listed to make known the richness of the Strawberry Hill Press collection gathered at Farmington before 1942, and since.

Columbia University, November 1972   A. T. H.

[v]

PREFACE

By W. S. Lewis

Messrs Dawsons of Pall Mall have made a notable contribution to bibliographical studies in general and to Walpolian studies in particular by reissuing Professor Hazen's Bibliography of the Strawberry Hill Press *with his additions and corrections to the edition of 500 copies published by the Yale University Press in 1942. As one hundred sets of sheets were torpedoed on their way to Oxford and the work has been out of print for years, it fetches some thirty times the original list price when a copy reappears in the market today.*

Professor Hazen's additions and corrections bring the Bibliography *down to the present by recording the migration of copies from their 1942 locations. What began as an ancillary volume to the Yale Edition of Horace Walpole's Correspondence has acquired the independent dignity accorded to a bibliographical landmark.*

Messrs Dawsons have also reissued Professor Hazen's Bibliography of Horace Walpole, *which was published by the Yale Press in 1948. Since the additions to it are comparatively few Professor Hazen has not recorded them in a supplement to the original work.*

BOOKS

1. ODES BY MR. GRAY. 1757.

In 1942 I was hesitant about dating Kirgate's reprints of the *Odes*, of Lady Temple's *Poems* (No. 12), and of the Detached Pieces. No evidence for an earlier date has appeared since 1942, so that instead of suggesting 1790 or later as a suitable date, it is safe to assume that all or most of Kirgate's reprints were prepared in 1797.

[p. 23] The large fleuron on the title-page was designed by Bentley.

[p. 25] On 1 February 1768, Gray wrote to Beattie: 'the two Odes printed at Strawberry Hill are very well . . . but the paper is rather too thin and transparent.'

[p. 28] An unperfected proof (dated July 16, 1757) of the first sheet, with five substantive readings not preserved by Gray in the published poem, and a copy of the whole piece (dated August 4th) are in HW's own collection of Detached Pieces; from the Crewe collection, April 1952, to WSL.

Copy 6. The copy bound with Bentley was never at Knowsley Hall; it was owned in 1956 by Mr. Jørgen Svitzer Lyngbye, in Copenhagen. Bull's copy of the *Odes* alone, from Lord Derby's collection at Knowsley Hall, was sold at Christie's, 20 October 1953, to WSL, £6.

ADDITIONAL COPIES NOW AT FARMINGTON

12. Disbound and untrimmed, in a cloth case. Given by Miss Annie Burr Jennings, 1929, to WSL.

13. In a volume of prints, drawings, and MSS, labelled 'Gray Miscellanies,' formed about 1850 by John Mitford. Sotheby's, 28 June 1933 (Rosebery Sale), lot 688, to Maggs for WSL, £20.

14. Modern calf by Zaehnsdorf. Brick Row, August 1939, to WSL, $65.

15. In modern wrapper, disbound, final leaf restored. Pickering & Chatto, Septeber 1939, to wsl, £8.9.0.

16. Marbled wrapper, in cloth case. Bookplates of Frank Brewer Bemis and R. B. Adam. Marginal notes transcribed by C. W. in 1845 from Gray's copy now in the Morgan Library (Copy 4 in *Bibliography*). Goodspeed, September 1944, to wsl, $275.

17. Interleaved and bound in modern half morocco, with inserted illustrations and clippings, one MS by Gray (extracts from Tellez's *Travels*), and an autograph of George Robins in 1842. Charles S. Boesen, from Bandler Library, May 1947, to wsl, $250.

18. Half calf; some leaves repaired and mounted; final leaf wanting. Gift of Mr. H. Wade White, February 1952, to wsl.

19. Calf by Riviere & Son. A note by Gray [to Mary Antrobus?] inserted. Bequeathed by Mrs. Frank F. Dodge of Stonington, Conn., August 1964, to Yale for the Lewis Walpole Library.

20. Modern mottled calf. With the 19th-century forgery of Garrick's Verses bound in. In the Gaskill collection, December 1939, to wsl.

21. Red morocco, with four sh books and other pieces bound in, with Charles Bedford's cypher and crest on spine, marked 'Poems, Strawberry Hill.' Many of the Detached Pieces derive from Kirgate and have his annotations, some being his reprints. Bookplates of Bedford and the 9th Earl Waldegrave. Lord Waldegrave, 1948, to wsl, £150.

22. *On thick paper*. Bound with other sh pieces in calf for Utterson. From the Kirgate Sale to Utterson to Lord Carlingford and later to Lord Strachie; Lord Strachie, September 1942, to wsl, in a collection.

23. *On thick paper*. Untrimmed and unbound, in a slip case. Templeton Crocker, December 1939, to wsl, in a collection.

2. HENTZNER'S JOURNEY. 1757.

[p. 33] The first copy listed, hw's own copy, was sold from the Glass Closet, sh SALE, vi.52. From Lord Waldegrave, 1948, to wsl, in a collection. (The copy sold in the Fourth Day's sale, lot 167, is almost certainly the copy in the Dyce Collection at the Victoria & Albert Museum.)

ADDITIONAL COPIES NOW AT FARMINGTON

10. Calf, with crest on sides. Presentation copy from hw, inscribed by Lord Strafford. Maggs, March 1949, to wsl, £3.3.0.

11. Original marbled boards, untrimmed. Armorial bookplate of Thomas Corbett. Quaritch, August 1939, to wsl, £5.5.0.

12. Original calf, with Phelips crest; name on fly-leaf: Ed. Phelips 1758. Stonehill, December 1939, to wsl, $7.50.

13. Bound in 19th-century red morocco. Note on fly-leaf to say that this copy was given by hw to Robert Dodsley, who gave it to Shenstone; the poet then

gave it to the writer of the note who signed it with his cypher; initials C. F. stamped on title-page. Sotheby's, 4 February 1953 (A. S. Fordham Sale), lot 609, to Maggs for WSL, £8.10.0.

14. Inlaid to folio size and extra-illustrated with about 200 plates; bound in russia about 1800, now rebacked. Gift of Mrs. Christopher Ward, of Greenville, Del., May 1956, to WSL.

15. Red morocco, bound for Charles Bedford with his bookplate; Christie's, 1 March 1861 (G. C. Bedford Sale), lot 2. Crest of T. Farmer Baily stamped on front cover and his bookplate. Maggs, July 1957, to WSL, £21.

16. Red morocco, about 1800. A faded inscription on title-page notes that it was the gift of the editor in November 1757. Given in 1820 by the Countess of Sutherland to her daughter, Charlotte Countess of Surrey, and her bookplate. Fletcher, March 1959, to WSL, £12.10.0.

17. Old russia. Given by HW to Lord Buckinghamshire (note by his daughter, Henrietta Hobart, who married Lord Ancram); bookplate of her husband, later Marquess of Lothian; another bookplate removed. Hodgson's, 6 June 1962 (Miscellaneous Sale), lot 497, to Maggs for WSL, £15.10.0 (with two other books).

3. CATALOGUE OF ROYAL AND NOBLE AUTHORS. 1758.

[p. 35] The small fleuron was designed by Müntz; Grignion's original plate was given to WSL in 1953 by Lewis Buddy's daughter, Mrs. Hugh McClure-Smith.

[p. 36] The edition listed as London 1763 was my error, for which I apologized in the *Bibliography of Walpole* in 1948. The edition of London 1796 is only a variant issue of the Edinburgh edition.

ADDITIONAL COPIES NOW AT FARMINGTON

17. Boards, untrimmed. D. Webster, April 1926, to WSL, £6.

18. Calf, broken. Lacking copyright notice. Brick Row, 1928, to WSL, $25.

19. Old calf. Presentation copy to James Whitchurch, a neighbor at Twickenham. Spencer, August 1933, to WSL, £2.

20. Boards, untrimmed. Inscribed: Sophie Schwerin-Dönhoff. Scribner's, January 1936, to WSL, $33.

21. Old calf, repaired. Presentation copy to Thomas Birch; sold as a British Museum duplicate in 1769. Bookplate of George Soaper. Christopher Blunt (through Elkin Mathews), August 1938, to WSL, £12.

22. Half calf, with marbled boards, by Mansell, successor to Hayday. Name: Matthew Smith, Welbeck Street. Label of Robert H. Walpole, Waburne Hall; bookplate of Joseph Manuel Andreini. Brick Row, August 1939, to WSL, $28.

23. Red morocco. Bookplate of H. Warburton, Caius College, Cambridge. Brick Row, August 1939, to WSL, $28.

24. Old mottled calf. Inscribed: C. H. Lewis, Reading; bookplate of Francis A. Gaskill. In the Gaskill collection, December 1939, to WSL.

25. Old calf. Inscribed 'From the author,' and armorial bookplate of Mooresfort, Tipperary. I. Kyrle Fletcher, February 1941, to WSL, £6.6.0.

26. Old mottled calf. Presentation inscription, by the recipient, Gregory Parry. Later inscription: Jane Elizabeth Hollis, the gift of her dear papa G. Parry Hollis. By exchange from WSL to R. W. Chapman in 1928; Chapman, May 1941, to WSL, $10.

27. Bound in vellum. Armorial bookplate of Lady Robert Manners [i.e. Mary Digges, d. 1829]. Elkin Mathews, July 1943, to WSL, £3.

28. Richard Bull's copy with his bookplates, extra-illustrated and bound about 1800 in citron morocco, 4 volumes. In the Bull Sale in 1880, lot 731; Thorp, April 1949, to WSL, £15.

29. Red morocco. Lacking copyright notice. Inscribed: J. Carlisle; armorial bookplate of Robert Heron [Sir Robert Heron, 2d Bart., 1765–1854]. Parke-Bernet, 11 January 1956 (Alfred B. Maclay Sale), lot 549, to Seven Gables for WSL, $12.50.

30. Old calf. Presentation copy to Lord Orrery. Bookplates of Marston House [Lord Orrery's seat] and Weston Library [Lord Bradford]. Lyon, May 1972, to WSL, £65.

31. Bound in 19th-century calf, with Sherborne arms on sides. Inscribed by Gen. Fitzwilliam that it was a present from HW in June 1780. With two notes by HW written perhaps in 1779 or 1780. Bookplates of Gen. Fitzwilliam, John Jeffreys, and the Sherborne Library. Christie's, 19 July 1972 (Sherborne Library Sale), lot 119, to Pickering & Chatto for WSL, $185.

32. *Second edition*, London, 1759. Old half morocco, with many corrections, additions, and new articles by HW, and his note: 'This copy is corrected and enlarged as I intend it should be printed for the last time.' Kirgate's note: 'These two volumes were given to me by my master Mr. Walpole, July, 1785.' In the Bull Sale in 1880; Christie's, 24 November 1971 (Lord Margadale of Islay Sale), lot 254, to Breslauer, £2,200. At Farmington are copies of the second edition presented to Lady Diana Beauclerk and Sir Horace Mann.

4. FUGITIVE PIECES. 1758.

[p. 40] The copy sold in SH SALE, iv.167, is in calf, without arms on sides; it passed from Thorpe to John Mitford. Later in the collection of Horatio William, 4th Earl of Orford of the new creation; inherited from him by Mrs. Colin Davy of Heckfield Place, and described in my *Catalogue of Walpole's Library*, No. 2527. The Spoor copy was sold iii.152 in 1842 and is correctly identified in my *Catalogue*, No. 1881.

ADDITIONAL COPIES NOW AT FARMINGTON

13. Red morocco. Bookplate of Ralph Edward Gathorne-Hardy; stamp of Williams Library, Streatham; notes copied by WSL from HW's copy now in the

Fitzwilliam Museum and from Cole's copy at Harvard. Elkin Mathews, April 1926, to WSL, £1.18.0.

14. Original boards, untrimmed. Maggs, January 1929, to WSL, £20.

15. Red morocco. Bookplate of Charles Bedford. Quaritch, July 1936, to WSL.

16. Red morocco by J. Wright. Bookplates of Dudley C. Marjoribanks and Vernon Watney. Brick Row, August 1939, to WSL, $45.

17. Bound in 19th-century calf. Bookplates of Charles Dexter Allen and Francis A. Gaskill. In the Gaskill collection, December 1939, to WSL.

18. Untrimmed, folded sheets, in a case. Parke-Bernet, 4 April 1941 (Property of a New York lady), lot 598, to Brick Row for WSL, $20.

19. Untrimmed, folded sheets, in a case. Parke-Bernet, 30 October 1945 (Hartshorne Sale), lot 390, to Brick Row for WSL, $25.

20. Old calf. Bookplate of Lord Harcourt when he was Viscount Nuneham and his note: 'Given to me by the author.' Bookplate of 9th Earl Waldegrave. Lord Waldegrave, 1948, to WSL, in a collection.

21. Red morocco, extra-illustrated by Kirgate and a few notes by him. Bookplate of 9th Earl Waldegrave. Lord Waldegrave, 1948, to WSL, in a collection.

22. Old calf. Given to James Bindley, 10 July 1776; with his note and bookplate. Sotheby's, 10 May 1949, lot 344, to Pickering & Chatto for WSL, £18.

23. Red morocco. Given to Sir David Dalrymple by HW in 1759, with Dalrymple's inscription. Bookplates of Peter Murray Hill and Michael Sadleir. Sotheby's, 25 May 1937 (Newhailes Sale), lot 382, to Elkin Mathews, £10; Sotheby's, 17 November 1958 (Sadleir Sale), lot 356, to Maggs for WSL, £38 (with Whitworth's *Russia*).

24. Old half calf. Some notes by Kirgate. Robinson, May 1959, to WSL, $100.

25. Calf, with bookplate and autograph of Mary, Lady Hervey. Notes by John Dillon and Peter Cunningham; bookplate of Sir William Augustus Fraser; extra-illustrated. Sold by Edgar Wells to Miss Elizabeth Hudson; given by her, April 1965, to WSL.

26. Red morocco. Charles Bedford's copy, with his cypher and bookplate. Sotheby's, 30 March 1971 (Christie-Miller Sale), lot 473, to Seven Gables for WSL, $96.

27. Bound, with HW's *Letter to the Editor of . . . Chatterton*, in red morocco by Jenkins & Cecil. Quaritch, August 1939, to WSL, in a collection.

5. WHITWORTH'S ACCOUNT OF RUSSIA. 1758.

[p. 42] Copy 1 has bookplate of Sir William Guise; later in the Phillipps collection. Robinson, August 1948, to WSL, £15.

[p. 44] Copy 4, Dalrymple's copy, with bookplates of Peter Murray Hill and Michael Sadleir, was sold at Sotheby's, 17 November 1958 (Sadleir Sale), lot 356, to Maggs for WSL (with *Fugitive Pieces*, Copy 23 above).

ADDITIONAL COPIES NOW AT FARMINGTON

6. Green morocco. Lower part of title-page supplied by a drawing of SH, and 'Strawberry Hill 1758' hand-lettered. From the Lowther Castle library; Quaritch, March 1937, to WSL, £6.6.0.

7. Half calf, untrimmed. Brick Row, August 1939, to WSL, $15.

8. Calf, rebacked. Extra-illustrated. Bookplate of T. Gosden. Quaritch, August 1939, to WSL, £3.3.0.

9. Old calf, repaired. Spencer, September 1939, to WSL, £1.10.0.

10. Old mottled calf. Bookplate of Francis A. Gaskill; in the Gaskill collection, December 1939, to WSL.

11. Calf, rebacked. Inscribed on fly-leaf: From Mr. Walpole. A bookplate removed. Parke-Bernet, April 1942, to Brick Row for WSL, $12.

12. Old calf. Armorial bookplate of Robert Pratt. Parke-Bernet, 8 October 1946 (Dr. Charles Thomas Silve Sale), lot 512, to Brick Row for WSL (with a copy of Spence below).

13. Old calf, rebacked, with original label. Bookplates of James Bindley and Henry Wade White. Gift of Mr. White, February 1952, to WSL.

14. Modern blue cloth; untrimmed; notes by John Loveday. Sotheby's, 8 June 1953 (Dr. Thomas Loveday Sale), lot 213, to Quaritch, £3.10.0; Quaritch, June 1953, to WSL, $16.80.

15. Old calf, rebacked. Inscribed: 'This book was given to Mrs. Clive by Mr. Walpole, and upon her decease, made a present of to me by her surviving brother Mr. Raftor, March 2, 1786. William Douglas.' Armorial bookplates of Douglas and Eric, Lord Reay. Catalogued by H. G. Commin in 1955; given by R. W. Ketton-Cremer, Christmas 1955, to Mr. & Mrs. Lewis.

16. Old calf, rebacked. Inscribed: William Whitworth 1766; armorial bookplate of Richard Whitworth. Walter Schatzski, February 1962, to WSL, $55.

6. SPENCE'S PARALLEL. 1758.

[p. 44] Copy 1, HW's own copy, has been in Lord Rosebery's library since 1875, as recorded in my *Catalogue of Walpole's Library*, No. 2516.

ADDITIONAL COPIES NOW AT FARMINGTON

7. Untrimmed and unopened; sewn, in paper cover. Quaritch, February 1933, to WSL, £4.14.6.

8. Bound in half calf by R. Wallis. A transcript of Pope's imitation of Horace, Ode 1 of Book 4, in Spence's hand inserted. Brick Row, August 1939, to WSL. $25.

9. Red morocco by Jenkins & Cecil. Quaritch, August 1939, to WSL, with other volumes.

10. Yellow morocco, with armorial bookplate of Robert Clutterbuck. T. Thorp, August 1939, to WSL, £1.15.0.

11. Untrimmed; sewn, in paper cover. In the Gaskill collection, December 1939, to WSL.

12. Old calf. George Montagu's copy, with his signature and bookplate. Parke-Bernet, 8 October 1946 (Dr. Charles Thomas Silve Sale), lot 512, to Brick Row for WSL (with a copy of Whitworth).

13. Half calf. Lord Harcourt's copy, inscribed: Newnham. Bound with a copy of Müntz's *Encaustic*, 1760. Sotheby's, 14 December 1948 (Harcourt Sale), lot 357, to Maggs for WSL (with other Harcourt tracts).

14. Untrimmed; sewn, in paper cover. John Loveday's copy, with his notes and corrections. Sotheby's, 8 June 1953 (Dr. Thomas Loveday Sale), lot 188, to Quaritch, £5.10.0; Quaritch, July 1953, to WSL, £10.

7. LUCAN'S PHARSALIA. 1760.

[p. 50] Copy 4, Bull's copy, was bequeathed to Yale by Dr. Fred T. Murphy of Detroit in 1947; deposited in the Lewis Walpole Library. Inserted are Edwards's bill and his letter· to Bull, 25 July 1784.

ADDITIONAL COPIES NOW AT FARMINGTON

12. Red morocco, with bookplate of Henry Labouchere. Michelmore, April 1925, to WSL, £9.9.0.

13. Old mottled calf, rebacked. Bookplate of Francis A. Gaskill. In the Gaskill collection, December 1939, to WSL.

14. Old mottled calf. Inscribed: 'To Sir Joshua Bernard from Mr. Bentley.' Bookplate of Kimbolton Castle. H. W. Pratley (for R. W. Chapman), November 1947, to WSL, $16.

15. Old calf, with Strafford arms on sides. Frank Hollings, July 1949, to WSL, £1.5.0.

16. Calf by Kalthoeber. John Mitford's copy, with his signature and notes. Bookplate of Battle Abbey. Rosenkilde og Bagger, Copenhagen, September 1957, to WSL, 650 Danish kronen.

8. CATALOGUE OF . . . THE HOLBEIN CHAMBER. 1760.

[p. 50] The copy preserved by HW in his own collection, *Loose Pieces printed at SH*, is now in the Lewis Walpole Library. A copy in MS, with a printed title-page, was in the SH SALE; offered by Thorpe in 1843 and 1844; then bound in HW's primary copy of his *Description of the Villa*, 1774, now at Farmington.

9. CATALOGUE OF . . . THE DUKE OF DEVONSHIRE. . . . 1760.

[p. 52] The three sale records, described as possibly the same copy, seem to have been exactly that; this copy has been in Lord Rosebery's library at Barnbougle Castle since 1875.

A copy in old gold-tooled vellum, with armorial bookplate of Thomas Walpole pasted over another plate probably that of George Townshend, was sold by David Holbrook, May 1955, to WSL, £120.

10. ANECDOTES OF PAINTING. 1762–71.

[p. 55] The intended Preface from the Eyton collection is in Lord Rosebery's library at Barnbougle Castle.

[p. 66] The notes in Copy 1 are not in HW's hand. Copy 4 is now WSL, from Lord Derby's library, 1953; the interchange in 1842 of the *Engravers* between this set and Copy 2 of the 2d edition is explained in my *Catalogue of Walpole's Library*, Nos. 2519–20. The *Catalogue of Engravers* mentioned under Copy 5 was purchased from Lord Waldegrave, 1948, by WSL. Copy 14, Sir Joshua Reynolds's set of the *Anecdotes*, is now in the Widener Collection in the National Gallery at Washington.

[p. 68] Of the 2d edition, Copy 3 (Kirgate) and Copy 4 (Cole— *Engravers* only) are now WSL.

ADDITIONAL COPIES NOW AT FARMINGTON

17. Red morocco by Riviere; bookplate of Arthur Kay. Extensive notes are probably by Richard Bull. Brentano's, February 1936, to WSL, $50.

18. Old calf. Armorial bookplate of Lord Dacre in each volume. Sotheby's, 7 November 1938 (Barrett-Leonard Sale), lot 35, to Maggs for WSL, £2.

19. Old calf. Armorial bookplate of Thomas Walpole, given in 1808 to A. B. Drummond. Pickering & Chatto, February 1947, to WSL, £12.

20. Bound in russia; inscribed H. Ancram [Lady Henrietta Hobart married William Kerr, Earl of Ancram and later Marquess of Lothian]. Christie's, 2 November 1951 (Lothian Sale), lot 220; Maggs, July 1952, to WSL, £12.15.0.

21. Volumes 1 and 2 only; old calf. Bookplates of the Duke of Leeds and Henry Wade White. Gift of Mr. White, October 1952, to WSL.

22. Red morocco. Christie's, 23 March 1954 (Derby Sale), lot 325, to Pickering & Chatto, £32 (with a Vertue letter); Pickering & Chatto, July 1955, to WSL, £55.

23. Nineteenth-century half calf. Wanting 4th volume. Bookplate of Earl

Fitzwilliam. Sotheby's, 12 November 1957 (Miscellaneous Sale), lot 471, to Maggs for WSL, £2.

24. Red morocco, attributed to Roger Payne; bookplate of Anthony Morris Storer. Maggs, October 1958, to WSL, £52.10.0.

25. Half calf. Gift of HW to Thomas Gray, with his note. Four volumes bound in two; wanting 4th volume. Bookplate of C. Alderson. Sotheby's, 14 April 1959 (Miscellaneous Sale), lot 328, to Maggs for WSL, £68.

26. Old calf. George Montagu's copy, apparently the set given him by HW in December 1764, with Montagu's bookplates and notes. (The final 4th volume, inscribed A. Fountayne, was perhaps purchased after Montagu's death.) Bookplate of Frederick J. O. Montagu in all volumes. H. W. Edwards, July 1959, to WSL, £20. The first two volumes are the reprinted sheets described on p. 60.

27. Old calf. Signature, notes, and bookplate of Paul Panton; wanting 4th volume. Major H. Lloyd-Johnes through Maggs, February 1960, to WSL, £25. (A letter from HW to his housekeeper, 24 June 1789, was included.)

28. Old calf. Inscribed: John T. Allen. Gift of Mr. J. William Middendorf, October 1962, to WSL. The first two volumes are the reprinted sheets described on p. 60.

29. Old calf. Henry Zouch's copy, given to him by HW; four volumes bound in two; wanting 4th volume. Lowther arms on sides, and Lowther bookplate. Richard Gilbertson, May 1964, to WSL, £45.

Copies of the 2d edition

Copy 3 is now WSL, from the Hartshorne Sale at Parke-Bernet, 29 October 1945, to Brick Row for WSL, $210. Green morocco by C. Smith. Notes both by Kirgate and by HW. The 4th volume has both the cancelled Advertisement of 1773 and the published one of 1780.

5. Old calf, rebacked. Sotheby's, 16 December 1929 (Powell Sale), lot 829, to Maggs for WSL, £2. Wanting 4th volume.

6. Old calf. Armorial bookplate of Charles Benjamin Caldwell, New Grange, Co. Meath. Last, August 1939, to WSL, £2.10.0.

7. Old calf, rebacked, with new labels. Armorial bookplate of Bernard Granville; each volume is inscribed: 'M. Delany the gift of the author,' and laid in is a letter from HW to her, 28 November 1786 [Mary (Granville) Delany, 1700–86]. Sotheby's, 19 July 1955 (Granville Sale), lot 475, to Maggs for WSL, £26.

8. Old tree calf; given by HW to Sir Thomas Cave; armorial bookplate of Lord de Braye; wanting 4th volume. Gift of Mr. H. W. Liebert, August 1970, to WSL.

11. LIFE OF EDWARD, LORD HERBERT OF CHERBURY. 1764.

[p. 72] The Ormerod copy in calf, mentioned under Copy 5, may derive from the SH SALE, v.208; it was offered by Quaritch in 1909 for £4.4.0; Goodspeed, *ca.* 1920, to William Zimmerman, Jr.; Scribner's (Zimmerman library), December 1968, to WSL, $300.

This copy has the corrected genealogical table. But the Orford bookplate is only a facsimile from Strong's announcement of 1843. Copy 4, Cole's copy, is at King's College, Cambridge. Copy 7, Warton's copy, was sold by Myers, April 1968, to WSL, £30.

ADDITIONAL COPIES NOW AT FARMINGTON

8. Old mottled calf. Given by HW to Lady Frances Erskine for James Erskine of Alva. Lacking genealogical table. Purchased in 1925 by WSL, £5.5.0.

9. Old green morocco. Bookplate of Thomas Grenville and his arms on sides. Given by Mrs. Lewis to WSL, 1929.

10. Old calf. Lionel Johnson's copy. T. Thorp, February 1939, to WSL, £4.4.0.

11. Old mottled calf. With arms of Duke of Newcastle on covers. Quaritch, August 1939, to WSL, £8.8.0.

12. Red boards, rebacked, untrimmed. With the corrected genealogical table. Goodspeed, November 1944, to WSL, $35.

13. Old calf. Given to Samuel Lysons in 1787. Evans, 9 June 1820 (Lysons Sale), lot 1052, £2.10.0; Sotheby's, 5 November 1947 (Col. Lloyd Sale), lot 920, to Maggs for WSL, £18.10.0.

14. Old calf. Gift of HW to Lord Nuneham, 21 August 1764, with his bookplate as Earl Harcourt. Sotheby's, 14 December 1948 (Harcourt Sale), lot 343, to Maggs for WSL, £10 (with Grammont).

15. Old calf. Gift of HW to Lord Nuneham, with his bookplate. Sotheby's, 14 December 1948 (Harcourt Sale), lot 342, to Pickering & Chatto, with two other books; Pickering & Chatto, April 1949, to WSL, £12.

16. Old calf, repaired. Walpole arms on sides. Gift of HW to Lord Powis, 13 July 1781; given by Lord Powis to Benjamin Booth; bookplate of Marianne Ford. Sotheby's, 18 December 1950 (Property of a Lady), lot 148, to Maggs for WSL, £19.

17. Old red morocco. Given by HW to Isaac Reed, with Reed's notes. Bound with Herbert's *Dialogue between a tutor and his pupil*, 1768. H. D. Lyon, May 1954, to WSL, £16.10.0.

18. Red morocco by Jenkins & Cecil. Given by HW to his cousin Horatio, later 1st Earl of Orford of the new creation. Christie's, 17 December 1957 (Mrs. Colin Davy Sale), lot 74, to Maggs for WSL, £62.

19. Old calf, rebacked. Given by HW to George Montagu, with his armorial bookplate and signature; bookplate of Frederick J. O. Montagu. H. W. Edwards, February 1959, to WSL, £12.10.0.

20. Green morocco, with HW's 2d bookplate inserted. Bookplate of Charles Butler. Seven Gables, February 1968, to WSL, $75. (Because of the report of HW's bookplate, I mentioned this copy in 1942 under Copy 5.)

12. COUNTESS TEMPLE, POEMS. 1764.

[p. 74] Another slight variant of Signature F lacks a comma in the last line on p. 21. In one copy now WSL, Signature E has been entirely reset, in the late spring of 1764 to judge from the paper, perhaps to complete a copy (or copies?) found imperfect.

As with Gray's *Odes*, I think it likely that Kirgate reprinted this piece in 1797.

Copy 7, Thomas Barrett's copy, was sold by Goodspeed, September 1955, to WSL, $175.

Copy 9, the Damer-Buddy copy, was sold at Parke-Bernet, 3 November 1945 (Hartshorne Sale), lot 391, to Brick Row for WSL, $55.

ADDITIONAL COPIES NOW AT FARMINGTON

12. Unbound and untrimmed, in a modern cloth case. Pickering & Chatto, August 1933, to WSL, £8.

13. Unbound and untrimmed, in a modern case. Brick Row, August 1939, to WSL, $15.

14. Modern boards. Bookplate of Ralph Edward Gathorne-Hardy. Pickering & Chatto, September 1939, to WSL, £2.5.0.

15. Unbound, in a paper wrapper. Pickering & Chatto, September 1939, to WSL, £2.5.0.

16. Richard Bull's copy, interleaved, with Bull's bookplate. Red morocco. Bookplate of Lewis Buddy, III. Anderson, 9 November 1909 (Buddy Sale), lot 567; given by Mrs. Jesse Metcalf of Providence, R.I., August 1944, to WSL.

17. Disbound, in a modern wrapper. Peter Murray Hill, July 1945, to WSL, £6.10.0.

18. Half brown morocco. Bound with other SH pieces; bookplate of FitzPatrick of Grantstown Manor. Includes: *Letters of Edward VI*, *Dorinda*, *Muse Recalled*, T. Walpole's *Letter*, *Bonner's Ghost*. Battersby, Dublin, 5 May 1938 (Castletown Sale), lot 188, £14; Maggs, July 1947, to WSL, £35.

13. HÉNAULT, CORNÉLIE. 1768.

ADDITIONAL COPIES NOW AT FARMINGTON

7. Wrappers, untrimmed, in a case. Maggs, March 1925, to WSL, 19/-.

8. Red morocco by Lewis. Sotheby's, 26 March 1928 (Holford Sale), lot 890, to Quaritch; Quaritch, August 1939, to WSL, £8.

9. Bound in 19th-century brown morocco. Bookplate of Francis A. Gaskill. In the Gaskill collection, December 1939, to WSL.

10. Eighteenth-century French blue morocco, bound with two other plays by Hénault and his bookplate; described in the Britwell Sale as the author's own copy. In the collection of Sir Mark Masterman Sykes; Britwell Sale, 8 April 1924; Maggs, June 1957, to WSL, £38.

11. Red morocco, attributed in the Wodhull Sale (1886) to Roger Payne, for Michael Wodhull; bookplate of Laurence Currie. Pickering & Chatto, September 1936, to WSL, £36.

12. Red morocco, interleaved, with Richard Bull's bookplate. In the Bull Sale, 29 April 1880, lot 728; Sotheby's, 15 February 1961 (Fairlie Sale), lot 741, to Maggs for WSL, £35.

13. Red morocco by Jenkins & Cecil, with Hoyland's *Poems* and the *Sleepwalker* bound in. Quaritch, August 1939, to WSL, £48.

14. THE MYSTERIOUS MOTHER. 1768.

[p. 81] A variant state exists (two copies now WSL), in which there is only a single Erratum; also at the end of the Postscript, some copies have three rules, while others lack the rules.

[p. 83] The 'forged' fleuron of 1791, Bewick's copy of the smaller fleuron, and Jeffery's copies about 1822 of both fleurons are also recorded in my introduction to the *Catalogue of Walpole's Library*, p. xxv. (Jeffery also prepared sets of plates to the *Description of the Villa* and a few other plates for collectors in 1822.)

[p. 84] Copy 2 was sold by Mrs. Courtauld, March 1953, to WSL, £100. Copy 3, Bull's copy, with his bookplate, was sold by Mrs. Dunn, February 1961, to WSL, $450. Copy 8, given to William Parsons in 1790, now WSL, is of the edition of 1781.

ADDITIONAL COPIES NOW AT FARMINGTON

10. The copy kept in the Beauclerk Closet; blue morocco. Thorp, September 1944, to WSL, £50. See *Catalogue of Walpole's Library*, No. 2528.

11. Green morocco by J. Clarke. Sotheby's, 20 May 1926 (Property of a collector), lot 821, to Maggs for WSL, £22.

12. Green morocco. With title-page ruled in red, and last leaf inlaid. Bookplate of Francis A. Gaskill. In the Gaskill collection, December 1939, to WSL.

13. Red morocco by F. Bedford. Goodspeed, July 1940, to WSL, $75.

14. Untrimmed, in half red morocco, with Storer's note: 'Never change the binding of this book.' Given by Mrs. Damer to A. M. Storer. Bookplates of Storer, Lord Orford, and Michael Sadleir. Pickering & Chatto, August 1955, to WSL, $60.

15. Red morocco by Lewis. Included is an undated letter from Richard Bull to Francis Annesley about showing the book to a friend. Sotheby's, 30 March 1928 (Holford Sale), £44; Ximenes, May 1972, to WSL, $650.

15. HOYLAND'S POEMS. 1769.

ADDITIONAL COPIES NOW AT FARMINGTON

4. Untrimmed, in original boards, rebacked. Dulau, September 1927, to WSL, £4.4.0.

5. Half green morocco. Bound with Mrs. Centlivre's *The wonder! a woman keeps a secret*, 1777. In the Gaskill collection, December 1939, to WSL.

6. Red morocco by Riviere & Son. Bookplate of John A. Spoor. Parke-Bernet, 3 May 1939 (Spoor Sale), lot 901; Walter M. Hill, April 1940, to WSL, $12.

7. Old mottled calf, rebacked. Inscribed: J. F. Fortescue. Bound with Anstey's *New Bath Guide*, 6th ed., 1766. Given by Allen T. Hazen, 1940, to WSL.

8. Old calf. Bookplate of George Simon Harcourt, Viscount Nuneham. Sotheby's, 13 December 1948 (Harcourt Sale), lot 342, with two other books; Pickering & Chatto, April 1949, to WSL, £8.

9. Untrimmed, folded and unsewn, in a case. Peter Murray Hill, November 1952, to WSL, £4.10.0.

10. Red morocco, interleaved. Richard Bull's copy, with his bookplate. In the Bull Sale, 29 April 1880, lot 730; Sotheby's, 15 February 1961 (D. O. Fairlie Sale), lot 742, to Maggs for WSL, £35.

11. Red morocco, with Charles Bedford's cypher and bookplate; in a volume with other SH pieces, including the *Sleepwalker* and *Postscript to R&NA*. Bookplate of 9th Earl Waldegrave. Lord Waldegrave, 1948, to WSL, in a collection.

16. WORKS. 1770.

[p. 94] Copy 5 may be the copy now at Yale. Copy 8, in half green vellum, was sold by Lord Strachie, September 1942, to WSL, £3.

The copy of *Historic Doubts*, from this proposed edition, preserved by HW and bound in mottled calf, was in the SH SALE, vii.33, and is now in Farmington.

17. REPLY TO DEAN MILLES. 1770.

[p. 95] Copy 2 is now in Lord Rosebery's library, Barnbougle Castle. Copy 3 was sold by Lord Waldegrave, 1948, to WSL, in a collection.

18. MÉMOIRES DU COMTE DE GRAMMONT. 1772.

[p. 98] Copy 6, old calf, rebacked, sold by George of Bristol, April 1963, to WSL, £20. The copy of the edition of 1746, with

HW's notes, is now WSL and recorded in my *Catalogue of Walpole's Library*, No. 2389.

ADDITIONAL COPIES NOW AT FARMINGTON

9. Old calf; with armorial bookplate of Lady Frances Scott. Christopher Blunt (through E. Matthews), August 1938, to WSL, in a collection.

10. Old mottled calf, rebacked. Bookplates of Mrs. Damer and Francis A. Gaskill. In the Gaskill collection, December 1939, to WSL.

11. Old calf, repaired. Gift of HW to Lord Nuneham, with his bookplate and two notes. Sotheby's, 14 December 1948 (Harcourt Sale), lot 343, to Maggs for WSL (with *Life of Lord Herbert*).

12. Old calf. Armorial bookplate of Westport House [Co. Mayo, seat of the Marquess of Sligo]. Maggs, August 1957, to WSL, £12.10.0.

19. LETTERS OF EDWARD VI. 1772.

[p. 101] Copy 1 is now WSL, from Lord Waldegrave, 1948, in a collection.

ADDITIONAL COPIES NOW AT FARMINGTON

6. Green morocco. Brick Row, August 1939, to WSL, $20.

7. Half calf, rebacked. Sir Henry Ellis's copy, with his notes. Bookplate of Francis A. Gaskill. In the Gaskill collection, December 1939, to WSL.

8. Disbound. Bequest of Mrs. Frank F. Dodge, Stonington, Conn., August 1964, to Yale for the Lewis Walpole Library.

9. Red morocco by Lewis, bound with other tracts. Apparently purchased from Kirgate by Francis Annesley; included are *Dorinda*, T. Walpole's *Letter*, the *Muse Recalled*, and *Bonner's Ghost*. Sotheby's, 26 March 1928 (Holford Sale), lot 893, to Quaritch; Quaritch, August 1936, to WSL, £200 (with the companion Annesley-Holford volume of Detached Pieces also from Kirgate).

10. Red morocco, with Charles Bedford's cypher; extra-illustrated. Bound with it are: *Miscellaneous Antiquities*, T. Walpole's *Letter*, *Essay on Modern Gardening*. Lord Waldegrave, 1948, to WSL, in a collection.

11. Old calf. Presentation copy to William Cole. Bound with it: *Miscellaneous Antiquities* (also presented to Cole, with his notes), and Ives's *Select Papers*. From the Phillipps Collection; Robinson, December 1952, to WSL, £40.

12. Bound in 19th-century calf. Bound with it: *Miscellaneous Antiquities*, with one note by Kirgate. Quaritch, September 1959, to WSL, $100.

20. MISCELLANEOUS ANTIQUITIES. 1772.

ADDITIONAL COPIES NOW AT FARMINGTON

9. Half calf, rebacked. John Wilson Croker's copy, with his note and a letter to him from Lockhart, quoting Mary Berry's answer to his inquiry concerning

the omission of these pieces from the *Works* in 1798. Elkin Mathews, September 1927, to WSL, £1.1.0.

10. Modern crushed red morocco, by Toof & Co.; untrimmed. Given by WSL to Mrs. H. D. Auchincloss in 1936; bequeathed by Mrs. Auchincloss to WSL. This is one of the 25 copies on writing paper.

11. Red morocco by Lewis; from the Holford library. Given by WSL to Miss Annie Burr Jennings in 1937, with her bookplate; bequeathed by her to WSL.

12. Half-calf, rebacked; untrimmed. From the Andreini library. Brick Row, August 1939, to WSL, $15.

13. Brown morocco, by Macnair of Queen Street. Bookplate of Francis A. Gaskill. In the Gaskill collection, December 1939, to WSL.

14. Half calf. Untrimmed; extra-illustrated, and Ives's *Select Papers* bound in. Myers, October 1944, to WSL, £5.10.0.

15. Sewn, untrimmed, in a case. The second number is on writing paper. Quaritch, July 1955, to WSL, £15.

16. Red morocco, extra-illustrated. Lord Carlisle's *Poems*, 2d ed., 1773, bound in. Bookplate of W. A. Foyle, Beeleigh Abbey. Sold by Mr. Foyle, July 1955 to WSL, £40 (with six other volumes of Walpoliana).

17. Red morocco, interleaved; Richard Bull's copy, with his bookplate and a few notes. In the Bull Sale at Sotheby's, 1 May 1880, lot 790; Christie's, 17 December 1957 (Mrs. Colin Davy Sale), to Sawyer, £50; Maggs, 1958, to WSL, £66.

21. DESCRIPTION OF THE VILLA.

[p. 105] Copy 1 was sold by Lord Waldegrave, 1948, to WSL, in a collection. It comprises 65 pp., with the plates prepared for the edition of 1784; also a copy of *Curiosities in the Glass Closet*. Both pieces are off-prints from the edition of 1774, perhaps intended only to be available to visitors in the public rooms as soon as they had been printed in 1773.

22. DESCRIPTION OF THE VILLA. 1774.

[p. 109] Copy 3 was sold by the New York Public Library, February 1950, to WSL, $2,000. Copy 6 was sold by Lord Waldegrave, July 1948, to WSL, in a collection.

ADDITIONAL COPIES NOW AT FARMINGTON

8. Red morocco, by Jenkins & Cecil. Sawyer, September 1927, to WSL, £9.9.0.

9. Rebound in half tan morocco by National Library Bindery. Jeffery's reprinted plates of 1822 bound in. Heffer, July 1930, to WSL, £3.10.0.

10. Old calf, rebacked with morocco. Owned in 1877 by Lady Waldegrave. In the Gaskill collection, December 1939, to WSL.

11. Bound in 19th-century half calf. Given by HW to Lord Harcourt. Bookplate of 9th Earl Waldegrave. Lord Waldegrave, July 1948, to WSL, in a collection. Appendix and Additions wanting.

12. Boards, untrimmed; on large paper. Bookplate of William Hardcastle. Maggs, November 1957, to WSL, £25.

13. Untrimmed, in folded sheets. One of the SH remainders described in my *Catalogue of Walpole's Library*, No. 3469:10. Sotheby's, 26 October 1959 (Hall Sale), lot 268, to Maggs for WSL, £18 (with the 1842 *Catalogue* and William Forster's letter to Mr. Manley transmitting the two catalogues).

14. Original wrappers, untrimmed, sewn, in a case. Seven Gables, September 1968, to WSL, $400. Appendix and Additions wanting.

25. DORINDA. 1775.

[p. 114] Copy 1 was sold by Lord Strachie, September 1942, to WSL, in a collection. This volume includes the *Muse Recalled* and *Bonner's Ghost*, as well as Kirgate's reprints of Gray's *Odes* and Lady Temple's *Poems*. All the pieces seem to derive from Kirgate, not from the sale in 1842.

ADDITIONAL COPIES NOW AT FARMINGTON

6. The untrimmed copy preserved by HW in his *Collection of all the Loose Pieces printed at Strawberry Hill*: from the Crewe collection, April 1952, to WSL.

7. Unbound. Myers, June 1937, to WSL, 10/-.

8. Half calf, bound with the *Muse Recalled*, *Bonner's Ghost*, T. Walpole's *Letter*, and some Detached Pieces. Bookplate of Lord Carlingford; later owned by Lord Strachie. Lord Strachie, September 1942, to WSL, £25.

26. THE SLEEP-WALKER. 1778.

[p. 116] Copy 1, the Cole-Bull copy, is now in Lord Rothschild's library.

ADDITIONAL COPY NOW AT FARMINGTON

4. Untrimmed, in paper wrapper, in a case. Pickering & Chatto, December 1925, to WSL, £11.7.0.

27. LETTER TO THE EDITOR OF . . . CHATTERTON. 1779.

[p. 118] Some copies read 'eloquence' on p. 22, presumably Kirgate's correction at press of the misspelling; later HW noticed the error and corrected many copies by hand to 'elegance.'

Copy 2 is in the Berg Collection at the New York Public Library. Copy 4, given to Miss Berry, bound in calf by Leighton, was in the Shirley Sale, Sotheby's, 28 April 1947, lot 205, to Maggs for WSL, £46.

ADDITIONAL COPIES NOW AT FARMINGTON

10. Untrimmed and unopened, in original wrapper. G. D. Smith, February 1925, to WSL, $40 (with a copy of the *Muse Recalled*).

11. Untrimmed, in calf-backed boards. Given by Father T. Lawrason Riggs, October 1931, to WSL.

12. Red morocco, untrimmed, with original blue wrapper bound in. Bookplate of J. A. Spoor. Parke-Bernet, 3 May 1939 (Spoor Sale), lot 909, to Brick Row, $12.50; Brick Row, August 1939, to WSL, $30.

13. Modern green cloth, untrimmed. Bookplate of F. A. Gaskill. In the Gaskill collection, December 1939, to WSL.

14. Red morocco, with Charles Bedford's cypher and bookplate; bound with other tracts connected with HW. Bookplate of 9th Earl Waldegrave. Lord Waldegrave, 1948, to WSL, in a collection.

28. WILLIAM JONES, THE MUSE RECALLED. 1781.

[p. 121] Copy 1, HW's copy with other pieces, appears to be the volume now in the Sterling Library at the University of London. But the copy offered by Thorpe was one of the SH remainders: see my *Catalogue of Walpole's Library*, Nos. 2508, 3469:4.

ADDITIONAL COPIES NOW AT FARMINGTON

4. The untrimmed copy preserved by HW in his *Collection of all the Loose Pieces printed at Strawberry Hill*: from the Crewe collection, April 1952, to WSL.

5. Untrimmed and unbound, in a case. From the Arbury Hall library. Brick Row, August 1939, to WSL, $12. Two similar untrimmed and unbound copies, probably from the SH remainders in 1842, are also at Farmington.

29. LETTER FROM THOMAS WALPOLE. 1781.

[p. 121] As pointed out under the *Muse Recalled*, Copy 1 is in the volume at the University of London. The other copy, offered by Thorpe in 1842 and 1846, seems to be the copy now in the Edward J. Sage bequest in the Stoke Newington Public Library. See my *Catalogue of Walpole's Library*, Nos. 2508 and 2529.

Copy 3, Bull's copy, was sold at Christie's, 17 December 1957 (Mrs. Colin Davy Sale), lot 77, to Maggs for WSL, £52.

BOOKS

ADDITIONAL COPIES NOW AT FARMINGTON

4. The untrimmed copy preserved by HW in his *Collection of all the Loose Pieces printed at Strawberry Hill*: from the Crewe collection, April 1952, to WSL.

5. Disbound, in a case. Two related pamphlets in French bound in. Purchased in 1928 by WSL.

6. Stitched, in a case. Another related pamphlet in French bound in. Peter Murray Hill, May 1964, to WSL, £45.

30.   DESCRIPTION OF THE VILLA.   1784.

[p. 126] The copy mentioned as owned by S. A. Courtauld in 1942, with plates on French paper, was sold by Traylen, February 1953, to WSL, £6.6.0.

[p. 127] Copy 1, HW's copy, is in Lord Rosebery's library, Barnbougle Castle. Copy 2 is bound with the 3d edition of *Aedes Walpolianae*, 1767: Lord Waldegrave, 1948, to WSL, in a collection. See my *Catalogue of Walpole's Library*, No. 3932. Copy 6, Pinkerton's copy, was purchased at Sotheby's, 3 July 1950, lot 40, by Maggs for WSL, £4. Copy 12, HW's extra-illustrated copy, is somewhat more fully described in my *Catalogue of Walpole's Library*, No. 3582.

ADDITIONAL COPIES NOW AT FARMINGTON

18. Calf-backed marbled boards, untrimmed. Bookplate of Francis Perrott; name on fly-leaf: P. Davis Cooke. Lowe Bros., Birmingham, 1928, to WSL, £9.9.0.

19. Unsewn and untrimmed, in a case; some leaves repaired. Spurr & Swift, 1931, to WSL, £8.

20. Red morocco, extra-illustrated; some plates have notes by Kirgate. Armorial bookplate of Mark Philips. Quaritch, July 1931, to WSL, £14.

21. Boards, untrimmed. Name on fly-leaf: S. S. Banks, 1812. Myers, June 1937, to WSL, £2.

22. Old calf, rebacked. Armorial bookplate [Caldecote]. Myers, December 1939, to WSL, £2.

23. Morocco-backed marbled boards. Armorial bookplates of Holland House and of Edward Cheney. Sotheby's, 25 June 1886 (Cheney Sale), lot 1904; Goodspeed, July 1940, to WSL, $15.

24. Boards, untrimmed; extra-illustrated. Given by Lord Carlingford, 1885, to Constance Strachey. Lord Strachie, September 1942, to WSL, £5.

25. Boards, untrimmed. Myers, October 1944, to WSL, £2.10.0.

26. Original wrappers, untrimmed; bequeathed to John Thomas Batt. Sotheby's, 10 April 1945 (Property of a Lady), lot 553, to Maggs for WSL, £26.

27. Mottled calf, rebacked. Mrs. Damer's copy, interleaved, with her notes. Christie's, 15 December 1947 (Waller Sale), lot 26, to Maggs for WSL, £50.

28. Old tree calf, rebacked. Bequeathed to William Pennicott. Bookplate of the Earl of Ellenborough. Mrs. Margaret Vincent-Smith, July 1948, to WSL, £5.

29. Red morocco. Bequeathed to Mrs. Keppel. Bookplate of Robert Foote. C. Marshall Spink, July 1948, to WSL, £12.12.0.

30. Green morocco. Bequeathed to John Carter, extra-illustrated and some notes by him. In Sir Thomas Phillipps's collection. Robinson, January 1949, to WSL, £20.

31. Half morocco. With Lord Wharncliffe's armorial bookplate and his arms on front cover. Given by Mrs. Damer to Mary Caroline Erne. Hodgson's, 21 April 1949, lot 31, to Maggs for WSL, £7.

32. Calf. Bequeathed to James Bindley; bookplate of Scottowe Hall Library. Pickering & Chatto, October 1949, to WSL, £55 (with additional plates laid in).

33. Brown morocco, gilt. Given by Mrs. Damer to Sir Wathen Waller; extra-illustrated; plates on French paper. Bookplate of John Hely-Hutchinson. Sotheby's, 14 March 1956 (Hely-Hutchinson Sale), lot 584, to Maggs for WSL, £75.

34. Worn calf, rebacked. Bequeathed to James Wyatt. Owned by Albert Landsberg, whose widow in 1965 gave it to Mr. Philip Hofer for WSL.

35. Red morocco by Riviere & Son, rebacked; untrimmed. Gift of Mr. Philip Ives, January 1968, to WSL.

36. Old half calf. Bequeathed to Rev. John Wheeler [Wheler]. Owned by Aubrey J. Toppin, York Herald. Paul Grinke, August 1972, to WSL, £150.

31. ESSAY ON MODERN GARDENING. 1785.

[p. 132] Copy 5, HW's copy, is in the Cincinnati Public Library; see my *Catalogue of Walpole's Library*, No. 2526. Copy 6 is not Thomas Barrett's copy; it was sold at Hodgson's, 30 April 1902 (Damer Sale), lot 156, to Denham, £9.5.0; Parke-Bernet, 30 October 1945 (Hartshorne Sale), lot 395, to Brick Row for WSL, $65. It is folded and untrimmed, marked on the wrapper by Kirgate: 'One pick'd Essay on Gardening'; in a case.

ADDITIONAL COPIES NOW AT FARMINGTON

8. Untrimmed, in a wrapper, in a blue cloth case. Inscribed: Robt. Blair 14–12–81. Purchased by WSL, £4.

9. Folded sheets; in a half-morocco case. Given by Mrs. Anna Roosevelt Cowles, January 1928, to WSL.

10. Calf, gilt, by Kalthoeber. Bookplates of Mrs. Damer and John A. Spoor. Parke-Bernet, 4 May 1939 (Spoor Sale, part 2), lot 910, to Brick Row for WSL, $22.50.

11. Boards, untrimmed, with bookplate of Francis A. Gaskill. In the Gaskill collection, December 1939, to WSL.

12. Old mottled calf, with bookplate of Sir Trevor Wheler. Given by HW, January 1786, to Rev. John Wheler. Maggs, October 1951, to WSL, £15.15.0.

13. Calf, rebacked, with armorial bookplate of the Earl of Lonsdale. Given by HW to Mary Carter. H. D. Lyon, January 1953, to WSL, £5.10.0.

14. Red morocco by Jenkins & Cecil. Given by HW to Caroline Georgina (Johnston) Anderson. Bookplate of Horace William, 4th Earl of Orford of the new creation. Christie's, 17 December 1957 (Mrs. Colin Davy Sale), lot 73, to Maggs for WSL, £98.

15. Old red morocco, elaborately gilt tooled, in leather case. Given by HW to Gen. Fitzwilliam, with his bookplate; HW's early bookplate also inserted. Two pages of MS additions by HW, and one page by Gen. Fitzwilliam. Bookplate of Mortimer M. Schiff. In the Benzon Sale at Sotheby's, 1875, and in a miscellaneous sale at Sotheby's, 1909. Given to Yale by Mr. John M. Schiff, December 1957, for deposit in the Lewis Walpole Library. (This copy is Copy 4 on p. 132, but I could record it only from the sale of 1909.)

16. Old blue boards, calf-backed; untrimmed. Bookplates of George Soaper and William F. Gable. American Art Assn., 5 November 1923 (Gable Sale), lot 716; Alston Deas of Mt. Pleasant, South Carolina, January 1958, to WSL, $25.

17. Boards, with cloth spine. Given by Nivernois to his secretary, M. Moreau, who gave it to J. Labour; owned in 1827 by Thomas Blaikie. Old Print Shop, September 1961, to WSL, $35.

32. HIEROGLYPHIC TALES. 1785.

[p. 134] Copy 4 is in Lord Rosebery's library at Barnbougle Castle. Copy 5 was sold at Parke-Bernet, 30 October 1945 (Hartshorne Sale), lot 396, to Brick Row for WSL, $125.

33. POSTSCRIPT TO ROYAL AND NOBLE AUTHORS. 1786.

[p. 135] In my *Catalogue of Walpole's Library*, No. 2521, I have indicated that the phrase 'postscript, with additions to ditto,' may well have signified only the 'Postscript, which provided additions to the *Catalogue*.'

34. HANNAH MORE, BISHOP BONNER'S GHOST. 1789.

ADDITIONAL COPIES NOW AT FARMINGTON

3. The untrimmed copy preserved by HW in his *Collection of all the Loose Pieces printed at Strawberry Hill*: from the Crewe collection, April 1952, to WSL.

4. Mottled calf by Zaehnsdorf. Quaritch to WSL, £3.

5. Half morocco, rebacked, with marbled boards. Crest and eagle, EH, on

spine. American Art Assn., 3 March 1925 (Gable Sale, part 7), lot 999, to WSL, $25.

6. Unbound and untrimmed, in a case. Heffer, January 1933, to WSL, in a copy of the SH sale catalogue of 1842.

7. Stitched and untrimmed, in a case. Anderson, 29 April 1921 (Arbury-Smith Sale), lot 314, to Brick Row; Brick Row, August 1939, to WSL, $20.

8. Stitched and untrimmed, in a case; bookplate of Henry Wade White. Given by Mr. White, February 1952, to WSL.

9. Red morocco, interleaved, with armorial bookplate of Richard Bull, and bookplate of Laurence Currie. In the Bull Sale in 1880, lot 793; Christie's, 15 June 1966 (Mrs. David Hargreaves Sale), lot 148, to Pickering & Chatto for WSL, £98.

10. Old calf. Bound with it is the Kirgate reprint of Lady Temple's *Poems*. Bookplate of Francis A. Gaskill. In the Gaskill collection, December 1939, to WSL.

11. Half green morocco, by Samuel Moore, Philadelphia; former owners include Edward Duncan Ingraham and Edward S. Buckley. Included are: *Description of the Villa* (1774), *Dorinda*, the *Muse Recalled*; and a number of Detached Pieces mostly deriving from Kirgate. Scribner's, July 1944, to WSL, $65.

12. Inlaid to folio size and bound in the Orford-Spoor copy of HW's *Reminiscences*. Red morocco by Riviere. Sotheby's, 14 March 1902 (Orford Sale), lot 211, to Stevens & Brown for John A. Spoor, £148; Parke-Bernet, 4 May 1939 (Spoor Sale), lot 1110, to W. M. Hill, $280; W. M. Hill, 1940, to WSL, $360.

APPENDIX A

35. RULES AND ORDERS FOR THE . . . FRIENDLY SOCIETY. 1774.

This is a genuine piece of SH printing, done by and for Kirgate, not for HW. Charles Bedford's copy, bound in red morocco with a number of books (Hoyland's *Poems*, *Sleep-Walker*, *Postscript to Royal and Noble Authors*) and Detached Pieces printed at SH, has Kirgate's note on it: 'Printed at Strawberry Hill by T. Kirgate.' It is in 8vo, 15 pp. Lord Waldegrave, 1948, to WSL, in a collection.

36. LAWS, RULES AND ORDERS BELONGING TO THE . . . FRATERNAL SOCIETY. 1779.

This is also a genuine SH production, done by and for Kirgate. The copy described on p. 142, with Kirgate's note, is in Lord Rosebery's library at Barnbougle Castle.

37. J. H. Müntz, Encaustic. 1760.

This fragmentary work is in Lord Rosebery's library at Barnbougle Castle.

DETACHED PIECES

No attempt is made in this *Supplement* to record each additional copy of any Detached Piece, at Farmington or elsewhere, that has been seen or reported since 1942; the effect would be confusing and not very meaningful, more especially since they would have to be subdivided to show originals, reprints by Kirgate in 1797, and the reprints made soon after 1818. Many of the additional copies are in collected volumes containing several different Detached Pieces, and the provenance of such volumes is always of interest, as with sets that surely derive from Kirgate. But the details of all individual pieces and of the various collected volumes are recorded in the shelf-lists at Farmington.

The one collection of crucial importance, HW's own collection of the Detached Pieces, was mentioned repeatedly in 1942 as a desideratum: it was in the 1842 sale, iv.150, but it was for many years in the library formed by Richard Monckton Milnes, later Lord Houghton, and unknown to Walpolians. It was sold by Lady Crewe, through the kind offices of Messrs. John Hayward and John Carter, April 1952, to WSL, $1,500. A quick summary of its evidence is on p. 12 of my *Bibliography of Walpole*; the same information is here recorded in somewhat more usable detail. The title-page (a variant of Detached Piece No. 63) is *A Collection of all the Loose Pieces printed at Strawberry Hill.*

[pp. 151, 198, &c.] The recovery of the original editions preserved in HW's collection proves or confirms my assertions about a goodly number of the Detached Pieces:

1. Vers sur 'Tuer le tems.' The copy illustrated and called probably a reprint is now certainly a reprint; HW's copy is a different setting.

2. THE PRESS SPEAKS, TO LADY TOWNSHEND. The copy in HW's collection is of the same setting as the Damer-Spoor copy, with a variant comma after 'you' in the 4th line.

3. THE PRESS SPEAKS, TO LADY ROCHFORD. Again, HW's copy is the same setting as the Damer-Spoor copy illustrated.

5. VERS QUE LOUIS XV. TROUVA. The copy illustrated is certainly a reprint, since HW's copy is a different setting.

7. GARRICK'S VERSES TO MR. GRAY, ON HIS ODES. The copy in HW's collection is the original setting.

9. [QUESTIONS TO THE SOCIETY OF ANTIQUARIES]. In 1942, I pointed out that this seemed to be an earlier, rejected form of No. 10. In his own collection, HW marked his copy of No. 9: 'This was not used.'

11. PORTRAIT OF JOHN EARL GRANVILLE. The copy in HW's collection is the original setting. The variant of Kirgate's reprint, signed W. H. in error for H. W., exists in at least two copies: in the Rothschild Library and in the Lewis Walpole Library.

13. VERSES SENT TO LADY CHARLES SPENCER. The copy in HW's collection is the original setting.

14. A SONG, 'THERE WAS A LITTLE MAN.' The copy in HW's collection is a different setting, so that the copy illustrated is proved to be a reprint by Kirgate, as I thought probable in 1942.

16. EPITAPH ON LORD WALDEGRAVE. The copy in HW's collection is a different setting, so that the copy illustrated (and rejected in Kirgate's MS note) is doubtless a later printing prepared in London and not necessarily by Kirgate.

18. VERSES BY THOMAS PENTYCROSS. The copy in HW's collection is the same setting but it is at the very end of his portfolio, to confirm my conjecture that this was printed not in 1768 but in 1797. Kirgate's note, on the Waldegrave-WSL copy of the piece, asserts that he found the MS among waste paper and printed it after HW's death.

21. THE PRESS TO THE EARL OF CHESTERFIELD. The copy in HW's collection is the same setting as that illustrated, so that the piece is genuine as described. I was misinformed in 1942: a copy of the Chesterfield verses is in the Bedford-Waldegrave collection, purchased in 1948 by WSL.

27. VERSES TO LADY CRAVEN. The copy in HW's collection is the same setting as the Damer-Spoor copy illustrated, but with the variant spaced colon in the 4th line.

33. RULES FOR OBTAINING A TICKET. The copy in HW's collection is of the original edition. But in Farmington in Paul Panton's set of the *Anecdotes* is a reprinted leaflet with the same text but in roman type; on it HW requests his housekeeper to show the house to Mr. Panton 'on Friday next'; this is dated 24 June 1789. Hence, it appears that No. 33 was reprinted in roman type in London in 1788 or 1789. Presumably No. 90, 'Lord Orford is very ready,' was also printed in London in 1792; in 1942 I interpreted Kirgate's note as a reference to the 'Lord Orford' version: 'The Rules in Roman Letter were not printed at Strawberry Hill.'

39. VERSES ON MRS. CLIVE and 40. EPITAPH. These two pieces are at the end of HW's portfolio, followed only by the Pentycross verses (No. 18). So these two are confirmed as productions by Kirgate, in 1791 or even later. Each has a note by Kirgate.

The five pieces that follow are not present in HW's collection; their absence increases my doubts as to whether HW planned the printing. (But any or all may have been printed by Kirgate.)

24. LABEL FOR THE PEDESTAL OF THE CHINA TUB.

26. THOMAS GRAY, THE CANDIDATE. The absence of this piece from HW's collection seems to me to increase the probability of its being a London printing; I have commented briefly on the matter in Appendix 7 to the Yale edition of HW's *Correspondence with Mason*.

32. TONTON TO MADAME LA VICOMTESSE DE CAMBIS.

34. LABEL FOR A SCREEN OF OLD TAPESTRY.

35. LABEL FOR THE FISHING EAGLE.

Five other items (Nos. 20, 23, 29, 31, and 38) not in HW's portfolio were not under suspicion.

It is clear now that Kirgate also reprinted a number of the separate title-pages, or preserved variants, and so was able to supply many of these to collectors.

[pp. 154–8] The ten detached pieces reprinted at one time, probably soon after 1818. Since 1942 I have seen some additional copies. They are likely to occur together: the set at Farmington described on p. 154; a complete set in the Barton collection at the Boston Public Library where it has been for one hundred years; a set of six in a volume at the University of Illinois. The paper used is consistently the same—several kinds of watermarked paper; in one piece, supposedly printed in 1775, the watermark is 1802. The bindings cannot be dated exactly, but the binding at Illinois is closer to 1818 than to 1840 or 1850. There can have been only a rather small number printed of each piece; I still do not know who was responsible for them.

49–63. TITLE-PAGES. Additional copies of some of these are now at Farmington, often with a different volume number. For No. 54, *Portraits of Painters*, some additional information is in my *Catalogue of Walpole's Library*, No. 3664; similarly, for No. 55, *Portraits in the Reign of King George the Third*, see my *Catalogue*, No. 3636. No. 58, the title to the *Description of the Villa*, exists in a variety of color combinations and with more than one variant in the type; some of these, to judge by the paper, were reprinted by Kirgate in 1797.

60–62. LYSONS's COLLECTANEA. Four volumes of the theatrical collections, *Collectanea Dramatica*, three of them with SH titles, are in the Folger Library.

64. BUNBURY's ETCHINGS. Copies of the labels prepared for the shelf-backs are in Lord Rosebery's library at Barnbougle Castle. The portfolios themselves, two volumes in marbled boards, were purchased in May 1952 by WSL, $225. Each volume has a title printed by Kirgate between 1776 and 1782; a fuller description is in my *Catalogue of Walpole's Library*, No. 3563.

65. SEVIGNIANA. A label is in Lord Rosebery's library. The portfolio was assembled by HW in 1783, and Kirgate printed a special title-page; a fuller description is in my *Catalogue of Walpole's Library*, No. 3631. A title-page only is in the Bedford-Waldegrave volume of miscellaneous *Poems* from the SH Press: Lord Waldegrave, July 1948, to WSL.

66. CROKER's DICTIONARY. Three labels for the three volumes are in Lord Rosebery's library. Two are in the Boston Public Library.

68. LOOSE PIECES PRINTED AT STRAWBERRY HILL. This label is on the spine of HW's *Collection of all the Loose Pieces*. Another copy is

on Kirgate's somewhat similar portfolio: Lord Waldegrave, 1948, to WSL.

69–77. CARDS OF ADDRESS. A complete collection of these is in Lord Rosebery's library. Several are in the Barton collection at the Boston Public Library. A set complete save for No. 75 was sold at Christie's, 13 December 1962 (Property of a Gentleman), lot 99, to Maggs for WSL, £62.

APPENDIX B

87. ETCHINGS BY AMATEURS. In 1942 I placed in the Appendix as a false attribution the title-page, *Etchings by Lady Louisa Augusta Greville*, reported to me by Lord Waldegrave from the collection of Detached Pieces formed by Kirgate. The paper was French, unlike any paper used at the Press in 1774–5. But later in 1942, the complete portfolio was sold at Sotheby's, 28 October 1942, to Maggs for WSL, £92; it has been for a long time in the library of John Waldie of Hendersyde, Kelso. The original volume is in a handsome red morocco binding, gilt, with HW's arms. (Possibly by Baumgarten.) The letter to Mason, 7 May 1775, describes the binding and points out that the titles have been printed at his own press. There are four titles in all, the general one, *A Collection of Prints*, and separate titles for Isabella Byron, Countess of Carlisle, for Lady Louisa Augusta Greville, and for Lord Nuneham. Other artists included are recorded in my *Catalogue of Walpole's Library*, No. 3588.

91. SEAL AS LORD ORFORD. In my *Catalogue of Walpole's Library*, pp. xxv–xxvi, I have corrected the identification of the two seals HW used as bookplates after 1792, and the very close copy made for Horatio William, 4th Earl of the new creation.

94. PROLOGUE AND EPILOGUE. Another edition of these two poems was printed in London on paper watermarked 1804.

PREFACE

THE *original plan for this book was to make it a catalogue of the imprints of the Strawberry Hill Press in my collection. Mr. Hazen soon discovered, however, that a wider view would be of more general interest and usefulness, and, accordingly, the book became a bibliography of the Press. This has enabled Mr. Hazen to include the imprints which I lack and to list interesting copies in other collections.*

The decision to print the prices, including the last one, is mine. I am aware that there has always been a certain reticence in printing these, a reticence which the collector does not always show in private conversation. It seems to me that this reticence is partly false modesty and partly affectation, for the price which books have fetched through the years is of the greatest interest to collectors and to booksellers. It may also be of interest to students of literature and to social historians: why, for example, have the novels of Surtees always fetched more than the novels of George Eliot? The price of a particular copy during many years has an even sharper interest, for linked with it is the name of its various owners, private and professional. Obviously, in the case of a pedigreed

[3]

book the most interesting price of all is the last one. I have discussed the publication of these figures with bookseller friends. They blanched slightly at the prospect, but invariably ended by saying that if I didn't mind, they didn't.

On one other point the trade will be in hearty agreement: it is not enough to own a single copy of the same edition. I have perhaps gone a little far in buying nineteen copies of the first edition of the Royal and Noble Authors *and fourteen copies of* Fugitive Pieces *(not all of them are listed here), but it was helpful to Mr. Hazen to spread out so many copies at once and the* Fugitive Pieces *did prove to have unrecorded variations. Mr. Hazen shows that 'duplicates' must be treated with respect—and caution, for they may turn out not to be duplicates, after all.*

This book makes waste-paper of virtually everything written about the Strawberry Hill Press since Walpole's and Kirgate's day. Collectors of the Press—and they have existed for nearly two hundred years—will be grateful to Mr. Hazen and to bibliography for fresh knowledge and a fresh stimulus to continue their collecting.

W. S. L E W I S

Farmington, July 1941.

CONTENTS

[5]

INTRODUCTION

I. History of Strawberry Hill collecting.—II. The function of bibliography.—III. Forgery. The rôle of Kirgate.—IV. Imperfections of the book.—V. Acknowledgments.—VI. Abbreviations. Arrangement and method of the book.

I

THE bibliographer of Walpole's Strawberry Hill Press follows a well-worn path. Ever since 1757, when Walpole recorded in his *Journal* the printing of Gray's two odes, the products of the Press have attracted bibliographers as unceasingly as they have attracted collectors. Nor is it entirely fair to attempt to separate the bibliographers from the collectors; the first formal bibliography of the Press was George Baker's Catalogue, printed in 1810, and Baker was one of the most ardent collectors of Strawberry Hill imprints. An even earlier bibliographer was Walpole's printer, Thomas Kirgate, who may be considered both as the villain and as the hero of this newest bibliography of the Press: it is clear that Kirgate collected not only everything given to him by Walpole but also everything he could find of Walpolian interest; and with a true collector's or bibliographer's zeal, he consistently added notes about the rarity or importance of the various pieces.

After Baker's Catalogue of 1810 comes Dibdin's list in the second edition of his *Bibliomania,* followed by the catalogues of two booksellers, Major in 1812 and McCreery in 1813. But a much more carefully compiled list is in John Martin's *Bibliography of Books Privately Printed,* 1834; here again the collector worked hand in hand

[7]

with the bibliographer, for most of Martin's information concerning the Press came from R. P. Cruden, a modest and retiring collector who bought extensively at the Kirgate and Baker Sales, and from Sir Alexander Johnston, whose wife had inherited the books and manuscripts that Walpole bequeathed to Mrs. Damer. George Robins's Catalogue of the Strawberry Hill Sale in 1842 is invaluable to the bibliographer, but is not in itself a praiseworthy addition to the bibliographies of the Press. The next major attempt was that of H. G. Bohn, in the Appendix to his revision of Lowndes's *Bibliographer's Manual,* 1864; Bohn's numbered list is still the most convenient guide to the bookseller and collector. Since 1864, Mr. H. B. Wheatley, Mr. Austin Dobson, and Dr. Paget Toynbee have all made valuable contributions to the study of the Press.

The sale records of various copies, placed at the end of each entry, have other purposes, but they do also serve in some sense as a roll of honor of collectors. I could have included more copies, but the multiplication of copies (even association copies) with only one or two appearances at auction seemed hardly worth while; even the association copies, therefore, are only a selection. I have been more inclined to include copies whose present owner is known—and the picture will not be wholly false if most of these copies seem to be at Farmington. (I ought also to admit that the comparative rarity of a book is not clearly represented by the number of copies listed, since some books have appealed to collectors more than others. In the bibliography of the books, a census of extant copies has been attempted only for the half-dozen rarest items; of most of the books dozens of copies are still extant.) Among collectors of Walpole's own time, the names of Thomas Barrett, Richard Bull, and William Cole take honored places, and notes of their copies have regularly been included. Selection in the nineteenth century is a difficult task, but in addition to Baker and Cruden, these records will be found to include books owned by E. L. S. Benzon, J. W. K. Eyton, Robert Holford, E. V. Utterson, and Lord Waldegrave. One interesting collection of Walpolian books was formed immediately after the sale of Kirgate's library, uniformly bound in green morocco by C. Smith, and offered in Longman's General Catalogue, July 1814 (41 volumes for £350); it was dispersed at Christie's in 1892. Since all these books came from Kirgate's collection, they are of considerable interest; unfortunately, the auctioneers have been unable to tell us the name of the consignor in 1892. In the twentieth century, any roll of honor must include Mr. F. A. Gaskill, Mr. Percival Merritt, Mr. Junius Morgan, and Mr. John A. Spoor. But many another well-known name will be found in these records. There are likewise the less resplendent collectors, men who could not buy in the expansive manner of Utterson and Beckford and Huntington but who deserve, and receive, equal commendation from the discerning for their scholarly interest in and love of their carefully chosen books.

The gravitational tendency of all valuable books toward public or university libraries is somewhat less pronounced in Walpolian collecting than in most fields. This may be because the important books, Gray's *Odes,* for instance, were printed in editions of considerable size and because most of the Detached Pieces are of slight literary importance, if any. Whatever the reason, it is true that very few public libraries have large or representative collections. So the collector may take heart, if he is not unnerved by the rather frightening accumulation at Farmington; and one function of this book is to help him decide whether he owns a piece that is wrongly attributed to the Press, a piece with a false or misleading title-page, a replica by Thomas Kirgate, a nineteenth-century forgery, or a genuine production.

The prices at which copies have been sold* will be of interest to some as matters of curiosity and to others as a part of the social and economic history of book-collecting. Individual prices, subject as they are to extraordinary fluctuations, can never be wholly reliable, but the general trend of prices cannot be falsified even if an occasional error has crept into these records. If it is true that the reported prices of the Kern Sale in 1929 were never actually paid by the purchasers, these prices nevertheless reflect accurately the strange enthusiasm of that sale and of that hectic era. Some readers will also be interested to

* The final price is omitted, in the case of books from the Gaskill Collection and a few others, because the collection was purchased as a whole.

observe the gradual but steady decline in value of extra-illustrated sets, sets 'with proofs on India paper,' and so on; of these, Major's edition of the *Anecdotes of Painting*, 1826–28 (sale records not listed in this volume), is an outstanding example. A somewhat analogous decline has been occurring in recent years among handsomely bound first editions, as collectors have increasingly demanded 'original' condition. The collection at Farmington, indeed, illustrates this tendency: aside from questions of provenance, volumes have usually been purchased not because they are handsomely bound but because they are in original wrappers or original boards. I have accordingly made only slight references to the bindings of the copies listed herein.

II

But I do not think of this bibliography as a mere guide-book to collectors. Scattered through these pages are illustrations of the methods of bibliographical deduction as I have applied them; and it is not improper to remind both bibliographers and scholars that bibliography is the scholar's servant, not his master. Two small examples may serve to explain my meaning: the proof that copies of Gray's *Odes* on thick paper have no standing will enable the scholar not only to eliminate a troublesome dispute about Gray's scholarship and his accuracy as a corrector of proof but also to choose the correct text without hesitation; and the identification of a cancel in the *Anecdotes of Painting* will illuminate some puzzling memoranda in one of Walpole's letters.

In my study of the bibliography of the Press, I have paid special attention to the paper on which the books and Detached Pieces are printed; possibly to some people the development of this method will be the most interesting part of the book. To examine the paper carefully is a time-consuming process, for one must look not only *at* the pages but *through* them into a strong light, and one must examine every related book or scrap of paper that is available; even then the way is beset with pitfalls for the unwary. But I have tried to be accurate, and I am confident that the method has been tested and approved by the results. One great advantage, obviously, is the fact that I have been dealing with a private press of limited output, since such a press will necessarily consume fewer and more homogeneous lots of paper. Since I have established a series of records from which I can suggest what paper might have been or ought to have been used at the Press at a given time, the burden of proof is on any suspected piece, which must show cause (undoubted contemporary association, for example) why it should not be rejected. The process is in practice not at all esoteric: if a piece is printed on paper that was not normally in use at the Press at the time of the authorized printing, the next move is to examine various copies to see whether they were distributed by Kirgate or whether their pedigree contains a legitimate line of descent from Walpole.

I hope that I have not been improperly technical in speaking of wove paper, Whatman paper, countermarks, chain-lines, and the like. I have indeed preferred to describe a watermark by its obvious design (crown, post horn, L V Gerrevink, for example) instead of calling it Dutch post paper; and the Maid of Holland design that was regularly used in eighteenth-century Dutch paper for the foolscap size, I have unashamedly referred to as Garden of Holland. It is perhaps well to add that the discussion of watermarks in the text is merely an exposition of the results obtained, without any consistent attempt to describe the steps, and errors, by which the proof was developed.

Unfortunately, we know comparatively little about the immediate sources of supply for Walpole's paper. Tonson was clearly acting as Walpole's agent in 1757 (Walpole to Grosvenor Bedford, 9 November 1757), and it is perhaps not unlikely that he supplied most of the Dutch and English paper used by the Press. The paper for Gray's *Odes,* however, was probably supplied by Gray's publisher, Dodsley.

The problems of types and type-faces are somewhat analogous. So far as we know, all the type came from the Caslon foundry, so that a piece printed in Wilson type, like a piece with the wrong watermark, must be examined carefully—and rejected. Similarly, Walpole's heavy purchases of Caslon's 'English' in 1768 (*Journal of the Printing Office,* pp. 95–96), for the printing of his *Works* in quarto, suggest that the Press had little or no 'English' before that date, and any earlier Detached Piece in type of that size is therefore under suspicion. Such problems of paper and of type are clearly a legitimate responsibility of the bibliographer.

The student will find comparatively few cancels recorded in this bibliography: one explanation is that it often seemed more satisfactory, for a limited edition at a private press, to reprint the half-sheet than to cancel a single leaf. A few unusual offsets may be the result of such reprinting, but certainty is not easy in such cases. Furthermore, some cancels have undoubtedly eluded me, since the stubs are seldom visible, and since a private press does not need to employ the telltale signature marks on its cancels.

III

THE desirability and relative rarity of books from the Strawberry Hill Press have always made reprinting (or forgery) attractive. In the proper places in the text can be found examples of various kinds: a half-sheet in the *Anecdotes of Painting* was reprinted after 1815; there were new impressions (after 1822) of the plates for the *Description of Strawberry Hill;* and Walpole himself reprinted two volumes of the *Anecdotes of Painting*. I have seen two copies of Gray's *Odes* with the last page in facsimile—a bit of twentieth-century 'improvement.' A discussion of a group of ten nineteenth-century forgeries will be found under the second Detached Piece, the Verses to Lady Townshend; probably only small editions of these, a dozen or so of each, were prepared.

The strangest forgeries (if that is the correct word) of all are the reprintings of which Thomas Kirgate stands accused in the text of this bibliography. (Walpole's troubles with his earlier printers are described in detail by Dr. Toynbee, in his edition of the *Journal of the Printing Office;* but for our purposes, Kirgate is more important than all the rest.) John Martin, in his *Bibliographical Catalogue of Books Privately Printed,* has a footnote (p. 489) that seems almost like dramatic irony: 'Kirgate was considered by his noble employer as the only honest printer he ever had. For this, and some other information, the Editor is indebted to the kindness of Miss Berry.' Now it may be that Walpole's faith in Kirgate was technically justified, for I am inclined to believe that all the reprints may have been produced in 1797, after Walpole's death but before Kirgate's departure from Strawberry Hill. This is a point not susceptible of proof by bibliographical evidence, however, and I have had to content myself in the text with the dates that are suggested by the watermarks. But since so many of these reprints are necessarily late, I think it likely that all (or nearly all) were done at one time; and the most likely time for him to undertake a series of reprints would be shortly before or just after Walpole's death. If this hypothesis is correct, Kirgate was in fact an honest printer until 1797.

Walpole's unexpectedly small legacy (£100 in return for thirty years of service as printer and secretary) does not justify a series of money-raising forgeries, but it may help to explain them.* For Kirgate to argue to himself that he had been 'neglected and forgot' and that he ought therefore to do what he could to provide for himself was a train of thought with a not unusual error in logic. But once that step had been taken, the various lies needed to cover his tracks were almost inevitable. It will be found in numerous instances that manuscript annotation by Kirgate is no proof of authenticity: he wrote notes about the scarcity of certain items, for example, on copies that he himself had reprinted. Richard Bull's fine collection of Detached Pieces, sold at Sotheby's in 1926 and now in the Huntington Library, illustrates the difficulty: many pieces are original, no doubt given to Bull by Walpole, but some of the pieces are Kirgate's reprints; on many pieces Bull has written short explanatory notes, but since one note, on the Verses printed for Mrs. Cloak, is copied exactly from the note Kirgate had supplied on a separate slip, it becomes probable that all the notes by Bull were furnished by Kirgate. Much of the information, nevertheless, is undoubtedly accurate. Bibliographically, the volume seems to divide at 1791, when it was bound: the pieces collected by Bull before this date are ruled in red, whereas the additions made after 1791—including some of Kirgate's later ac-

* In his *Forlorn Printer* (Privately printed, 1931), Mr. Lewis suggested that the legacy was purposely made small because Walpole knew that Kirgate had appropriated extra copies of the various books with the hope of selling them later.

knowledged printing and some of his unacknowledged reprints—are ruled in black. Now it is always possible that Kirgate sold these reprints (three shillings for a copy of Gray's *Odes,* and so forth) for what they were—reprints of the scarce originals; we have always to keep that possibility in mind. But the weight of evidence makes such exoneration very difficult; i.e., we have found no instance of an admitted reprint except *Cockey's Address,* Detached Piece, No. 43 (that of Lady Temple's *Poems,* No. 12, is at best ambiguous), and there is abundant evidence that experienced collectors bought these reprints from him, and from one another, as originals. In at least one instance, furthermore, Kirgate is certainly a liar: on the copy of Tonton (Detached Piece, No. 32) at Harvard he wrote, 'But this and one more printed,' and yet two copies of the same printing are at Farmington.

That Kirgate should have been weak enough to be led into such forgeries is perhaps understandable, for human nature has often failed under such stresses; perhaps there will be forgeries as long as there are collectors. But if he was unscrupulous in the way he undertook to satisfy the demand, he was never bibliographically uninteresting, and all his work can be called, by a moderate extension of the term, 'genuine' Strawberry Hill printing.

IV

THAT this bibliography is imperfect in many ways will soon be apparent. Numerous puzzles have remained unsolved, and I have been forced into almost tiresome repetition of words like 'presumably.' The spreading war has made impossible any further study of the great English collections: most of the information on English collections was gathered by Mr. Kirby and Mr. Lewis before 1939. But the omissions of this sort are not great in bulk, however many in number. To be unable to see what is described as a large paper copy of the *Description of Strawberry Hill* (1784) is a disappointment, but our inability to see it now provides an opportunity for a test of bibliographical ingenuity, a test that is very real even if we are to learn of success or failure only in the happier days to come.

The books that seem to have disappeared are likewise a matter of regret. If we could recover Walpole's set of Detached Pieces [Strawberry Hill Sale in 1842; Utterson Sale in 1852, bought by Monckton Milnes later created Lord Houghton], for example, nearly all traces of 'presumably' could be eliminated from the text. Or what has become of the rarities from Eyton's collection: the 'intended preface' to the *Anecdotes?* the Catalogue of the Duke of Devonshire's Pictures? the Book of Club Orders begun in 1779? But it may be ill-natured to cry for the moon when we have so much.

Walpole's *Journal of the Printing Office* has been constantly useful, and yet even in that we have found puzzles. Some of the entries (the MS is now at Farmington) seem to have been made by Walpole long after the event, when he had forgotten the details. Thus, he says that of the first edition of the *Anecdotes of Painting* six hundred copies were printed; since he could not have made this error (it must be counted an error, I think) at the time of printing, one can only conclude that he inserted the number (600 copies) years later, after six hundred had been printed in the two Strawberry Hill editions. The quotations from the *Journal,* therefore, are a primary source, but wherever possible they have been supplemented or confirmed by letters and manuscript notes.

V

A PLEASANT part of any bibliographical work is its unceasingly co-operative nature. Whereas a reader of Keats may, if he chooses, withdraw into solitude to study the text of his author, no bibliographer can work without examining or inquiring about other copies of each book. Every page of this bibliography will show how largely I have depended on the collection at Farmington, and I am proud to add that Mr. Lewis has read over with me, and improved, nearly every page. And Mrs. Lewis has saved us, at critical moments, from many of the lapses that do continually afflict bibliographers and collectors. But wherever I have turned, I have been made welcome, in libraries public and private; and the response to appeals sent through the mails has been equally cordial. The names of many of these assistants are represented throughout the book by the names of the present owners, private collectors or public libraries, of various copies.

Help in time of need has come, in the way of notes about their own copies, from: Mr. James T. Babb; Mr. R. W. Chapman; Mr. Frederick Coykendall; Mr. Philip B. Daghlian; the Earl of Derby, K.G.; Mr. W. M. Elkins; Mr. Robert Hartshorne; Mr. Frederick W. Hilles; Mrs. Augustus Loring; Mr. Nathan van Patten; Mr. Carleton R. Richmond; Sir Wathen A. Waller, Bt.; and Mr. Joseph Widener. Others have helped with information about books entrusted to their care: Mr. A. W. Aspital and Mr. A. J. Watson of the British Museum; Mr. Lawrence C. Wroth of the John Carter Brown Library; Miss Katharine M. Hall of the Library of the University of Chicago; Miss Cora Sanders of the William Andrews Clark Memorial Library; Mr. Charles M. Adams of Columbia; Miss Ruth Granniss of the Grolier Club; Mr. William A. Jackson and Miss Carolyn E. Jakeman of Harvard; Mr. Louis B. Wright, Mr. Lyle H. Wright, and the staff of the Huntington Library; Miss Belle da Costa Greene of the Morgan Library; Mr. Karl Küp and Mr. Paul North Rice of the New York Public Library; Mr. Lawrance Thompson of Princeton; and Mr. William McCarthy, formerly of Texas and now of Harvard. For particular help requested and received, it is also a pleasure to thank the following: Mr. John Carter; Mr. Robert Claus of the Class of 1943 at Yale; Mr. George Goodspeed; Mr. Walter N. H. Harding of Chicago; Mrs. Ragnhild Hatton; Mr. George L. Lam; Mr. Hellmut Lehmann-Haupt; Mr. Shane Leslie; Mr. F. G. Ludwig; Mr. E. L. McAdam; Miss Julia McCarthy; Mr. Maynard Mack; Mr. A. N. L. Munby, formerly of Quaritch's; Mr. J. M. Phillips; Mr. C. P. Rollins; Mr. A. S. W. Rosenbach; Mr. Rudolph Ruzicka; Mr. Theodore Sizer; Mr. Warren H. Smith; Mr. Arthur Swann of the Parke-Bernet Galleries; Mr. Emerson Tuttle; Miss Rosamond Tuve; the late Mr. Leonard Whibley; and Mr. W. K. Wimsatt.

Lord Waldegrave has replied, patiently and accurately, to Mr. Kirby's numerous inquiries about the pieces at Chewton Priory. What was apparently Kirgate's most complete set of Detached Pieces is now at Chewton, having passed successively through the hands of

George Baker, William Upcott, and George Smith; the reader will find notes from that set frequently quoted. The bibliography would have many more serious imperfections had it not been for Lord Waldegrave's help.

Mr. Kirby has done the larger share of the work on the Detached Pieces, much of it long before I became interested in Strawberry Hill. The final responsibility, especially on bibliographical problems, has been mine, and I have changed his conclusions in some cases, when I have been able to study the Detached Pieces in connection with the books. But his materials are the basis of each article, and the census of recorded copies is almost wholly his work. From far and near, he gathered accurate information on each small piece, and then spread before me the records that I needed to fill out the bibliographical picture presented by the books.

Most of the work has been done at Farmington, but the interest of friends at Yale, in the library and on the teaching faculty, has been unfailing; and they have always responded when I have asked for help.

VI

To shorten the references in the body of the work, we have made use of the following abbreviations:

HW. Horace Walpole.

JPO. *Journal of the Printing Office,* edited by Dr. Paget Toynbee, London and Boston, 1923.

Lowndes. *The Bibliographer's Manual of English Literature,* by W. T. Lowndes, revised by H. G. Bohn. The name Lowndes followed by a number refers to the numbered list of items printed at the Strawberry Hill Press contained in the Appendix first published by Mr. Bohn in 1864.

Martin. John Martin, *A Bibliographical Catalogue of Books Privately Printed,* 1834.

SH. Strawberry Hill.

SH Sale. *Catalogue of the Classic Contents of Strawberry Hill,* 25 April–21 May 1842 (sold by George Robins). The roman and arabic numerals indicate the day and lot number. (A parenthetical 'London Sale' refers to the prints and illustrated books of the Seventh and Eighth Days' Sale; these were withdrawn and recatalogued for sale in London, 13–23 June 1842.)

'Short Notes.' Horace Walpole, 'Short Notes of the Life of Horatio Walpole,' reprinted by Mrs. Paget Toynbee at the beginning of the first volume of her edition of *The Letters of Horace Walpole,* Oxford, 1903–5.

wsl. W. S. Lewis.

The works have been numbered in two series, one for the books and one for the Detached Pieces. This arrangement has some conveniences, and it does not seem likely to cause any difficulty in the use of the book; in cross-references, the first series is called the *Bibliography,* or the books, and the second series is called the Detached Pieces. Within each series, the arrangement is chronological, save that the title-pages, labels, and cards of address have been gathered at the end of the Detached Pieces.

Since the full title is available in the facsimiles, the titles in the text have been kept very short. The facsimiles are the same size as the originals, except for the seven largest pieces; the amount of reduction can be discovered by comparing the width of the facsimile with the measurement of the widest line of the original as recorded below each of these seven pieces. Most of the facsimiles have been made from copies at Farmington. A few have been made, with the kind permission of the libraries concerned, from other copies, as follows: The Duke of Devonshire's *Catalogue,* No. 9 (British Museum); *Hieroglyphic Tales,* No. 32 (Princeton); *The Magpie and her Brood,* reprint of Detached Piece No. 17 (Clark Memorial Library); *The Candidate,* Detached Piece No. 26 (Eton College); *Epitaph on King of Corsica, Questions for the Society of Antiquaries, Tristes Regrets,* and reprint of verses to the Berry sisters, Detached Pieces Nos. 6, 10, 15, 36 (Harvard); *Portrait of Lord Granville* and verses by Mrs. Cloak, Detached Pieces Nos. 11 and 41 (Huntington Library). No facsimiles have been prepared for the offprints (Nos. 17, 23, 24), for three awkwardly shaped Detached Pieces (Nos. 20, 31, 35), for the miscellaneous title-pages, labels, and cards of address (Detached Pieces Nos. 49–77), or for items in the two Appendices. The frontispiece has been reproduced in collotype from the water-color in Richard Bull's copy of the *Description of Strawberry Hill,* 1784.

For each piece we have included the number in Lowndes's list of Strawberry Hill imprints, since this is such a well-known and convenient guide. For the Detached Pieces, which are somewhat more confusing, we have also included a page-reference to Martin.

In quotations from the JPO, we have normalized the dates and the spelling, since the quotations are included as references and not as specimens of Walpole's writing. Similar liberties have been taken with other quotations.

The method of bibliographical description is I hope easily understood: the total is always the same in the collations by signatures and by pagination, but the semicolons (inserted for convenience) do not necessarily agree in the two collations. A bracketed signature is used only when no leaf of that gathering is signed.

At Farmington there is an untrimmed copy of nearly every book, and the measurements, unless a special note is included, are taken from copies at Farmington. I have no great faith in the value of measurements, whether in inches or centimeters, but every collector is proud to own a copy 'taller than the one recorded in the bibliography,' and the measurements may serve a useful purpose in dispelling certain misconceptions about copies on large paper. Since I have given an overall measurement of the book's apparent size, the figures vary slightly, because of irregularities of handmade paper and of folding, even among the books printed (in 1758, for example) on the same paper.

The records of sales have been compiled from numerous sources: from marked copies of catalogues, from *Book Prices Current* and the other annual compilations, from Mr. Lewis's notes, and from other sources; some errors are inevitable, but I believe the records will be found generally reliable. The date is intended to be the day on which the book was actually sold, but a good many references have been included from secondary sources and some of these record only the first day of the sale in question. Whenever possible, the name of the sale and the lot number have been included; the date will then furnish an accurate reference to libraries sold in more than one part.

The census of Detached Pieces, unlike the records of the books, is intended to be inclusive: there is of course no such thing as perfection in such a compilation, but all copies known to us have been included. The sale prices of the Detached Pieces are of little value, since copies are difficult to trace and since neither dealers nor collectors have had any clear notion of relative rarity among the various pieces; I have therefore ordinarily omitted the prices.

This *Bibliography of the Strawberry Hill Press* is complete in itself, but we hope that it will be the first of several books of Walpolian bibliography, all based in large part on the collection at Farmington. Mr. Lewis and Mr. Kirby have made considerable progress in a study of the books from Walpole's library; and it is my hope that I can soon continue, despite the uncertainties of our epoch, with a bibliography of Walpole's own writings.

A. T. H.

Yale University, July 1941.

BIBLIOGRAPHY OF THE STRAWBERRY HILL PRESS

BOOKS

ODES

BY

Mr. GRAY.

ΦΩΝΑΝΤΑ ΣΥΝΕΤΟΙΣΙ——————

PINDAR, Olymp. II.

PRINTED AT STRAWBERRY-HILL,
For R. and J. DODSLEY in Pall-Mall.
MDCCLVII.

1. REDUCED SLIGHTLY. WIDTH OF ORIGINAL 12.9 cm.

BOOKS

1. ODES BY MR. GRAY. 1757.

Lowndes 1.

JPO, p. 3: '25 June 1757. The Press was erected. Wm. Robinson, printer. 16 July. Began to print. The first work was an edition of two new Odes by Mr. Gray: one, on the power and progress of Poetry; the other, on the destruction of the Welsh Bards by Edward I. 3 August. 1000 copies of the Odes finished. 8 August. 2000 copies published by Dodsley.'

JPO, Appendix A, p. 77 [HW's rough notes]: 'To Mr. Grignion for engraving the fleuron, £2.12.6. . . . 1000 of Mr. Gray's Odes finished Aug. 3d. 2000 in all: published Aug. 8th.'

HW to John Chute, 12 July 1757: 'On Monday next the Officina Arbuteana opens in form. The Stationers' Company, that is, Mr. Dodsley, Mr. Tonson, &c. are summoned to meet here on Sunday night. And with what do you think we open? *Cedite, Romani Impressores*—with nothing under *Graii Carmina*. I found him in town last week: he had brought his two Odes to be printed. I snatched them out of Dodsley's hands, and they are to be the first-fruits of my press.'

HW to George Montagu, 16 July 1757: 'Elzevirianum opens to-day; you shall taste its first-fruits.'

Gray to James Brown, 25 July 1757: 'As there is but one hand employed, you must think it will take up some time to dispatch 2000 copies. As soon as may be, you will have a parcel sent you, which you will dispose of, as follows: [recipients].'

HW to John Chute, 26 July 1757: 'The press goes on as fast as if I printed myself. I hope in a very few days to send you a specimen. . . . Gray has been gone these five days.'

Gray to William Mason, 1 August 1757: '[The *Odes*] had been out three weeks ago, but Mr. Walpole having taken it into his head to set up a Press of his own at Twickenham, was so earnest to handsel it with this new pamphlet, that it was impossible to find a pretence for refusing such a trifle. You will dislike this, as much as I do, but there is no help. You understand, it is he, that prints them not for me, but for Dodsley.' Dodsley paid Gray forty guineas for the copyright of the *Odes,* 29 June 1757; the receipt is now in the Huntington Library.

HW to Sir Horace Mann, 4 August 1757: 'I send you two copies (one for Dr. Cocchi) of a very honourable opening of my press—two amazing Odes of Mr. Gray.'

HW to Charles Lyttelton, 4 August 1757: 'I cannot send you *our Odes* by the post, they are too large: I shall leave two copies in Hill Street to be sent to Hagley; I must beg you to desire my Lord [Lyttelton, Charles Lyttelton's brother] to accept one; and if he likes the type and paper, I should hope that the next life he writes of Henry the Second (the present being I know engaged) he would let me print it.'

Gray to HW, 10 August 1757: 'Dodsley sent me some copies last week: they are very pleasant to the eye, and will do no dishonour to your Press.'

Gray to Wharton, 17 August 1757: 'I hear, we are not at all popular. The great objection is obscurity, nobody knows what we would be at.'

Gray to Mason, 7 September 1757: 'I would not have put another note to save the souls of all the *Owls* in London. It is extremely well, as it is. Nobody understands me, and I am perfectly satisfied. . . . If you chance to call [at Dodsley's] yourself, you might enquire, if many of my 2000 remain upon his hands. He told me a fortnight ago about 12 or 1300 were gone.'

Two thousand copies were printed: HW's list in the *Description of SH* (1784), giving 1000 copies as the number printed, has often been reprinted and accepted without question. (Pinkerton in *Walpoliana* says 1100—perhaps a misprint.) But the evidence of Gray's letters and of the JPO seems conclusive. HW was apparently careless when he prepared the list twenty years later, or forgetful.

Much speculation has arisen about the printing arrangements, however, because of the existence of copies on thick paper as well as on ordinary paper. The two printings were first differentiated, so far as I am aware, in the catalogue of Mr. Jerome Kern's library, sold at the Anderson Galleries in January 1929. In 1934, Mr. I. A. Williams examined the *Odes* (in his *Points in Eighteenth Century Verse,* p. 75) and concluded that the two forms were merely variant issues of the same setting of type. Then in 1936, in response to a query, Mr. John Carter's careful study (*Bibliographical Notes and Queries,* May 1936) showed that the two issues were in fact two completely different settings. But Mr. Carter, puzzled by the conflict between the evidence of HW's list and of the JPO, postulated two editions, as follows: 1000 copies printed at Strawberry Hill, on thick paper, the 'first issue'; and 2000 copies printed in London, in the same fount of type, on ordinary paper, the 'second issue.' This solution seemed possible because copies on ordinary paper are much more common to-day than those on thick paper, and because the ordinary paper is unlike anything used by HW in his other books. In April 1938 (also in *Bibliographical Notes and Queries*), Mr. Carter described the watermarks of several early SH pieces (including, as it happened, one forgery), to show that these Dutch papers were similar to the paper used in the thick-paper copies of the *Odes*. In the same number of *Bibliographical Notes and Queries*, however, Mr. Leonard Whibley pointed out that Gray's own copy and the copy sent by HW to John Chute are both on thin paper. In November 1938, faced by this evidence and by the fact that HW's own copy is also on thin paper, Mr. Carter saw at once that his hypothesis was wrong and that the thick-paper copies must represent the *second* setting; he was unable to explain why a second setting of type had been necessary or why thick-paper copies are so much rarer to-day than those on ordinary paper. But now that the copies on thick paper can be established as a much later, independent printing by Thomas Kirgate [see below, STATES AND VARIANTS], these difficulties are resolved: two thousand copies were printed by William Robinson between 16 July and 8 August, and a much smaller edition on thick paper was printed by Kirgate, about 1790 or later.

Quarto in half-sheets; approximately 27.7 x 22 cm. uncut.
Signatures: [A]–E²; one leaf.
Pagination: [1] half-title, with verso blank; [3] title-page, with verso blank; 5–21 text; [22] blank.

Some booksellers have occasionally caused uncertainty by offering copies of the *Odes* 'with the blank leaf at end wanting.' I have no record of a blank leaf at the end, nor do I believe that a perfect copy requires any. Since this error seems to be caused by the belief (strongly held by Dr. Greg in the *Library* in 1934) that only even index numbers are allowable in collation, it is perhaps not inappropriate to point out again that odd numbers may occur in collation even in commercial printing; and in private undertakings such as that at SH, a single leaf is not uncommon. It would have been possible for Robinson to set up page 21 twice, so that he could print two copies of this leaf on one half-sheet—perhaps as part of the sheet containing Signature E. But I do not hesitate to believe it possible that this final leaf, of the first work printed at the Press, was imposed separately.

STATES AND VARIANTS

The first printing is on a good 'trade' paper, in which the watermark is a small lily. Textually, this printing can be identified by the correct spelling of 'Ilissus' on p. 8. (The spelling in the reprint is 'Illissus,' and on p. 16 the reprint omits the comma after 'Swarm.') The reprint is on a fine, heavy Dutch paper, in which the watermark is a crown surmounting a lily in a shield, with the initials 'J H & Z'; the countermark is 'J HONIG & ZOONEN.' The evidence that these thick-paper copies are a late reprint follows:

(a) *The evidence of the paper itself*. The thin paper of the original edition, though not at all sumptuous, is a good 'trade' paper; and it seems to me entirely suitable for an edition printed at one shilling a copy. This paper was probably supplied by Dodsley, who was both the publisher and the holder of the copyright; after paying forty guineas to Gray for the copyright, Dodsley's profit could not have been great in any case.

The thick-paper copies are on a much heavier paper, the kind on which engravings are usually printed. Much of the paper that HW used at the Press, especially in the earlier years, was of Dutch origin, and I have seen some MSS by both Kirgate and Walpole, about 1790, on Honig paper; but no paper from the Honig firm appears in any other work printed at SH. Furthermore, so far as I can judge from a few samples, the firm was 'J Honig & Zoon' until about 1767, when the plural 'Zoonen' first appears. Finally, among the various watermarks used by Messrs. Honig, the only one I have found that agrees exactly with the mark in the thick-paper copies of the *Odes* occurs in an engraved plate in the *Catalogue des livres de M. Pierre-Antoine Bolongaro-Crevenna,* printed at Amsterdam in 1789. It is therefore certain that this particular paper was available in Amsterdam in 1789, and probable that Kirgate printed some copies of the *Odes,* perhaps a hundred, on this paper in 1790 or at some date near that time—quite possibly as late as 1797.

(b) *Provenance of copies*. Every copy that is known to have belonged to Gray or Walpole or that can be traced to an early date is on thin paper. Here is a list of these copies; other copies belong in it, but I have not such complete information about them: (1) Gray's copy (now Morgan Library) with his MS annotations; (2) HW's copy (now Lord Rothschild) dated 'Aug. 4' by him in MS; (3) William Cole's copy (now wsl) presented by HW, inscribed and dated on verso of title-page by Cole in 1757 (the half-title of this copy is on thick paper, interesting proof that a bookseller or collector early in the nineteenth century was anxious that his copy should collate perfectly); (4) William Cole's copy (now Lord Rothschild) presented by Gray, inscribed and dated on the title-page by Cole in 1757; (5) a copy (now wsl) bound with Countess Temple's *Poems* (this volume contains HW's bookplate, and the poems by Lady Temple contain MS annotations in HW's hand); (6) a copy (now owned by Mr. C. L. Chute of 'The Vyne' near Basingstoke) presumably, though not certainly, the copy sent by HW to John Chute in 1757; (7) a copy inscribed 'The Gift of the Author,' formerly owned by Dr. Roderick Terry; (8) a copy (now wsl) inscribed on the half-title 'Samuel Watson 1758'; (9) a copy (owned by Dr. A. S. W. Rosenbach in 1939) inscribed on title-page 'The Gift of the Author. Nic. Bonfoy' (Bonfoy is one of a number of recipients named by Gray in his letter to James Brown, 25 July 1757); (10) Michael Wodhull's copy (now Yale) bound with other Odes in 1766; (11) a copy (now wsl) inscribed (probably by George Grenville) 'From the Honble. Mr. Walpole, Nov. 12, 1781.'

On the other hand, no copy of the thick-paper *Odes* is known, save those from the library of Thomas Kirgate, with any record of eighteenth-century ownership; three copies can be traced with reasonable certainty to Kirgate's Sale in 1810. (1) E. V. Utterson's copy (now wsl) bound in a volume of miscellaneous pieces, with Utterson's note, 'The greater part, if not the whole of these desultory pieces was purchased by me at Kirgate's Sale in 1816.' (Kirgate's library was sold in December 1810, six months after his death. Utterson's error in date may have been caused by his reliance on Martin: Martin, perhaps by a typographical error, says that Kirgate died in 1816.) (2) A copy (now Princeton) bound about 1814 by C. Smith, with a pencil note on the fly-leaf, 'From the library of Thomas Kirgate (Walpole's printer).' (3) A copy (now WSL) bought by William Upcott at the sale of George Baker's library in 1825; because of Baker's purchases from Kirgate in 1798 (Kirgate's bills, now WSL) and his purchases at the Kirgate Sale in 1810, it seems safe to assume that any copy of the *Odes* in Baker's collection came from Kirgate.

(c) *Condition of copies.* Thin-paper copies are likely to be heavily trimmed, with half-title or last leaf defective (if not supplied in facsimile); they frequently occur bound with other poems of the period. But thick-paper copies are likely to be offered in immaculate condition, often with original gray-blue wrappers, and very often with edges untrimmed: these are not copies that were read with bewilderment in 1757 by the purchasers of whom Gray wrote to Wharton and Mason.

(d) *Kirgate's copies.* Thomas Kirgate was first employed by HW in 1765, nearly eight years after the original edition had been published, and sold, by Dodsley. I think it very unlikely that HW held back (or received later from Dodsley) any considerable number of copies: a dozen copies would be a sufficient supply from which to make an occasional gift (like that to Grenville in 1781). Dodsley was the publisher, he held the copyright, and presumably he supplied the paper on which HW printed the *Odes.* (HW's mention of Tonson as his paper merchant, in the letter to Grosvenor Bedford, 9 November 1757,* I take as a reference to the Dutch paper on which Hentzner's *Journey,* the *Catalogue of Royal and Noble Authors,* and succeeding works were printed.) It is therefore unlikely that any remainder would have been returned to HW, even if the *Odes* had not sold well; but we know from Gray's letter to Mason, 7 September 1757, that twelve or thirteen hundred copies were sold before the end of August, and it therefore seems possible that the whole edition of two thousand copies was sold eventually. Nevertheless, forty years later, in 1798, Kirgate sold a copy of the *Odes* to George Baker for three shillings (Kirgate's bill, now WSL), and in 1810 thirty-five copies of the *Odes,* grouped in five lots of seven copies each, were sold to collectors for two shillings a lot (2/6 for one lot). These copies, sold for

* Misdated 9 May 1759 by Cunningham: see Vol. xvi of Mrs. Toynbee's edition of the *Letters,* p. xxvi, note 1.

five pence each in 1810, have in recent years been so eagerly sought by collectors that a top price of $1250 at auction (Kern Sale, 1929) has been recorded.

Four separate, but related, kinds of evidence, therefore, point to one conclusion: records of provenance indicate that only the thin-paper copies have any standing as the original edition, and this decision is supported by records of condition; the thick-paper copies seem to have been prepared later to satisfy the demands of collectors. Kirgate's connection with these later copies is sufficient proof, I think, that he himself printed them; and the particular paper that he used indicates 1790 or later as a suitable date for this reprinting. (For a similar reprint, that of the Countess Temple's *Poems,* see below, No. 12.)

OTHER EDITIONS

The *Odes* were reprinted in Dublin in 1757, in octavo; Northup in his bibliography of Gray also records an edition at Cambridge in 1769, but this entry appears to be an error.

COPIES

1. HW's copy, with his bookplate and MS annotations, gray wrapper, uncut, now bound in cloth with a morocco case; reviews and a copy of Garrick's Verses bound in. Hodgson's, 30 April 1902 (Mrs. Damer's Sale), lot 121, to Sabin, £171; Anderson's, 8 December 1924 (Chew Sale), lot 183, to Rosenbach for Mr. Frank Bemis, $3900; now (1940) Lord Rothschild.

2. Presentation copy from HW to William Cole, inscribed by Cole on verso of title: 'Donum Hon. Horatii Walpole 1757. Gulo. Cole Rectori de Blecheley.' A few annotations by Cole; the half-title has been supplied from a thick-paper copy. Bound (about 1820) with Cole's copy of Lady Temple's *Poems* (No. 12 below), presentation copies (not to Cole) of *Miscellaneous Antiquities* (No. 20 below), the *Muse Recalled* (No. 28 below); and Lady Temple's *Verses to Lady Charles Spencer* (No. 13 of Detached Pieces); red morocco with arms of Viscount Valentia (died 1841) on sides; bookplates of James Bindley, John Trotter Brockett, and Francis A. Gaskill. Offered by T. Thorpe, in his General Catalogue for 1844, lot 1801, for three guineas; re-offered by Thorpe in 1845; offered by Sotheran, 1885, for £2.10.0; Sotheby's, 24 July 1906 (Miscellaneous Sale), lot 446, to B. F. Stevens, £13; bought by WSL in the Gaskill Collection, December 1939.

3. Presentation copy from Gray to William Cole, inscribed by Cole on title: 'Wm. Cole Cantabr. ex dono Authoris 1757.' Unbound, half-title and last leaf frayed, signature of Wm. Baker on title. Hodgson's, 14 December 1928 (Mis-

cellaneous Sale), lot 496, to Pickering, £16; Hodgson's, 24 July 1935 (Miscellaneous Sale), lot 83, to Robinson, £10; now (1940) Lord Rothschild.

4. Gray's copy, with his MS notes. Interleaved, and bound in olive morocco by Clarke and Bedford, morocco case. Sotheby's, 28 August 1851 (Gray Library), lot 53, with a large collection of MSS, £500; Sotheby's, 4 August 1854 (Gray Library), lot 241, to George Daniel. Mr. Daniel's note says that Mr. Penn paid one hundred guineas at Evans's for the *Odes* alone; Daniel added portraits of Gray, the MSS of the Song for Miss Speed, etc., and Gray's letter to Dr. Brown. Sotheby's, 22 July 1864 (Daniel Sale), lot 746, to Harvey, £110; Sotheby's, 22 April 1901 (Sir W. A. Fraser Sale), lot 749, to Harvey, £370; now in the Morgan Library. (A second letter to Dr. Brown was added in 1922.)

5. Uncut and unbound, in a morocco case, with Garrick's Verses, a portrait of Gray with MS note by HW, a letter from William Mason, and a MS copy of two poems by Gray with MS note by HW. Sotheby's, 10 April 1902 (Hibbert Sale), lot 351, to Pickering, £23; Sotheby's, 18 May 1903 (Miscellaneous Sale), lot 512, to Sabin, £40. The MS of the poems is now in the Huntington Library.

6. Richard Bull's copy, with his bookplate; inlaid to folio and bound with Bentley's *Designs for Poems by Mr. Gray*, 1753; half-title wanting. Red morocco; offered by Quaritch, Catalogue 372 (1922), lot 210, £7; now Lord Derby, Knowsley.

7. Bound with Lady Temple's *Poems, Miscellaneous Antiquities, Letters of Edward VI* (No. 19 below), and the *Muse Recalled;* inscribed: 'From the Honble. Mr. Walpole, Nov. 12, 1781'; presented probably to George Grenville. Red morocco, stamped with arms of Duke of Buckingham and Chandos. Sotheby's, 28 July 1933 (Lady Mount-Stephen Sale), lot 607, to Robinson (with other books), £31; bought by WSL from Robinson for £20.

8. Modern blue levant morocco, with name on half-title: 'Samuel Watson, 1758.' Brentano's, January 1940, to WSL, $100.

9. *On thick paper*. In a collection of miscellaneous pieces formed by E. V. Utterson at the sale of Kirgate's library in 1810; bound in half morocco. Sotheby's, 20 January 1909 (Miscellaneous Sale), lot 197, to Pickering, £14.10.0; Hodgson's, 13 June 1934 (Butler Sale), lot 422, to Maggs for WSL, £116.

10. *On thick paper*. Sotheby's, 8 June 1825 (Baker Sale), lot 826, to William Upcott (with *Notes to the Portraits at Woburn Abbey*), 14/–; Evans's, 16 June 1846 (Upcott Sale), lot 517, to Bohn, 16/–. In the Catalogue of Upcott's books, this is called Large Paper, uncut; with it were a copy of the Directions for seeing the house (No. 33 of the Detached Pieces) and a MS epitaph on Jane Clerke by Gray, said to be in HW's hand: these two items were removed from the volume at some time between 1932 and 1939. The volume was bound in red morocco by Jenkins and Cecil, probably for E. L. S. Benzon; the half-title is missing. Sotheby's, 25 May 1875 (Benzon Sale), lot 239, to Sabin, £4.4.0; Ritter-Hopson Galleries, 13 December 1932 (Mrs. Davenport Sale), lot 87, $110; Brick Row, August 1939, to WSL (without the Directions for seeing the house or the MS), $140.

11. *On thick paper*. Pencilled note on fly-leaf, 'From the library of Thomas

Kirgate (Walpole's printer).' Green morocco (about 1814) by C. Smith; two portraits inserted. Offered in Longman's General Catalogue (July 1814, lot 1645), in a collection of 41 volumes, £350; Christie's, 1 March 1892 (Property of a gentleman), lot 113, to Nattali, £2.8.0. One portrait was later removed, and a copy of Garrick's Verses [Kirgate's reprint; see Detached Pieces, No. 7] inserted. Now in the Morgan Collection at Princeton.

2. HENTZNER'S JOURNEY INTO ENGLAND. 1757.

Lowndes 2.

HW to John Chute, 12 July 1757: 'An edition of Hentznerus, with a version by Mr. Bentley and a little preface of mine, were prepared, but are to wait [for Gray's *Odes*].'

JPO, pp. 3–7: '8 August 1757. Began to print Hentznerus's account of England, with a translation by Rich. Bentley; the advertisement by H. Walpole. . . . 13 October. Fifty copies of Hentznerus finished. 17 October. The whole number, being 220 copies, completed. . . . 11 November 1758. Eight imperfect copies of Hentzner, perfected.'

Octavo in half-sheets; approximately 19.6 x 12 cm. uncut.

Signatures: [A]–Ee⁴.

Pagination: Title-page, with verso blank; Dedication, with verso blank; [i]–x Advertisement (by HW); fly-title; 103 pp. of Latin text printed on versos (beginning with verso of fly-title) to face the corresponding 103 pp. of English text on rectos; one blank page; one blank leaf (often missing).

STATES AND VARIANTS

In some copies, rather more than half of those examined, the '9' of p. 39 (recto) has dropped out, producing an unimportant variant.

The entry in the JPO, 11 November 1758, makes me believe that eight copies may exist in which some pages have been reset, but I have not identified any such copy.

OTHER EDITIONS

Hentzner's *Journey* was reprinted by Jeffery in 1797, by T. E. Williams at his private press in 1807, and by the Aungervyle Society in 1881. It was also included in the second volume of Dodsley's *Fugitive Pieces on Various Subjects*, 1761; Third edition 1771. Some extracts were printed in the *London Magazine* for December 1757 (JPO, p. 76).

A
JOURNEY
INTO
ENGLAND.
BY
PAUL HENTZNER,
IN THE YEAR M.D.XC.VIII.

PRINTED AT STRAWBERRY-HILL.
MDCCLVII.

2.

COPIES

1. HW's copy, with a MS note; calf, with his arms on sides. SH Sale, iv.167, to Thorpe, £2.18.0 (with HW's copy of *Fugitive Pieces*). Now Lord Walde-grave, Chewton Priory.

2. Boards, uncut; described as having pencil notes by HW. Sotheby's, 22 May 1848 (Eyton Sale), lot 1438, to Lilly, 2/–.

3. Presentation copy to David Dalrymple, Lord Hailes, in 1758, inscribed by him 'Editoris Donum'; with his MS notes. Red morocco. Sotheby's 25 May 1937 (Dalrymple Sale), lot 380, to Quaritch, £6.10.0; Quaritch, 1937, to WSL, £9.

4. Presentation copy to Richard Bull, with presentation letter (26 March 1783) from HW. Blank leaf lacking. Bound in two volumes, interleaved and extra-illustrated; blue morocco. Sotheby's, 29 June 1926 (Burgh Sale), lot 159, to Quaritch, £24; Quaritch, February 1927, to Frank B. Bemis, £35; estate of Mr. Bemis (through Goodspeed) to WSL, 1937, $45.

5. Presentation copy in 1781 to Lord Ossory, according to a pencilled note. Red morocco binding attributed to Roger Payne; title-page ruled in red; blank leaf wanting. Quaritch, 1937, to WSL, £25.

6. Presentation copy to Thomas Walpole, with his initials on title-page; he gave it to his daughter, Catherine Margaret; she died in 1876; bookplate of Thomas Sanderson. Original boards, uncut. Maggs, 1925, to WSL, £5.15.0.

7. Green morocco by C. Smith (about 1814); blank leaf wanting; bookplate of F. A. Gaskill. Probably one of the copies in the sale of Kirgate's library in 1810; offered in Longman's General Catalogue (July 1814, lot 1645), in a collection of 41 volumes, £350; Christie's, 1 March 1892 (Property of a gentle-man), lot 114, to Toovey, £1.16.0; from the Gaskill Collection, December 1939, to WSL.

8. David Garrick's copy; contemporary calf (broken); inscribed on fly-leaf: 'This book was given to me by Mr. Hor. Walpole. D. Garrick.' Bookplate of John A. Spoor. R. Saunders, 26 April 1823 (Garrick Sale), lot 1017, £2.3.0; Hodgson's, 20 February 1902 (Miscellaneous Sale), lot 476, £9.10.0; offered by a bookseller (clipping inserted) for £20; Parke-Bernet, 4 May 1939 (Spoor Sale), lot 887, to W. M. Hill, $85; Hill, April 1940, to WSL, $100.

9. William Cole's copy, with MS notes; morocco. T. King, 20 May 1800 (Steevens Sale), lot 1141, to Malone, £1.16.0; King and Lochée, 5 March 1807 (Waldron Sale), lot 389, £3.16.0.

3. CATALOGUE OF ROYAL AND NOBLE AUTHORS. 1758.

Lowndes 3.

'Short Notes,' p. xlii: 'In April, 1758, was finished the first impression [i.e., edition] of my *Catalogue of Royal and Noble Authors,* which I had written the preceding year in less than five months.'

JPO, pp. 6, 7: '17 October 1757. Began to print the Catalogue of Royal and Noble Authors. . . . 27 January 1758. Finished first volume of the Catalogue

A

CATALOGUE
OF THE
ROYAL
AND
NOBLE AUTHORS
OF
ENGLAND,
With LISTS of their WORKS.

*Dove, diavolo! Meſſer Ludovico, avete pigliato
tante coglionerie?*
CARD. D'ESTE, to ARIOSTO.

VOL. I.

PRINTED AT STRAWBERRY-HILL.
M DCCLVIII.

3.

of Authors, except dedication, preface, and index. 30 January. Began to print the second volume. 11 April. Finished 50 copies. Mr. Müntz took off the copper plates, which (being the frontispiece, fleuron, and coin of Queen Elizabeth) were engraved by Grignion. [Grignion received one guinea for engraving the coin and two guineas for the fleuron, according to the entry in the JPO, p. 77.] Half of the whole number of copies have a variation in the second page of the dedication, which was corrected after part were printed off. 13 April. 50 more copies finished. 15 April. The whole 300 finished.'

Two volumes, octavo in half-sheets; approximately 19.7 x 12.5 cm. uncut.

Signatures: Vol. I. Quarter-sheet; plate; A (two quarter-sheets, quired), b, B–Ee⁴; Ff²; quarter-sheet.

Vol. II. Quarter-sheet; B–Ee⁴; half-sheet.

Pagination: Vol. I. 'This work is entered in the HALL-BOOK of the COMPANY of STATIONERS, according to Act of Parliament,' on fourth page, preceded by three blank pages; frontispiece by Grignion; title-page, with verso blank; Dedication on 4 pp.; [i]–viii Advertisement; fly-title to Royal Authors, with verso blank; [1]–219 text; [220] blank; [221–223] Index; [224] blank.

Vol. II. Title-page, and fly-title to Noble Authors, with versos blank (these two leaves frequently reversed); [1]–215 text; [216] blank; [217–222] Index; one blank leaf.

In the second volume, B₁ is a cancel; in the first volume, signature R, because of the engraving on p. 126, is composed of two quarter-sheets, quired.

All copies were printed on the same paper, I believe, despite an occasional offer by a bookseller of a copy on large paper. Since the book was printed with wide margins, and copies are likely to be heavily trimmed, an untrimmed copy seems noticeably larger.

The *Postscript* of 1786 (No. 33 below) is not infrequently bound at the end of the second volume.

STATES AND VARIANTS

In the Dedication (Vol. I, A₂ verso) the first state 'to be partial' was corrected at press to read 'to have a bias.' (See the entry in the JPO, 11 April 1758, quoted above.) The second state seems to be slightly more common, but I think HW, after making the change while the work was in the press, attempted no consistent separation of the two states, inasmuch as presentation copies of both states are known.

OTHER EDITIONS

On 30 April 1758, HW sold the copyright for two years to Graham and Dodsley. (JPO, p. 7.) On 5 December 1758, an edition of 2000 copies was published, dated 1759. HW's proof sheets of this edition (now WSL) contain the original title-page to the first volume of this edition, dated 1758. Published copies have a cancel title-page, to correct the imprint. The work was also reprinted in Dublin 1759, London 1763, Edinburgh 1792, Edinburgh 1796, London 1796, and (enlarged by Thomas Park) London 1806. Silvester Harding published a series of portraits to illustrate the *Catalogue* in 1803, the prints having been issued at intervals from 1798 to 1803.

For the SH quarto edition, 1787, see *Works*, 1770, No. 16 below.

COPIES

1. HW's copy; calf, with his bookplate and 3 MS notes; A₂ verso in second state. SH Sale, iv.165 (probably; the *Postscript*, a separate volume, was included), to Bohn, £3.3.0; Sotheby's, 7 May 1904 (Ford Sale), lot 547, to B. F. Stevens, £7.5.0. Bookplate of John A. Spoor; Parke-Bernet, 4 May 1939 (Spoor Sale), lot 890, to Brick Row for WSL, $85.

2. Paper covers, uncut; Countess (later Duchess) of Northumberland's copy, signed 'E. Northumberland' in first volume; A₂ verso in second state; two leaves of text wanting. R. W. Chapman, August 1937, to WSL, in a collection.

3. Presentation copy to Mrs. Clive; given by her brother, James Raftor, to William Douglas in 1786. A₂ verso in second state; copyright notice wanting. Calf. Douglas Sale, 1792, to G. Huddesford, £3; Maggs, September 1925, to WSL, £4.14.6.

4. Presentation copy to Soame Jenyns; inscribed by him, 'Given me by the Honble. Horace Walpole Esq. the Author.' A₂ verso in second state; blank leaves wanting. Calf. Hodgson's, 10 December 1937 (Miscellaneous Sale), lot 463, to Maggs for WSL, £2.

5. Presentation copy to Lord Dacre; inscribed inside front cover, 'The Gift of the Honorable & accomplished Author.' A₂ verso in second state; blank preceding copyright notice wanting. Half calf, with Dacre bookplate. Sotheby's, 7 November 1938 (Barrett-Lennard Sale), lot 23, to Maggs for WSL, £1.18.0.

6. Presentation copy to Henry Zouch; inscribed by him on verso of title-page. A₂ verso in first state; blank leaves wanting. Calf. Sotheby's, 14 July 1937 (Lowther Castle Sale), lot 505, to Maggs for WSL, £4.

7. Frontispiece and title vignettes colored, and six original drawings by Harding inserted. A₂ verso in second state; blank leaves wanting. Red morocco by

Lewis, with *Postscript* bound at end of second volume. Sotheby's, 30 March 1928 (Holford Sale), lot 886, to Quaritch, £27; Quaritch, August 1939, to WSL, £31.10.0.

8. Presentation copy to David Dalrymple, inscribed on fly-leaf, 'Regum aequabat opes animis. Dav. Dalrymple Auctoris Donum. 1758.' A_2 verso in first state; blank preceding copyright notice wanting. Contemporary red morocco. Sotheby's, 25 May 1937 (Newhailes Sale), lot 381, to Quaritch, £9. Quaritch, August 1939, to WSL, £12.

9. Presentation copy to Lady Ossory; inscribed by her on fly-leaf, 'A present from the Author to Lady Ossory 1771'; note by R. Vernon Smith identifying the handwriting of the inscription. A_2 verso in first state; copyright notice wanting. Contemporary red morocco; bookplates of HW and of Harold Murdock. Goodspeed, December 1939, to WSL, $30.

10. Presentation copy inscribed by Kirgate, 'Given by Mr. Walpole, in 1787, to his Printer, T. Kirgate,' and a similar inscription in the second volume. A_2 verso in first state. Early nineteenth-century calf, uncut, with *Postscript* bound at the end of the second volume. Bookplate of George Soaper. Offered by Quaritch, Catalogue 432 (1930), lot 232, £25; from the Gaskill Collection, December 1939, to WSL.

11. Presentation copy to Lord Harcourt; now at Nuneham.

12. Presentation copy (in 1762) to William Cole, inscribed by him. This is probably the copy he gave to Dr. Glynn; cf. Cole to HW, 1 March 1780; it is now in the Bodleian Library.

13. Presentation copy to William Cole, inscribed by him, 'William Cole, 1780'; cf. HW to Cole, 6 March 1780. Calf; with autograph of George Steevens. (Probably) B. White, 1784 (Cole Sale), lot 5616, £1.1.0; King, 20 May 1800 (Steevens Sale), lot 1142, to Waldron, £1.10.0; King and Lochée, 5 March 1807 (Waldron Sale), lot 386, £2.3.0; King and Lochée, 4 December 1810 (Kirgate Sale), lot 341, to Lowndes, £1.11.6; offered by Lilly in his Catalogues, 1856, 1863, 1868. Since 1868 this copy seems to be unrecorded.

14. A copy from Kirgate's sale, according to a note on the fly-leaf; four copies, in addition to Cole's, were offered in the sale. Bound about 1814 in green morocco, probably by C. Smith. Offered in Longman's General Catalogue (July 1814, lot 1645) in a collection of 41 volumes, £350. (Probably) Christie's, 1 March 1892 (Property of a gentleman), lot 116, to Nattali, £1.13.0; bookplate of Wilhelmus Mynderse; Anderson, 29 October 1909 (Mynderse Sale), lot 504, $14; Anderson, 18 February 1920 (Sherer Sale), lot 841, $22.50.

15. Bookplate of David Garrick; contemporary red morocco. Puttick and Simpson, 16 July 1902 (Miscellaneous Sale), lot 139, to Maggs, £8; S. V. Henkels, 12 November 1903 (Goodwin Sale), lot 157, $40; Anderson, 20 November 1916 (Jones Sale), lot 556, $20.

16. Proofs of the second edition, with HW's corrections; half calf. Arms of Owen family and name 'Penrhos' inside front cover. Sotheby's, 20 May 1926 (Property of a nobleman), lot 700, to Maggs for WSL, £17.

FUGITIVE PIECES

IN

VERSE and PROSE.

Pereunt et imputantur.

PRINTED AT STRAWBERRY-HILL.
M DCC LVIII.

4.

4. FUGITIVE PIECES. 1758.

Lowndes 4.

JPO, p. 7: '24 April 1758. Began to print my own Fugitive Pieces. . . . 13 July. The Fugitive Pieces were finished. 200 copies printed.'

'Short Notes,' p. xliii: '17 March 1759. I began to distribute some copies of my Fugitive Pieces, collected and printed together at Strawberry Hill, and dedicated to General Conway.'

Octavo in half-sheets; approximately 19.7 x 12.5 cm. uncut.

Signatures: 4 leaves, the second signed 'A2'; B–Ee⁴; 2 leaves.

Pagination: Title-page, with verso blank; iii–iv Dedication; v–vi Contents; blank leaf (often missing); [1]–219 text; [220] blank.

An inserted leaf, usually after p. 216, contains a 'Note' about the Countess of Desmond's picture, with verso blank. This leaf is often missing (see below).

The title-page and Dedication were printed together as a quarter-sheet, and a detached quarter-sheet so printed is now at Farmington (in Utterson's collection of Detached Pieces); similarly, the Contents leaf and the blank (when present) form a quarter-sheet. Signature M, on the other hand, consists of two quarter-sheets, quired; the quarter-sheet was perhaps found convenient because the engraving of Theodore's coin was to be printed on p. 88 (M₄ verso).

STATES AND VARIANTS

Copies that lack the inserted 'Note' have often been described as the first issue. I have not found an exact date for the printing of the 'Note', but the evidence suggests that HW prepared it before beginning the general distribution of the book in March 1759. HW's copy (now wsl), presumably one of the first to be completed, lacks the 'Note' and might therefore seem to support the believers in a first issue; but the 'Note' is likewise lacking in three wsl copies that are certainly a later state (see below): copies presented to Thomas Pennant in 1774 and to Lady Ossory probably in 1771, and Richard Bull's copy. William Cole's copy, presented in 1762, also lacks the 'Note.' On the other hand, the copies that belonged to Lord Dacre and to Rev. Henry Zouch, both probably presented in 1759, contain the 'Note.' From these facts one might suggest that the 'Note' was inserted carefully in the copies that were distributed immediately after it had been prepared, and that it was neglected later; but more than this can hardly be assumed with any certainty. The presence or absence of the 'Note,' therefore, does not indicate a 'state' or issue.

There is, however, a second state in which four leaves are printed from a new setting of type, but not all these leaves are reset in every copy of the second state. The four leaves are: (a) title-page, (b) Dedication, and (c) pp. 81–2, 87–8 (M_1 and M_4).

(a) The new title-page can be identified by the flat-topped 'T' in Fugitive.

(b) The 'F' of Friendship and the 'A' of Affinity (p. iv) are large caps. (In the first state both words are set wholly in small caps.)

(c) On p. 81, line 4, the exclamation point is under the 'r' of for. (In the first state it is under the 'f' of for.)

This second state probably represents Pratt's completion of imperfect copies in the spring of 1762 [JPO, 28 June 1762; in Cole's copy, presented in 1762, all four leaves are in the first state], after he had reported to HW that there were 86 perfect copies of *Fugitive Pieces* in stock, and 50 copies 'wanting Title ½ sheet and M' [JPO, p. 86]. The press work is distinctly inferior in these leaves, and the use of a large-cap initial (Friendship and Affinity) is at variance with the practice in the text, pp. 131 ff. Furthermore, the watermark in these leaves (JW) first appears in the reprinted portions of the first two volumes of the *Anecdotes* (No. 10 below) in 1762.

OTHER EDITIONS

The *Fugitive Pieces* were not reprinted until HW undertook a quarto edition of his *Works* in 1768.

COPIES

1. HW's copy, with his MS annotations; portraits inserted. Original calf, with HW's arms on sides; lacks 'Note.' SH Sale, iv.167, to Thorpe, £2.18.0 (with Hentzner's *Journey*); owned by Peter Cunningham, 4 July 1854 (his MS note); Sotheby's 1860 (Cunningham Sale), lot 3677, to Elkins, £2.11.0; Sotheby's, 21 June 1904 (Miscellaneous Sale), lot 368, to B. F. Stevens, £8.15.0. Bookplate of John A. Spoor; his sale, Parke-Bernet, 4 May 1939, lot 893, to Brick Row for WSL, $30.

2. Henry Zouch's copy, inscribed on verso of title-page, 'H. Zouch—Ex dono acutissimi Viri—Authoris.' Original calf; lacks blank leaf after Contents. Bequeathed by Zouch to the family of his nephew, Sir William Lowther, Bt. (afterwards Earls of Lonsdale), in whose possession it remained until 1937; with

Lowther bookplate. Sotheby's, 14 July 1937 (Lowther Castle Sale), lot 506, to Maggs for WSL, £7.10.0.

3. Presented by HW to T. Kirgate, according to a later note on fly-leaf; contemporary calf. Bought, with other pieces, by WSL from Mrs. Curtis, Langford Hall, Newark, Notts, August 1937.

4. Thomas Pennant's copy, inscribed on fly-leaf in his hand, 'The Gift of the Author. April 14th 1774.' Calf; lacks 'Note' and blank leaf after Contents. Offered by Maggs, Catalogue 406 (1921), lot 472, £4.4.0; Sotheby's, 28 July 1933 (Lady Mount-Stephen Sale), lot 611, to Last, 10/–; Last, September 1933, to WSL, £1.15.0.

5. Richard Bull's copy, with his bookplate. Red morocco, extra-illustrated; lacks 'Note' and blank leaf after Contents. Sotheby's, 29 June 1926 (Burgh Sale), lot 160, to Quaritch, £24; offered by Quaritch, Catalogue 405 (1927), lot 3066, £36; Quaritch, March 1937, to WSL, £14.

6. Lady Ossory's copy. Contemporary red morocco; lacks 'Note'; a plate loosely inserted (from the collection of Sir Edward Astley), inscribed by HW, 'Humours of Oxford.' Bookplate of Arthur John Kennedy Clark Kennedy (1857–1926). From the Gaskill Collection, December 1939, to WSL.

7. A copy with HW's MS corrections and his note on fly-leaf: 'This copy is corrected as I intend it should stand, if ever reprinted. H. W.' Calf. Sotheby's, 10 July 1862 (Hawtrey Sale), lot 3116, £2.6.0; Puttick and Simpson, 1 May 1884 (Gosford Sale), lot 3065, to Harvey, £3.3.0; now in the Fitzwilliam Museum, Cambridge.

8. Presentation copy to Eliza Farren, actress, afterwards (1797) Countess of Derby, with her name on title-page; inscribed on fly-leaf, 'The gift of my revered friend Mr. Horace Walpole.' Now the Earl of Derby, K.G., Knowsley Hall, Lancs.

9. Extra-illustrated, ca. 1800, with prints and drawings; MS notes by Kirgate; lacks 'Note' and blank leaf. Blue morocco by C. Lewis; bookplate of E. V. Utterson. King and Lochée, 4 December 1810 (Kirgate Sale), lot 350, to Utterson, £2.7.0; Sotheby's, 27 April 1852 (Utterson Sale), lot 1829, £5.5.0; Sotheby's, 15 December 1941 (Miscellaneous Sale), lot 140, to Maggs for WSL, £15.

10. Presentation copy to Gray, calf, inscribed on title-page, 'Tho. Gray the gift of the Author.' Sotheby's, 28 August 1851 (Stoke Poges or Penn Sale), lot 132, to Pickering for Daniel, £1.19.0; Sotheby's, 27 July 1864 (Daniel Sale), lot 1719, to Forster, £1.12.0; now in Forster Collection at South Kensington.

11. Presentation copy to William Cole, with his notes; inscribed by him, 'Wm. Cole, ex Donis hon. Autoris, 1762, Horatii Walpole Arm.' Old calf, with fore-edge painting; lacks 'Note.' King, 20 May 1800 (Steevens Sale), lot 1144, to Waldron, £1.5.0; King and Lochée, 5 March 1807 (Waldron Sale), lot 388, £2.10.0; offered by Lilly in 1863 and 1868, £2.12.6. Bookplate of Mrs. John V. L. Pruyn; now in the Merritt Collection, Harvard.

12. Presentation copy (probably to George Grenville) inscribed on title-page, 'From the Author, Nov. 12, 1781.' Red morocco; bookplate of John Towneley. (Probably) T. Thorpe, Catalogue for 1847, lot 1052, £1.5.0; Sotheby's, 26 June

1883 (Towneley Sale), lot 2518, to Bain, £1.10.0; Anderson, 12 November 1919 (Avery Sale), lot 960, $41; Anderson, 16 February 1926 (Adam Sale), lot 409, $60.

5. WHITWORTH'S ACCOUNT OF RUSSIA. 1758.

Lowndes 5.

JPO, p. 7: '24 July 1758. Began to print Lord Whitworth's account of Russia. 29 September. Finished Lord Whitworth's book. 700 copies printed, 600 sold, for the benefit of the poor of Twickenham, at 3s. a volume but deducting 3d. for binding in blue paper, and 3d. to the bookseller for selling them. Sold by Graham.'

HW says in his *Advertisement* that the MS was purchased by Richard Owen Cambridge, with a collection of books on Russia, from Monsieur Zolman, Secretary to Stephen Poyntz.

Octavo in half-sheets; approximately 19.7 x 12.5 cm. uncut.
Signatures: A (2 quarter-sheets, quired), b, c, B–X⁴.
Pagination: [i] title-page, with verso blank; [iii]–xxiv Advertisement by HW; [1]–158 text; [159] Errata; [160] blank.

Leaf F_2 is incorrectly signed 'E_2.' The Errata leaf, of course, is regularly present, being part of the last signature. (I have seen one copy in which signature X is composed of two quarter-sheets, quired.)

STATES AND VARIANTS

Of two uncut copies, now WSL, in original bindings, one is bound in blue-gray boards, and the other sewed in a blue paper wrapper.

OTHER EDITIONS

Whitworth's *Account* was reprinted in the second volume of Dodsley's *Fugitive Pieces on Various Subjects,* 1761; Third edition, 1771.

COPIES

1. HW's copy; calf. SH Sale, iv.164, to Thorpe, 14/– (with Spence's *Parallel*); offered in Thorpe's General Catalogue, 1845, lot 2006, £1.5.0.

2. Presentation copy (1758) to Henry Zouch, inscribed by him on verso of title-page; calf. Sotheby's, 14 July 1937 (Lowther Castle Sale), lot 507, to Maggs for WSL, £4.

3. Richard Bull's copy, with his bookplate and MS notes. Red morocco, extra-illustrated. Sotheby's, 29 June 1926 (Burgh Sale), lot 161, to Quaritch, £28; Quaritch, March 1937, to WSL, £13.

AN
ACCOUNT
OF
RUSSIA

AS IT WAS

IN THE YEAR 1710.

BY

CHARLES LORD WHITWORTH.

PRINTED AT STRAWBERRY-HILL.
M DCC LVIII.

5.

4. Presentation copy to David Dalrymple, inscribed, 'Donum editoris. 1759. Dav. Dalrymple.' Red morocco. Sotheby's, 25 May 1937 (Newhailes Sale), lot 383, to Quaritch, £4.10.0; offered by Quaritch, Catalogue 546 (1938), lot 706, £6.6.0.

5. Inscribed on fly-leaf, 'From the library of Thomas Kirgate (Walpole's printer).' Green morocco (*ca.* 1814) by C. Smith. Offered in Longman's General Catalogue (July 1814, lot 1645), in a collection of 41 volumes, £350; Christie's, 1 March 1892 (Property of a gentleman), lot 118, to Nattali, 16/–; now in the Morgan Collection at Princeton.

6. SPENCE'S PARALLEL IN THE MANNER OF PLUTARCH. 1758.

Lowndes 7.

JPO, pp. 7, 8: '2 October 1758. Began to print Mr. Spence's parallel of Magliabechi and Mr. Hill. 11 November. It was finished. 700 copies printed. Sold by Dodsley, for the benefit of Mr. Hill. In the title-page, a head of Magliabechi from a medal, engraved and printed off at Strawberry Hill by Mr. Müntz. . . . [Newspaper cutting advertising 'This day was published, price sewed, 1*s.* 6*d.*' pasted in by HW and dated by him 'Feb. 2, 1759'] 600 of these being sold in a fortnight, a second edition was printed in London.'

'Short Notes,' p. xliii: '2 February 1759. I published Mr. Spence's Parallel of Magliabechi and Mr. Hill, a tailor of Buckingham; calculated to raise a little sum of money for the latter poor man. Six hundred copies were sold in a fortnight, and it was reprinted in London.'

Octavo in half-sheets; approximately 19.7 x 12.5 cm. uncut.

Signatures: A (2 quarter-sheets, quired); B–N⁴.

Pagination: [1] title-page, with verso blank; [3]–104 text. On p. 104 there is also a request for contributions to relieve Mr. Hill's distresses.

Other Editions

The collation of the second edition, printed in London in 1759, is the same as that of the first edition. Quaritch's Catalogue 546 (1938), lot 726, asserts that this second edition consists of the original SH sheets with a cancel title-page; but the whole volume was reprinted on different (though similar) paper.

The *Parallel* was reprinted in the second volume of Dodsley's *Fugitive Pieces on Various Subjects,* 1761; Third edition, 1771.

Copies

1. HW's copy; calf. SH Sale, iv.164, to Thorpe, 14/– (with Whitworth's *Ac-*

A PARALLEL;

In the manner of PLUTARCH:

Between a moſt celebrated

Man of FLORENCE;

And ONE, ſcarce ever heard of, in

E N G L A N D.

By the Reverend Mr. SPENCE.

--------*Parvis componere magna.*------VIRGIL.

PRINTED AT STRAWBERRY-HILL,
By WILLIAM ROBINSON;
And Sold by Meſſieurs DODSLEY, at Tully's-
Head, Pall-Mall ;
For the Benefit of Mr. HILL.
M DCC LVIII.

6.

count of Russia); offered in Thorpe's General Catalogue, 1845, lot 1693, £1.5.0. Perhaps the copy bought in 1871 by the Library of Congress.

2. William Cole's copy, with his MS notes. King, 20 May 1800 (Steevens Sale), lot 1146, to Waldron, £2.6.0; King and Lochée, 5 March 1807 (Waldron Sale), lot 387, £2.5.0.

3. Presentation copy to Thomas Pentycross (see, concerning Pentycross, No. 18 of Detached Pieces below); inscribed inside front cover, 'The Gift of the Honorable Horace Walpole to Thomas Pentycross.' Calf, rebacked; book-label of Fitz-James Watt. Pickering and Chatto, August 1927, to WSL, £4.15.0.

4. Richard Bull's copy, with his bookplate; red morocco, interleaved. Sotheby's, 29 June 1926 (Burgh Sale), lot 162, to Quaritch, £10; offered by Quaritch, Catalogue 405 (1927), lot 3063, £13.13.0; Quaritch, March 1937, to WSL, £5.10.0.

5. Calf, with medallion of Magliabechi (1633–1714) inlaid in cover; a letter inserted of Magliabechi to Vincenzio Giraldi, 1 December 1663; bookplate of Sir Edmund Antrobus (1818–1899). Anderson, 12 November 1919 (Avery Sale), lot 896, $60; Sotheby's, 7 July 1938 (Schiff Sale), lot 1243, to Maggs for WSL, £10.

6. Original wrapper, uncut; from the Geoffrey Madan Collection. Quaritch, August 1939, to WSL, £2.10.0.

7. LUCAN'S PHARSALIA. 1760.

Lowndes 8.

JPO, pp. 7–9: '11 December 1758. Began to print Lucan in quarto with Dr. Bentley's notes. . . . 7 November 1759. Lucan was postponed. But . . . soon after . . . resumed Lucan. . . . 4 October 1760. Finished Dr. Bentley's Lucan. . . . 8 January 1761. Published Lucan. 500 copies printed.'

HW to Henry Zouch, 27 November 1760: 'My Lucan is finished, but will not be published till after Christmas.'

HW to William Mason, 30 January 1780: 'Mr. Cumberland, full as ingenuous as he is ingenious, has barely mentioned [in the article on Dr. Bentley in *Biographia Britannica,* Second ed. 1780] the edition of his grandfather's Lucan, which, with singular veracity, he says that he, Mr. Cumberland, published. The truth of which veracity is exactly this: the MS of the notes, I believe, was in Cumberland's possession, who gave it to his uncle for the latter's benefit, and for the latter's benefit I printed it at Strawberry Hill, entirely at my own expense, found the paper, and as it was at least a year printing, and I had but one printer at a guinea a week, it cost me above fifty guineas. Mr. Bentley alone selected and revised the notes, and he and I revised the proof-sheets; and as Mr. Bentley did not choose, for reasons best known to himself, or to his nephew, to appear the editor, Cumberland's name was affixed to the dedication, which, with the gift of the MS, entitled him, I suppose, to the right of calling it *his* publication. . . . Did I ever tell you a ridiculous blunder that happened to our edition by Mr. Bentley's and my carelessness? He had chosen for the motto a note out of the MS, in which were these words, *Multa sunt condonanda in*

M. ANNAEI LUCANI

PHARSALIA

Cum Notis HUGONIS GROTII,

ET

RICHARDI BENTLEII.

Multa funt condonanda in opere poftumo.

In Librum iv. Nota 641.

STRAWBERRY-HILL, MDCCLX.

7. REDUCED. WIDTH OF ORIGINAL 14.3 cm.

opere postumo, so they stand in the title-page; but, alas! Mr. Bentley had rejected the note, and thus the motto quotes a note not to be found in the edition.'

An earlier form of the edition of Lucan was begun, in octavo. See JPO, p. 7: '14 July 1758. Began to print some sheets of Dr. Bentley's notes on Lucan. . . . 11 December 1758. Began to print Lucan in quarto with Dr. Bentley's notes. At first it was intended to print only the notes in octavo without the text.' A Preface to Lucan was in Kirgate's collection of Detached Pieces, owned in turn by Baker, Upcott, and George Smith; since this collection is now owned by Lord Waldegrave, it is to be hoped that a rejected preface, in octavo, can be recovered at Chewton after the war.

A letter, now WSL, from Bentley to Dodsley, 20 November 1758, discusses the printing arrangements: 'If we print the Lucan in quarto, it is to be considered that the notes are not complete, and it will be called an imperfect edition, to remedy which I think it will be advisable to revert to my Father's design of printing Grotius's notes along with his own. . . . No doubt you are the best judge of how many we are likely to dispose at home, but when I talked to Mr. Franklyn [probably Thomas Francklin, 1721–84, the classicist] upon our first scheme of printing it in octavo, he said he had no doubt but half the edition might be disposed of in Holland. I should be glad to know your opinion. Suppose therefore we were to print 500 at twelve shillings each, the Trade to sell again at sixteen shillings, I imagine the account would stand thus:

Paper	£ 84.
Advertisements	10.
500 books at 12*s.* each	300.
Profit to the bookseller	

If you agree to this proposal, we can begin upon it immediately.'

In selling the published edition, in quarto, Dodsley seems to have acted merely as HW's agent. An undated memorandum, *ca.* 1761, is printed in the JPO, p. 39: '350 Lucan received by Mr. Dodsley; 186 remain in hand; 51 delivered to Mr. Walpole; 33 delivered to Mr. Bentley and Mr. Cumberland; 80 sold.' Of the 186 copies left, I judge that some more were sold in the next few years, for on 1 January 1765 Bentley wrote a receipt (MS now at Harvard) to James Dodsley for £35, in full payment for 118 copies of Lucan. I assume that this payment represents the profit, since Alexander Chalmers in the *General Biographical Dictionary* (1812) says that Bentley received the profit from the sale of this edition, amounting to about £40.

Quarto; 29.5 x 23.5 cm. (no untrimmed copy examined).
Signatures: Half-sheet; one leaf; A–3T⁴; 3U (half-sheet); one leaf.
Pagination: Title-page, with verso blank; Dedication, with verso blank; 'Ad Lectorem' and vignette by Grignion, with verso blank; [1]–525 text; [526] blank.

[48]

HW's collection of 'Drawings by Mr. Bentley,' a folio scrapbook, now WSL, contains the originals of the two vignettes by Grignion.

This volume is perhaps the most distinguished piece of printing to come from the Press at Strawberry Hill.

STATES AND VARIANTS

There is a second setting of the three preliminary leaves, showing small differences on all three pages. (The easiest means of differentiating the two states is perhaps the spacing of the text in the notice to the reader: in the original the second comma in line 8 is directly under the 'B' of Burmannum; in the reprint this comma is under the first 'u' of Burmannum.) The second state probably represents Pratt's completion of imperfect copies in June 1762. (See Pratt's undated note, JPO, p. 86: 'May it please your Honor. There are ninety-one books, excepting titles and dedications, op. Lucani.') Pratt's memorandum indicates that, out of five hundred copies, less than one hundred should be in the second state. Since three copies, of more than a dozen examined, have this second state, I should judge that the ratio of one to four is approximately maintained.

OTHER EDITIONS

Another edition of Lucan with notes by Grotius and Bentley was printed at Glasgow in 1816.

COPIES

1. With a letter from Bentley (and note by HW) to Dodsley, concerning the arrangements for publication, laid in. Red morocco. Sir Robert Abdy, Bt., August 1938, to Maggs for WSL, £12.

2. Extra-illustrated with plates of Worlidge's *Antique Gems;* portraits of Bentley, Cumberland, and Worlidge. Green morocco. Sotheby's, 14 May 1903 (Baker-Wilbraham Sale), lot 271, to Maggs, £5.15.0; Brick Row, August 1939, to WSL, $60.

3. HW's copy; uncut, and folded ready for binding. Offered by T. Thorpe, General Catalogue for 1845, Part II, lot 3731, £5.5.0.

4. Contemporary red morocco. Bookplate of (probably) Benjamin Way (1740–1808); also signature and bookplate of Charles Harcourt Chambers, and bookplate of Augustine Birrell; from the Geoffrey Madan Collection. Quaritch, August 1939, to WSL, £3.

5. Presentation copy to William Cole; calf by Payne; Cole gave it to Lord Montfort (see Cole's letter to HW, 19 May 1763). Sotheby's, 20 December 1882 (Beckford Sale), lot 1927, to Bain, £5.17.6.

6. Richard Bull's copy, bound in vellum by Edwards, with fore-edge painting. Sotheby's, 28 June 1926 (Burgh Sale), lot 66, to Edwards, £99; offered by Tregaskis, Catalogue 925 (1927), lot 234, £265.

7. George Montagu's copy, with his bookplate and autograph, bound in calf, is now at Harvard in the Merritt Collection.

8. Presentation copy from Richard Cumberland to William Duer. Now at Cornell.

9. Syston Park copy, in contemporary red morocco. Sotheby's, 17 December 1884 (Thorold or Syston Park Sale), lot 1180; Sotheby's, 4 March 1893 (Buckley Sale), lot 2002; Sotheby's, 26 March 1917 (Miscellaneous Sale), lot 597, to Dobell, £2.12.0; offered by Edwards, Catalogue 405 (1920), lot 564, £8.10.0; American Art–Anderson, 3 December 1930 (Lehmann Sale), lot 911, $130.

10. With bookplate of Lord Shelburne (died 10 May 1761); contemporary calf, rebacked, with his arms on sides. Bookplate of John A. Spoor. Sotheby's, 14 March 1902 (Orford Sale), lot 130; Parke-Bernet, 5 May 1939 (Spoor Sale), lot 896, to Hill, $15; Hill, April 1940, to WSL, $20.

11. Bound (about 1814) in green morocco, probably by C. Smith; offered in Longman's General Catalogue (July 1814, lot 1645), in a collection of 41 volumes, £350; Christie's, 1 March 1892 (Property of a gentleman), lot 119, to Maggs, 10/–; now in the Morgan Collection at Princeton.

8. CATALOGUE OF PICTURES AND DRAWINGS IN THE HOLBEIN CHAMBER. 1760.

Lowndes 10.

JPO, p. 9: '20 October 1760. Printed a few catalogues of the pictures in the Holbein chamber.'

Octavo; approximately 19.5 x 12.5 cm. uncut.

Signatures: One half-sheet, unsigned.

Pagination: [1] title-page; [2] Note; [3]–8 text.

COPIES

This is HW's first printed catalogue of any part of his collections. With the exception of No. 9, it seems to be the rarest of the Strawberry Hill books; copies are recorded as follows:

1. British Museum, bound in red morocco with No. 9. It was in the bequest of C. M. Cracherode in 1799.

2. Harvard (Merritt Collection); unbound, without wrapper. This is perhaps the copy sold at Christie's, 1 March 1892, bound in a volume of Detached Pieces.

3. Princeton (Morgan Collection). This is perhaps Mrs. Damer's copy, sold at Hodgson's, 30 April 1902, to Sotheran, £28.10.0.

4. An uncut copy inscribed on title-page, 'Printed by Horace Walpole at Strawberry Hill and presented by Charles Walpole Esq. 1767.' Offered by Tre-

CATALOGUE

OF

PICTURES

AND

DRAWINGS

IN THE

Holbein-Chamber,

AT

STRAWBERRY-HILL.

M DCC LX,
8.

gaskis, Catalogue 673 (1909), lot 585, £10.10.0; bound in red morocco, probably by Mr. Spoor; Parke-Bernet, 4 May 1939 (Spoor Sale), lot 895, to Brick Row for WSL, $15.

5. [In Thomas Thorpe's *Catalogue of Manuscripts* (1844), lot 396, a manuscript catalogue was offered, with notes by HW, and printed title-page from the SH Press, for £1.1.0.]

9. CATALOGUES OF THE COLLECTIONS OF PICTURES OF THE DUKE OF DEVONSHIRE, GENERAL GUISE, AND THE LATE SIR PAUL METHUEN. 1760.

Lowndes 11.

JPO, p. 9: '1 November 1760. Printed some catalogues of the collections of pictures of the Duke of Devonshire, General Guise, and Sir Paul Methuen, taken from a new work called *London and its Environs,* in six volumes.'

HW to George Montagu, 24 October 1761: 'The catalogue of the Duke of Devonshire's collection is only in the six volumes of the Description of London. I did print about a dozen, and gave them all away so totally, that on searching, I find I had not reserved one for myself. When we are at leisure, I will reprint a few more, and you shall have one for your Speaker. [Montagu had asked for a copy to give to Speaker Ponsonby of the Irish House of Commons.]'

HW to George Montagu, 8 December 1761: 'Lord Farnham . . . brings you the list of the Duke of Devonshire's pictures.'

Unless HW sent a MS list to Montagu, this letter seems good evidence that he found another copy of the *Catalogue* after his letter of 24 October or that he reprinted the *Catalogue;* but it is curiously hard to find now. I have the following records of copies: (1) SH Sale, 1842, iv.168, bound in calf with the *Sleep-Walker, Hieroglyphic Tales,* Hoyland's *Poems,* and *An Account of the Giants;* (2) Sotheby's 1848 (Eyton Sale), unbound, notes by HW and a note on the fly-leaf by HW: 'This catalogue was printed from Dodsley's London and the Environs, solely for Mr. Walpole's own use. Farmer, his then printer, secretly printed another copy, and sold it.' (3) Sotheby's 1875, bound in half red morocco, with Spence's *Parallel* and Whitworth's *Account of Russia,* HW's copy, with MS notes. Two of these (or even all three) may be the same copy. The only copy now known to me is in the British Museum, where it is bound with No. 8 in red morocco; it was bequeathed to the BM by C. M. Cracherode in 1799. Mr. A. J. Watson has furnished the collation.

Octavo in half-sheets; approximately 17.2 x 10.6 cm. trimmed.

Printed on recto only, the first leaf of each gathering signed; signature marks A and C omitted.

Signatures: [A]–K⁴; L³.

Pagination: Title-page; [3]–44 text.

CATALOGUES

OF THE

COLLECTIONS

OF

PICTURES

OF

The Duke of DEVONSHIRE,

General GUISE,

AND THE LATE

Sir PAUL METHUEN.

STRAWBERRY-HILL,
MDCCLX.

9.

ANECDOTES

OF

PAINTING in ENGLAND;

With some Account of the principal Artists;

And incidental NOTES on other ARTS;

Collected by the late

Mr. GEORGE VERTUE;

And now digested and published from his original MSS.

By Mr. HORACE WALPOLE.

Multa renascentur quae jam cecidere.

VOL. I.

Printed by THOMAS FARMER at STRAWBERRY-HILL,
MDCCLXII.

10.

10. ANECDOTES OF PAINTING IN ENGLAND. 1762–71.

Lowndes 12.

Lowndes also has the following entry (No. 82) under 'Detached Pieces in Octavo et infra': 'Part of the intended Preface to the *Anecdotes of Painting,* pp. 8. Mr. Walpole originally designed to print the work in this form, but changed his plan and printed it in quarto.' The entry seems to have been copied directly from Martin (who took it, no doubt, from Baker's Catalogue of 1810), but it may be correct. In the Eyton Sale at Sotheby's in 1848, among the Detached Pieces, there is the following item: 'Part of intended Preface to *Anecdotes,* 8 pp.' Another copy (or more probably the same one) was sold at Sotheby's in 1875: 'Part of intended Preface with autograph corrections.' Beyond these references, I have no knowledge of this piece; it seems difficult to believe that HW printed the Preface before he undertook the text, but the records all agree in calling it an intended Preface. The JPO makes no mention of it.

Gray furnished some notes for the work; see letters of Gray to HW, 2 September 1760 and 28 October 1760. William Cole also helped. HW bought Vertue's MSS from his widow in 1758, for £100; they were sold in 1842 (London Sale, 21 June, lot 1110) for £26.10.0, and are now in the British Museum.

THE FIRST EDITION

'Short Notes,' pp. xliv–xlvi [Dates of composition]: '1 September 1759. I began to look over Mr. Vertue's MSS, which I bought last year for one hundred pounds, in order to compose the lives of English Painters. . . . 1 January 1760. I began the lives of English Artists, from Vertue's MSS. . . . 14 August. Finished the first volume of my *Anecdotes of Painting in England.* 5 September. Began the second volume. 23 October. Finished the second volume. 4 January 1761. Began the third volume. . . . 29 June. Resumed the third volume of my *Anecdotes of Painting,* which I had laid aside after the first day. . . . 22 August. Finished the third volume. . . . 2 August 1762. Began the *Catalogue of Engravers.* 10 October. Finished it.'

JPO, pp. 9–12 [Dates of printing and publication]: '24 November 1760. Began to print my *Anecdotes of Painting in England.* . . . 20 June 1761. Finished the first volume of my anecdotes on painting. 600 copies. 22 June. Began to print the second volume. 28 November. Finished the second volume. 600 copies printed. . . . 15 February 1762. The two first volumes were published. . . . 28 June. Began to print the third volume of my *Anecdotes.* . . . 8 October. Finished the third volume. 9 October. Began the volume of engravers. . . . 9 May 1763. Finished the volume of engravers. [6 February 1764. The third volume of *Anecdotes* and the *Catalogue of Engravers* were published.]'

HW to William Cole, 8 October 1763: 'The volume of engravers is printed off and has been for some time; I only wait for some of the plates.'

NUMBER PRINTED

In the JPO, HW says that 600 copies of the first volume were printed, and

600 of the second volume. Since no figures are given for the third volume and the *Catalogue of Engravers,* one must assume that the size of the edition was planned to match the first two volumes. The list in the *Description of SH* (*Anecdotes,* 3 volumes, and *Engravers,* 1 volume, 1761–600 copies) seems to confirm this figure. Nevertheless, I believe that HW added these figures later, and that they include the second edition, for the following reasons: (1) the MS of the JPO shows that HW did occasionally amplify his original entries, although it is difficult to be certain that he did so in this particular case; (2) 600 copies of the fourth volume were printed in 1771 (JPO, p. 19, quoted below); since sets of either edition normally include the fourth volume, I conclude that enough copies of this volume were printed to equal the number in the two editions combined; (3) neither the JPO nor the *Description of SH* has any indication of the size of the second edition; (4) HW's letter to Cole, 30 November 1780, seems to me explicit and accurate: 'The first edition of the *Anecdotes* was of three hundred, of the two first volumes; and of as many of the third volume and of the volume of *Engravers.* Then there was an edition of three hundred of all four. . . . Of my new fourth volume, I printed six hundred.'

DIFFICULTIES OF PUBLICATION

The demand for the first edition of the *Anecdotes* quickly forced the price up, and HW makes more than one embarrassed but amused reference to the premium they command. (William Bathoe in the Strand sold the *Anecdotes,* but whether as HW's agent or as publisher I do not know. Unfortunately, we have no records of HW's dealings with Bathoe, and I can give no explanation of the actions that caused HW's complaint to Dalrymple; nor do I know what Bell had done to cause the letter to Lady Ossory in 1789.) The stated price was thirty shillings for each two volumes, and for the second edition, containing a few additions, three guineas for the four volumes. But on 17 April 1763, before the publication of the later volumes, George Montagu wrote to HW: 'Do you know your *Anecdotes* are become very scarce, and that they sell for ten shillings more than they did?' A few of HW's comments follow:

HW to David Dalrymple, 23 February 1764: 'The London booksellers play me all manner of tricks. If I do not allow them ridiculous profit, they will do nothing to promote the sale; and when I do, they buy up the impression, and sell it at an advanced price before my face. This is the case of my two first volumes of *Anecdotes,* for which people have been made to pay half a guinea, and a guinea, more than the advertised price.'

HW to William Cole, 30 November 1780: 'Of my new fourth volume, I printed six hundred; but as they *can* be had, I believe not a third part is sold. This is a very plain lesson to me, that my editions sell for their curiosity, and not for any merit in them.'

HW to Lady Ossory, 6 February 1789: 'Bell is a rascal. . . . He cheated me literally of above £500 on my last volume of the *Anecdotes of Painting,* and now sets me at defiance because he found I would not arrest him.' [Bell was the publisher of Vol. IV in 1780.]

HW to Thomas Walpole, 26 June 1792: 'Some years [ago] Count Potocki brought me a message from the present King of Poland, . . . desiring my *Anecdotes of Painting*. It distressed me, as they were out of print; and I had only my own set. In short, I was reduced to buy a second-hand set (yet in good condition), and, though the original set sold for less than thirty shillings, I was forced to pay thirteen guineas from their scarcity.'

Quarto in half-sheets; approximately 24.5 x 19.5 cm. uncut.

Volume I, 1762. *Signatures:* Half-sheet, unsigned; A, B²; C¹; A–Aaa²; one leaf.

Pagination: [i] title-page, with verso blank; [iii–iv] Dedication; [v]–xiii Preface; [xiv] Contents; [1]–168 text; [169–182] Appendix; [183–188] Indexes; [189] Errata; [190] blank.

Y$_1$, a cancel in all copies, is printed on paper watermarked 'JW': this was probably prepared early in 1762, just before publication. (See below, STATES AND VARIANTS.) HW presumably made some alteration in his remarks on Holbein.

The Errata leaf was probably printed with C$_1$ of the Preface.

Volume II, 1762. *Signatures:* One leaf; A–Hhh².

Pagination: Title-page, with verso blank; [1]–158 text; [159–209] Appendix; [210–215] Indexes; [216] Errata.

The *Additional Lives* for Volume II, published in January 1768, may be bound at the end, with three new plates (see below).

Occasionally included at the end (but not an integral part) of Volume II is a leaf containing advertisements of Vertue's catalogues of pictures prepared for the press by HW and published by Bathoe: James I, Charles I, Duke of Buckingham, and his description of the works of Hollar.

Volume III, 1763. *Signatures:* One leaf; A–Ss²; Tt (one leaf).

Pagination: Title-page, with verso blank; [1]–155 text; [156–158] Appendix; [159–166] Indexes.

The *Additional Lives* for Volume III, published in January 1768, may be bound at the end, with one plate; or the *Additional Lives* for both volumes may be bound at the end of Volume III (see below).

Catalogue of Engravers, 1763. *Signatures:* Half-sheet, unsigned; A–Tt²; one leaf.

Pagination: Title-page and 'Direction to the Binder' printed on one forme of a half-sheet, with versos blank (the 'Direction to the Binder' may precede or follow the title-page, according to the folding); [1]–128 text; [1]–14 Life of Vertue; [1]–20 List of Vertue's works; [21–27] Indexes of Engravers; [28] blank.

Occasionally included at the end (but not an integral part) of the volume is the advertisement leaf mentioned under Volume II.

PLATES

HW employed several artists (Bannerman, Chambars, Grignion, Miller, Walker) to engrave the plates for the *Anecdotes,* but he was never wholly satisfied with their work. His letter to Dalrymple, 23 February 1764, may serve as an illustration of his attitude: 'I am disgusted with paying great sums for wretched performances. I am ashamed of the prints in my books, which were extravagantly paid for, and are wretchedly executed.'

Volume I. 16 plates, placed opposite (or near) the following pages: title-page, 31, 33, 47, 50, 61, 122, 126, 128, 137, 140, 143, 144, 148, 152, 163. One WSL copy contains a proof, on India paper before lettering, of the portrait of Sir Nathaniel Bacon, p. 163.

Volume II. 25 plates, opposite (or near) pp. 3, 4, 7, 12, 23, 31, 48, 55, 78, 87, 101, 104, 105, 106, 110, 113, 115, 117, 120, 127, 134, 135, 142, 155 (two). Three plates with the *Additional Lives* when these are bound at the end, though one (of Henry Gyles) is occasionally inserted opposite his name on p. 16.

Volume III. 37 plates, opposite (or near) pp. 4, 8, 11, 13, 15, 21, 24, 28, 29, 34, 42, 43, 55, 59, 61, 64, 67, 80, 82, 89, 99, 102, 103, 107, 116, 118, 122, 125, 127, 129, 130, 133, 134, 142 (two), 143, 151. One plate with the *Additional Lives* to Volume III when these are bound at the end, though it may be inserted opposite p. 126.

Catalogue of Engravers. 9 plates, opposite (or near) pp. 13, 42, 57, 71, 76, 87, 92, 100, and p. 1 of Life of Vertue.

STATES AND VARIANTS

JPO, p. 10: '2 December 1761. Thomas Farmer ran away for debt. I thought he had finished the two volumes [the first two of the *Anecdotes*], but he had left 19 sheets not printed off. Took one Pratt to finish the work. . . . 28 June 1762. Till this day Pratt had been employed in completing imperfect copies of former editions [i.e., the first two volumes of *Anecdotes,* the edition of Lucan, and *Fugitive Pieces*].'

HW to George Montagu, 23 December 1761: 'Just when I thought my book finished, my printer ran away, and had left eighteen sheets in the middle of the book untouched, having amused me with sending proofs.'

HW to George Montagu, 30 December 1761: 'My printer ran away and left a third part of the two first volumes unfinished.'

HW to William Cole, 20 May 1762: 'For the faults of impression, they were owing to the knavery of a printer, who when I had corrected the sheets, amused me with revised proofs, and never printed off the whole number, and then ran away. This accounts too for the difference of the ink in various sheets, and for some other blemishes.'

Since one-third of the two volumes is about eighteen or nineteen sheets, depending somewhat on how the preliminary leaves are counted, HW's various accounts of the matter agree tolerably well. It is less easy to determine which parts were left unfinished by Farmer, but some attempt at differentiation is possible. Since most of the first volume is printed on the same Gerrevink paper that had been used for earlier SH books (or similar paper—a slight variation begins at or near signature T), but only a small part of the second volume is on this paper, I believe that the parts printed by Pratt in the winter of 1761–62, to complete what Farmer had left imperfect, will be found generally among the sheets watermarked 'JW,' a paper that first appears in SH books at this time.

In most copies of Volume I, this paper marked 'JW' is used for signatures C, H, K, M, O, P, R, Aa, and Aaa, plus the cancel Y_1 and all the preliminaries—six and three-quarter sheets in all. But since nearly all the second volume is printed on this paper, it seems clear that Farmer had begun to print on the new stock before he departed. On other evidence, therefore, chiefly that of the irregular inking and offset, I suggest that some or all copies of the following signatures (in some cases only the inner forme) in Volume II were reprinted by Pratt: signatures D, F–S, Oo, Pp, Rr, 3E–3H, ten and one-half sheets in all. Hence, seventeen and one-quarter sheets can be identified with reasonable accuracy as those reprinted by Pratt (eighteen and one-quarter when the variants discussed in the next paragraph are included), and HW's accuracy is happily established.

At least two signatures, X and Ii, in the first volume exist in two states, representing two separate settings of type; presumably Farmer left these partly printed. Signature X (outer forme) in the first state has p. 84 numbered at the left of the page; in the second and commoner state, the page is numbered at the right. Signature X (inner forme) in the first state has p. 83 numbered at the right of the page; in the second and commoner state, the page is numbered at the left. I have seen one copy (George Montagu's, now wsl) with the outer forme in the first state, and one copy (Robert Long's, now wsl) with the inner forme in the first state; I suppose a copy may be found with the whole half-sheet in the first state. The first state of signature Ii (the outer and inner formes seem to be matched consistently in one state or the other) can be recognized by the erroneous running-title on p. 127, 'Painters in the reign of Queen Elizabeth.' The second state of this half-sheet, with the running-title corrected, seems to be slightly rarer than the first state. In each case, the question of priority between the two states is determined by the evidence of the paper and of the inking.

The first two volumes were also reprinted, from a new setting of type, on paper watermarked 'crown, post horn, L V G.' (The earlier paper is similar but has 'L V Gerrevink' instead of initials.) Since this watermark first appears in the *Catalogue of Engravers,* printed October 1762 to May 1763, I think it likely that Pratt was authorized to reprint the two volumes (perhaps to enable HW to answer requests for copies) at some time in the late winter of 1762–63, before the second edition had been decided upon in May 1763. (I take the entry in the JPO, 23 May 1763, 'Began to reprint the *Anecdotes of Painting,*' to refer to the second edition that was not published until 1767.) I think only a few copies were so reprinted, for I have seen only three, one at Harvard, one at the Clark Memorial Library, and one at Farmington, plus a few scattered sheets in a copy of the first edition owned by Mr. P. B. Daghlian; the authenticity of this reprinting is vindicated by the Harvard copy, which is filled with MS notes in HW's writing. This printing can be differentiated from the original by the watermark and by the following points: in the first volume, Y_1 is not a cancel; on p. 57 the signature, P, is under the 's' of was, whereas in the original the signature is under the 'w'; in the second volume, Campbell (line 20 on p. 153), correctly spelled in the original, is misspelled 'Campbel' in the reprint. But every page has been reset.

In Samuel Lysons's copy (now wsl), the final half-sheet, 3A, of the Index to Volume I has been supplied in different (probably Wilson) type on paper watermarked '1815.' Since the verso of Zz$_2$ shows off-set from the Errata leaf, I think it probable that the original signature 3A was accidentally omitted from this copy.

ADDITIONAL LIVES

The JPO contains no reference to the printing of the *Additional Lives*, and it is my belief that they were printed in London. The evidence for this belief, tenuous though it is, follows: (1) if HW's dates in the JPO for the closing and reopening of the Press are correct, the *Additional Lives*, to be printed at SH, must have been prepared in the summer of 1765, before HW closed the Press on 24 August; (2) if printed in the summer of 1765, the paper used would normally be the same as that used for the second edition of the *Anecdotes*; (3) the paper is entirely different from that used in the *Anecdotes*, but it is the same as the paper used in 1768, in the next productions of the Press, *Cornélie* and the *Mysterious Mother*, Nos. 13 and 14 below; (4) the *Additional Lives* were certainly printed before HW reopened the Press and reëmployed Kirgate in April 1768 (the date given by HW in the JPO), since they were noticed in the *Critical Review* for January 1768 and advertised (price: three shillings) in the *Daily Advertiser*, 5 December 1767; (5) since the second edition of the *Anecdotes* (published in June) was noticed in the *Critical Review* for July 1767, the later entry for the *Additional Lives* seems an indication that they had just been published; (6) Lowndes (under 'Walpole,' pp. 2819–20) records the *Additional Lives* as 'London 1771,' an entry that may come from correct knowledge of the place of printing despite the error in date; (7) in the life of George Jamesone a completely different monogram is used to reproduce the painter's 'GJ'—a change that one would hardly expect if both the *Additional Lives* and the second edition of the *Anecdotes* were printed at SH. (Perhaps this last point is the strongest evidence for a London printing.) It seems to me likely, therefore, that the *Additional Lives* were prepared in the summer or autumn of 1767, to satisfy purchasers of the first edition; possibly HW purchased enough paper then to supply his own press the next spring.*

The *Additional Lives to complete the first edition* contain three half-sheets, quarto, pp. 1–12 (with three plates), for Volume II; and

---

* I am not greatly perturbed by the advertisement saying that the *Additional Lives* are 'Printed at Strawberry Hill, and sold by Bathoe in the Strand,' since this imprint can be taken to refer to the *Anecdotes*: '*Additional Lives* to complete the first edition of the *Anecdotes of Painting*. By Horace Walpole. Printed at Strawberry Hill.' Some further evidence that the *Additional Lives* were printed at London and not at SH is contained in George Baker's letter to Francis Annesley, 14 March 1800 (now WSL), in which he tells of his attempts to find a copy of the *Additional Lives* for Annesley: 'I have likewise applied to Collins the other person who divided the remainder at Bathoe's Sale.' Bathoe died 2 October 1768; if the *Additional Lives* had been printed at SH, I think any remainder would have been returned to HW.

one-half sheet, quarto, pp. 1–4 (with one plate), for Volume III. They may be bound: (1) at the end of the proper volume; (2) both at the end of Volume III; (3) by themselves in a separate pamphlet.

THE SECOND EDITION

JPO, pp. 12–13: '23 May 1763. Began to reprint the *Anecdotes of Painting*. 22 September. Finished the first volume. . . . 30 January 1764. Began to reprint the second volume of the *Anecdotes*. . . . [HW to William Cole, 8 November 1764: 'It is printed to past the middle of the third volume.'] 18 March 1765. Took T. Kirgate, a new printer, and continued reprinting of the *Anecdotes*. 24 August. Finished everything, and discharged printer, as I was going abroad. 1767. Second edition of the *Anecdotes of Painting* published in June.'

This was the only Strawberry Hill work to be issued from the Press in an acknowledged second edition.

Quarto in half-sheets. The title-pages of all four volumes were printed last (as the watermarks show) and are dated 1765, when Kirgate completed the edition.

Volume I. *Signatures:* Half-sheet, unsigned; A, B²; half-sheet, with the two leaves signed C and A, respectively: B–Eee².

Pagination: [i] title-page; [ii] blank; [iii–iv] Dedication; [v]–xiii Preface; [xiv] Contents; [1]–182 text; [183–196] Appendix; [197–202] Indexes.

Volume II. *Signatures:* One leaf; A–Ooo².

Pagination: Title-page, with verso blank; [1]–182 text; [183–233] Appendix; [234–239] Indexes; [240] blank.

Volume III. *Signatures:* One leaf; A–Xx²; Yy¹.

Pagination: Title-page, with verso blank; [1]–167 text; [168–170] Appendix; [171–178] Indexes.

Catalogue of Engravers. Signatures: Half-sheet, unsigned; A–Yy²; one leaf.

Pagination: Title-page and 'Direction to the Binder' as in the first edition; [1]–140 text; [1]–14 Life of Vertue; [1]–20 List of his Works; [21–27] Indexes of Engravers; [28] blank.

PLATES TO THE SECOND EDITION

Since the plates of the first edition were used in this new edition, the page numbers on the plates are incorrect. Their position in the text is therefore likely to vary even more than in the first edition.

Volume I. 16 plates, placed opposite (or near) the following pages:

title-page, 34, 37, 50, 54, 64, 130, 134, 136, 147, 150, 154, 155, 160, 164, 177.

Volume II. 25 plates as in first edition, plus three from *Additional Lives*, opposite (or near) pp. 3, 5, 8, 13, 18 [Gyles from *Additional Lives*], 25, 34, 52, 60, 86, 96, 110 (or 127), 112, 113, 116 [Jamesone from *Additional Lives*], 120, 125, 129, 131, 133, 136, 141 [Petitot-Matthews-Torrentius from *Additional Lives*] (or 150), 144, 156, 158, 166, 179, 180.

Volume III. 37 plates as in first edition, plus one from *Additional Lives*, opposite (or near) pp. 4, 8, 11, 14, 15, 22, 25, 29, 30, 35, 44, 45, 58, 61, 64, 67, 71, 84, 86, 94, 106, 109, 110, 114, 126, 128, 132, 134, 136 [Sevonyans from *Additional Lives*], 137, 138, 140, 143, 146 (or 154), 154, 155, 159 (or 154), 164.

Catalogue of Engravers. 9 plates, opposite (or near) pp. 13, 44, 63, 79, 85, 96 (or 55), 101, 111, and p. 1 of Life of Vertue.

THE FOURTH VOLUME. 1771 (published 1780).

HW to William Cole, 20 August 1768: 'I intend next summer to set about the last volume of my *Anecdotes*, and to make still further additions to the former volumes.'

HW to William Cole, 15 November 1770: 'If you see Bannerman, I should be glad you would tell him that I am going to print the last volume of my *Painters*, and should like to employ him again for some of the heads.'

HW to William Cole, 20 November 1770: 'My last volume of *Painters* begins to be printed this week, but as the plates are not begun, I doubt it will be long before the whole is ready.'

HW to William Cole, 20 December 1770: 'The last volume of my *Anecdotes*, of which I was tired, is completed [i.e., written].'

JPO, pp. 16–19: '13 April 1771. Finished printing the last volume of the *Anecdotes of Painting*. . . . 9 October 1780. Published the last volume of the *Anecdotes of Painting*, which had been printed nine years, 600 copies.'

This final volume had been planned at least as early as 1763, since the Direction to the binder in the *Catalogue of Engravers* reads: 'This volume should not be lettered as the fourth, but as a detached piece; another volume of the Painters being intended, which will complete the work.' Opposite this, in one copy now WSL, is written in an unidentified hand: 'This completion Mr. Walpole told me, he had no design of publishing himself—perhaps he might leave it behind him. Truth, said he, which I am determined to adhere to, might offend the near relations and friends of some of the artists that are dead, and prejudice those that are living.'

HW wrote an apologetic preface in 1773, and in 1780 he substituted a new preface in which he included high praise of Reynolds and Gainsborough, Lady

Lucan and Lady Diana Beauclerk. But the delay was caused chiefly by his unwillingness to publish what he had said about Hogarth's Sigismunda (p. 78); when he finally published the volume in 1780, he not only made some additions to his catalogue of Hogarth's work, but also wrote a conciliatory letter to Mrs. Hogarth, 4 October 1780.

Quarto in half-sheets; the title-page is dated 1771, the first Advertisement 18 October 1773, and the published Advertisement 1 October 1780.

Signatures: One leaf; a¹; b²; c¹; one leaf; A–Pp²; Qq (in brackets)¹; Qq²; Rr¹.

Pagination: [i] title-page; [ii] blank; [iii]–iv Dedication; [v]–x Advertisement (1 October 1780); Contents, with verso blank; [1]–151 text; [152] Errata; [153–154] Appendix of additional Hogarth prints; [155–160] Indexes.

Plates: 22 plates, placed opposite (or near) pp. 3, 6, 15, 20, 27, 31, 34, 35, 38, 44, 48, 55, 64, 66, 69, 91, 95, 99, 100, 107, 108, 111.

The title-page was printed with the Contents leaf, and in a few copies the half-sheet is intact, preceding the Dedication.

Y_1 and Z (the half-sheet) are cancels, on paper that was first used in the second volume of *Miscellaneous Antiquities,* September 1772. Y_1 was perhaps cancelled to add to or alter the long footnote on p. 86. Signature Z contains the life of Liotard: HW's MS sketch (now Harvard) of this was in Mrs. Damer's collection, and because of the existence of this separate MS, I suggest that the whole life was perhaps recast after the volume had been printed. Furthermore, in HW's memoranda for his letter to Mme. du Deffand, 14 December 1772 [printed in the Yale edition, iii.439], are the names Aubrey de la Mottraye and Liotard; Hogarth's prints for La Mottraye's Travels are listed on p. 82, and the life of Liotard is on pp. 90–91. I therefore think it likely that in December of 1772 HW was considering corrections in this part of the volume, and that he made at least these two changes soon afterwards, or perhaps when he printed the Advertisement in October 1773. Additional proof of the cancellation of signature Z can be obtained from the record of a sale at Hodgson's, 22 October 1902: a copy of Volume IV was offered with three proof pages [perhaps the cancelled Advertisement?] loosely inserted, and a note by HW on the cover: 'Perfect all but the cuts and cancelled leaf of Liotard.'

I judge that Pp$_2$, containing the Errata, is also a cancel; in any case, Pp$_1$, Pp$_2$, and Rr$_1$ are single leaves. Probably Rr$_1$ was printed immediately after signature Qq; then the list of Errata was compiled, and printed on the blank verso of a new Pp$_2$.

Qq (in brackets), the Appendix of additional Hogarth prints, was imposed with c$_1$, as the watermarks show: this Appendix was therefore added in 1780, with the new Advertisement.

The Advertisement, on half-sheet b and leaf c$_1$, dated 1 October 1780, was printed just before the volume was published. The cancelled Advertisement, comprising leaf a$_2$ and half-sheet b (pp. [v]–ix, and [x] blank), was printed in October 1773. George Baker's copy of the cancelled Advertisement was sold at Sotheby's in 1825 and the same copy (probably) was in Eyton's collection, sold at Sotheby's in 1848. A different copy (probably) was in Mrs. Damer's collection, sold at Hodgson's in 1902, and is now WSL.

OTHER EDITIONS

Among numerous supplements to the *Anecdotes* are the following:

1. The *Works of Jonathan Richardson*, quarto, 1792, 'The whole intended as a supplement to the Anecdotes of Painters and Engravers.' The title-page, containing an imitation of the large SH fleuron, exists in two states: (a) with 'Printed at Strawberry-Hill' above the fleuron, and with 'B. White and Son' the first name in the imprint; (b) without 'Printed at Strawberry-Hill,' and White's name omitted in the imprint.

2. *An illustrative supplement to Pilkington's Dictionary of Painters principally taken from the Anecdotes of Painting*, quarto, 1805.

3. *Anecdotes of Painters*, by Edward Edwards, 'intended as a continuation to the *Anecdotes of Painting*,' quarto, 1808.

4. Mark Noble's *Continuation of the Catalogue of Engravers*, a small quarto MS of 250 pages, now WSL.

5. *Anecdotes of Painting*, 'Volume the Fifth and last,' edited from HW's 'Books of Materials' (now in Folger Library) by Frederick W. Hilles and Philip B. Daghlian, and published by the Yale University Press, in 1937.

Later editions of HW's work follow:

1. 'The third edition, with additions' [Volume IV, 'Second edition'], 5 volumes, octavo, 1782.

2. 'The fourth edition, with additions' [Volume IV, 'Third edition'; *Catalogue of Engravers*, 'Second edition'], 5 volumes, octavo, 1786.

3. *Catalogue of Engravers*, one volume, octavo, 1794.

[65]

4. 'The fourth edition,' 4 volumes, octavo, 1796. This edition, apparently never published, is known to me only from a title-page of Volume IV now at Farmington and a similar title-page of Volume II in the Widener Collection at Harvard. It bears the imprint of J. Dodsley below an imitation of the large SH fleuron; the price was to be three guineas. (For a discussion of the forged SH fleuron, see No. 14 below, the Dublin edition of *The Mysterious Mother*, 1791.)

5. Edited with additions by Rev. James Dallaway, 5 volumes, octavo, 1826–28. Reissued in 5 volumes, 1828. Proofs of the illustrations were also published on India paper.

6. Edited by Ralph N. Wornum, 3 volumes, octavo, 1849. This edition was reprinted in 1862, 1876, 1879, 1888, and one impression is undated.

A French translation was prepared, by M. Mariette, in 1765, but never published. The MS is in the Bibliothèque Nationale. (See Yale edition of HW's *Correspondence with Mme. du Deffand*, v.269.)

COPIES (First edition)

HW seems to have annotated numerous copies. Furthermore, many sets with association interest have been combined in different ways by dealers and collectors, so that they are difficult or impossible to identify. A selection, for which reasonable accuracy only can be hoped, is included here.

1. Extensive MS notes by HW throughout; eleven autograph letters to Benjamin Ibbot and a presentation copy of *Dorinda* (No. 25 below) bound in Volume IV; bookplate of Hon. R. Fitz-Gibbon. Blue morocco, 5 volumes. Evans, 21 March 1834 (Hanrott Sale), lot 1372, to Hon. R. Fitz-Gibbon, £15.15.0; Sotheby's, 31 January 1881 (Clare, i.e., Fitz-Gibbon, Sale), lot 143, to H. Stevens, £175; now in the Morgan Library, New York. The letters to Ibbot have now been removed from the volume.

2. With MS notes by HW; Volume II inscribed by HW, 'This copy is prepared for the second edition. H. Walpole'; Volume III imperfect. Offered by White, 1850, £3.13.6 (in a collection of 20 items).

3. HW's copy, with MS notes communicated by him; calf, 6 volumes (including second edition of *Catalogue of Engravers* 1765), with the *Additional Lives*. Bought at Gen. Walpole's Sale, Eccles, Norfolk, 1 October 1835; offered in H. G. Bohn's Catalogue, 1841, lot 22614, for £5.5.0 (five volumes); probably bound in red morocco by E. L. S. Benzon; Sotheby's, 25 May 1875 (Benzon Sale), lot 252, to Harvey, £25; offered by Maggs, Catalogue 168 (1899), lot 861, £9.9.0.

4. With HW's note in the first two volumes, 'My own copy'; extra-illustrated. SH Sale, iv.139, to Boone, £33.12.0; now Lord Derby, Knowsley Hall.

5. HW's copy, with his MS notes; calf, with his arms on sides, rebacked. Mr. Merritt thought this was not the original binding, but it does not seem suspicious to me. (The *Catalogue of Engravers* is from a different set, in a different binding, and without notes; HW's copy of *Engravers*, calf, with his arms on sides, is now Lord Waldegrave, Chewton Priory.) Owned by Olin L. Merriam,

but not included in the Merriam Sale at Anderson Galleries, 1920; Goodspeed, 1923, to Mr. Merritt; now in the Merritt Collection, Harvard. Volumes I and II of this set are the reprinted form described above.

6. Five volumes, uncut, with HW's MS corrections in Volumes III and V; Volume III inscribed by HW 'This volume ready for the new edition.' Hodgson's, 30 April 1902 (Damer Sale), lot 133, to Denham, £32. (The *Catalogue of Engravers* was second edition, 1765, with the cancelled Advertisement for Volume IV loosely inserted.) Offered by Denham, 1902, for £42; offered by Maggs, Catalogue 423 (1922), lot 2190, for £25. The *Catalogue of Engravers* only, with the cancelled Advertisement for Volume IV, was sold by Maggs, 1925, to WSL, £4.14.6.

7. Volume IV (1771) only, sewed, uncut; 3 proof pp. (perhaps the cancelled Advertisement) loosely inserted; inscribed by HW, 'Perfect all but the cuts and cancelled leaf of Liotard.' Hodgson's, 22 October 1902 (Supplement to Damer Sale), to Maggs, £1.11.0. Possibly this copy was combined with Volume III and the second edition of the *Catalogue of Engravers*, for the three volumes, wrappers uncut, with HW's MS corrections, are recorded at Sotheby's, 17 June 1903 (Miscellaneous Sale), lot 107, to Dobell, £3.

8. Garrick's copy, with his bookplate; Volumes I and II only. Calf. Sotheby's, 16 December 1908 (Sale of Garrick's library), lot 514, to Walford, 19/–.

9. Presentation copy to Lord Harcourt; now at Nuneham.

10. Sir John Fenn's copy: Volumes I and II inscribed by Fenn in 1771; Volume III and *Catalogue of Engravers* inscribed by Fenn, 'The gift of the Honorable Horace Walpole, the Author, to his obliged humble servant Jn. Fenn. 9 Feby. 1774'; Volume IV inscribed by Fenn in 1781; *Catalogue of Engravers* inscribed by HW, 'Mr. Fenn is desired to accept these volumes [i.e., Volume III and *Engravers*] from his obliged humble Servant. Horace Walpole.' The set includes *Life of Lord Herbert* 1764, *Historic Doubts* 1768, *Miscellaneous Antiquities* 1772, *Essay on Modern Gardening* 1785, *Postscript to Royal and Noble Authors* 1786, and some pieces not by HW. Seven volumes, original calf; bookplates of Sir John Fenn and of his nephew, William Frere (1775–1836). Sotheby's, 3 December 1907 (A. H. Frere Sale), lot 340, to Dobell, £6.17.6 (with Fenn's copy of Granger's *Biographical History*); offered by Tregaskis, Catalogue 642 (1908), lot 599, 30 guineas; T. Thorp, April 1934, to WSL, £35.

11. Samuel Lysons's copy, inscribed: 'Saml. Lysons 1787. The two first volumes given me by Walter Hill Esqr. the three last by the Author the Honble. Hor: Walpole.' (Probably) Evans, 5 June 1820 (Lysons Sale), lot 1706, £9.9.0; described as 5 volumes, russia. Rebound in half calf, and *Catalogue of Engravers* wanting; Edwards, 1927, to WSL, £2.10.0.

12. Bookplate of C. G. M. Gaskell; many MS notes transcribed from the third edition; *Catalogue of Engravers* inscribed (in a different hand), 'Given to me by the Honble. Mr. Hor. Walpole Aug. 16, 1781.' Contemporary red morocco, six volumes (including Richardson's *Works*, 1792). Hodgson's, 28 February 1924 (Milnes-Gaskell Sale), lot 96, to Spencer for WSL, £15.10.0.

13. Presentation copy to Lord Strafford, with proof plates and bookplate of John Maude of Moor House, Yorks. Five volumes bound in four, calf; sold at Sotheby's in 1882 for £8.5.0; Sotheby's, 19 July 1926 (Miscellaneous Sale), lot 52, to Parsons, £8.15.0; now Major-General Sir John Hanbury-Williams.

14. Four volumes; Sir Joshua Reynolds's copy, with a few MS notes in his autograph. Owned in 1938 by Mr. Joseph E. Widener of Philadelphia.

15. Five volumes, with bookplate of Thomas Barrett of Lee; original red morocco. Not in the Barrett Sale, 1859; Sotheby's, 2 March 1921 (Paul Butler Sale), lot 506, to Howell, £7.15.0; now in Clark Memorial Library. Volumes I and II of this set are the reprinted form described above.

16. *Catalogue of Engravers* only; extra-illustrated; MS corrections by HW. Most of the plates are wanting, but proofs of two (Hoefnagle, van Voerst) are inserted. Half morocco; Spencer, 1933, to wsl, £15.

Copies (Second edition)

1. Extra-illustrated, chiefly by Kirgate, and bound in green morocco about 1814 by C. Smith; a few MS notes; 5 volumes (first edition of Volume IV). Offered in Longman's General Catalogue (July 1814, lot 1645), in a collection of 41 volumes for £350; Christie's, 1 March 1892 (Property of a gentleman), lot 122, to Harvey, £48 (with Richardson's *Works* 1792 and Edwards's *Anecdotes* 1808); Spencer, 1936, to wsl, £9.

2. HW's copy, with his bookplate in the *Catalogue of Engravers;* MS notes by HW at iii.145, iv.111, and at end of *Catalogue of Engravers.* Calf, with the arms of Ralph Sneyd stamped on sides (the arms perhaps added by Sneyd in 1842). SH Sale, iv.140, to Thorpe for Ralph Sneyd, £8.18.6; Sotheby's, 1 December 1927 (Sneyd Sale), lot 898, £6.15.0; Halliday, 1929, to R. W. Chapman, £6.6.0; bought by wsl from Dr. Chapman, in a collection, July 1937.

3. A copy with MS notes by Kirgate. (Probably) King and Lochée, 4 December 1810 (Kirgate Sale), lot 386, to Denley, £11.10.0; now Mr. Robert Hartshorne, Highlands, New Jersey.

4. *Catalogue of Engravers* only; presentation copy to William Cole, with his MS notes and inscription at end, dated 'Febr. 1, 1768.' Calf, with Cole's bookplate. Hodgson's, 26 June 1930 (C. Whibley Sale), lot 485, to Pickering, £3.15.0.

11. LIFE OF EDWARD, LORD HERBERT OF CHERBURY. 1764.

Lowndes 13.

HW to Charles Lyttelton, 10 July 1763: 'I have got a most delectable work to print, which I had great difficulty to obtain, and which I must use while I can have it. It is the life of the famous Lord Herbert of Cherbury, written by himself—one of the most curious pieces my eyes ever beheld.'

The story of the acquisition of the MS, and of the way in which the owner, Lord Powis, was conciliated, is amusingly told in greater detail by HW in a let-

THE
LIFE
OF
EDWARD Lord HERBERT
Of *CHERBURY*,

Written by himfelf.

STRAWBERRY-HILL: Printed in the Year MDCCLXIV.

11.

ter to George Montagu, 16 July 1764 (printed in JPO, pp. 42–43). The present Lord Powis has part of the MS that HW printed; see an interesting article by Mr. R. L. Aaron in *Modern Language Review,* April 1941, pp. 184–94. While HW was editing the work, he called on Gray for help, and Gray responded with numerous notes; see his letters to HW, 12 and 19 September 1763.

'Short Notes,' p. xlvii: '1763. Beginning of September wrote the Dedication and Preface to Lord Herbert's *Life.*'

JPO, p. 12: '23 September 1763. Began to print Lord Herbert's life, 200 copies. 27 January 1764. Finished Lord Herbert's life.'

For some reason HW did not begin the distribution of the book until July, although he recorded the printing as finished in January. Perhaps the delay was caused by the preparation of the pedigree (see below). HW to William Cole, 16 July 1764: 'I want to know how I may send you Lord Herbert's *Life,* which I have just printed.' Gray to Wharton, 10 July 1764: 'There will be only 200 copies of Lord Herbert's *Life* printed. . . . If I happen to have two (which I do not expect) he [Stonehewer] shall have one of them.'

HW to William Pitt, 29 August 1764: 'There are but two hundred copies, of which only half are mine.'

HW to Dr. Birch, 3 September 1764: 'I have no hope that Lord Powis will permit any more to be printed. There were indeed so very few, and but half of those for my share, that I have not it in my power to offer you a copy, having disposed of my part.' Despite this refusal, however, HW wrote to Thomas Warton, 30 October 1764 (misdated 1767 in Mrs. Toynbee's and earlier editions of the *Letters*): 'You will permit me, I hope, . . . to send you a most singular book, of which I have lately been permitted to print two hundred copies (half only indeed for myself). It is the *Life* of the famous Lord Herbert of Cherbury.'

HW to George Montagu, 24 December 1764: 'If you lose it, I have not another to give you.'

HW to Lord Ossory, 23 June 1771: 'In two years one copy was sold at an auction for four guineas.'

Quarto in half-sheets; approximately 24.7 x 18.7 cm.

Signatures: One leaf; a–b²; A–Uu².

Pagination: Title-page, with verso blank; [i–ii] Dedication to Lord Powis; [iii–viii] HW's Advertisement; [1]–171 text; [172] blank. Folded portrait of Lord Herbert as frontispiece, and folded pedigree following the Advertisement.

THE PEDIGREE

HW worked hard at the pedigree of the Herbert family; in his letter to George Montagu, 16 July 1764, he wrote: 'Pray take notice of the pedigree, of which I am exceedingly proud.' Yet it contains numerous inaccuracies, of which HW must have become aware, for (according to T. F. Dibdin in the Second edition of his *Bibliomania*, 1811, p. 718) it was later suppressed by HW because of its inaccuracy. Martin (p. 498), when referring to the suppression of the pedigree, adds: 'In the collection of Sir Alexander Johnstone, who possesses Mrs. Damer's books, printed at this press, there are a considerable number of copies of this pedigree.' Two copies were with Mrs. Damer's books when they were sold at Hodgson's in 1902.

Although the pedigree is usually referred to as rare or suppressed, it is present in about two out of every three copies that are sold; HW seems, therefore, to have distributed a good many copies of the book in the summer of 1764 before he became aware of its faults (and presumably the hundred copies he sent to Lord Powis contained the pedigree). At least one attempt to supply the deficiency was made by a later collector or dealer, for at Sotheby's in 1875 (Benzon Sale) a copy was described as having the pedigree in facsimile, and a copy (perhaps the same one) in the Merritt Collection at Harvard has the pedigree in facsimile.

What seems to be an attempt by HW to correct the pedigree is known to me from one copy (Syston Park–Schiff copy, now WSL) in which the pedigree has been altered: this corrected state can be identified at once by the presence of an extra generation, 'Percy Herbert, Second Lord Powis, married Elizabeth Craven.' The corrections are all in the ancestry of Lord Powis's wife; perhaps HW's most embarrassing error was in this line of descent where he had confused her uncle with her grandfather.

But other errors remain even in this state of the pedigree, and I think it possible that HW finally decided to remove the plate from the copies still in his hands. It is perhaps worth recording that Thomas Warton's copy (presented 30 October 1764—see letter quoted above) contained the pedigree when it was sold at Sotheby's, 20 July 1906; it would be interesting to know whether this was of the corrected state.

OTHER EDITIONS

A second edition was printed by Dodsley (without the pedigree) in 1770. For his copy of this edition, Sir John Fenn prepared a MS pedigree, one that is rather more accurate than HW's. The third edition was published by Dodsley in 1778; the fourth edition in 1792. Since 1800 it has been reprinted many times, edited by Walter Scott, Sidney Lee, Henry Morley, and C. H. Herford, among others.

COPIES

1. Presentation copy to Henry Zouch, with his inscription dated 1764 on verso of title-page; letter from HW, sent with the book, bound in. Tree calf, with Lowther monogram on sides and bookplate of Lowther family. Sotheby's, 14 July 1937 (Lowther Castle Sale), lot 508, to Maggs for WSL, £17.12.0.

2. Bookplate of Lord Auckland; inscribed on fly-leaf, 'W. Eden, D. D. Vc. Beauchamp.' [William Eden, 1744–1814, was created Baron Auckland in 1789; Viscount Beauchamp was Francis Seymour-Conway, 1742–1822.] Red morocco. Parke-Bernet, 3 May 1939 (Spoor Sale), lot 898, to Brick Row for WSL, $15.

3. Syston Park bookplate; letter (formerly in the Morrison Collection) from Lord Herbert to Hugo Grotius inserted; green morocco by Derome le jeune, ca. 1782–83; blue morocco case by Rivière; described in Seymour De Ricci's Schiff Catalogue, I, 90–91. (Probably) Evans, 4 May 1829 (George Hibbert Sale), lot 3905, to Pickering, £2.8.0; probably bought by Thorold soon afterwards; Hodgson's, 13 July 1926 (Miscellaneous Sale), lot 115, to Pearson, £31; offered by Pearson for £300; Sotheby's, 6 December 1938 (Schiff Sale), lot 2203, to Maggs for WSL, £32.

4. William Cole's copy, with his MS notes. King, 20 May 1800 (Steevens Sale), lot 1148, to Waldron, £1.17.0; King and Lochée, 5 March 1807 (Waldron Sale), lot 396, £2.12.6.

5. HW's copy, extra-illustrated, with MS notes; calf. SH Sale, iv.143, to Strong, £7.17.6. Perhaps the same copy, calf, with bookplates of HW and George Ormerod, Sotheby's, 16 August 1875 (Ormerod Sale), lot 967; offered by Quaritch, Catalogue 282 (1909), £4.4.0. A different copy, green morocco, with HW's bookplate, was offered by W. M. Hill of Chicago, Catalogue 40 (1912), $40.

6. A copy presented to James West (1704?–1772), inscribed (probably by West), 'The gift of the Honorable Horatio Walpole Esq.' It was probably bought at West's Sale, 1773, by Lord Cowper, for £2.12.6; now at Panshanger in Hertfordshire. See R. W. Chapman in *Bodleian Quarterly Record*, vii (1933), 174.

7. With the autograph of T. Warton; calf. Sotheby's, 20 July 1906 (Property of a gentleman), lot 366, to Pickering, £2.2.0.

12. COUNTESS TEMPLE, POEMS. 1764.

Lowndes 14.

HW to the Countess Temple, [January 1764]: 'More than slight corrections in measure would destroy the chief merit of the poems, which consists in the beautiful ease and negligence of the composition.'

POEMS

BY

ANNA CHAMBER

COUNTESS TEMPLE.

STRAWBERRY-HILL:

PRINTED in the YEAR MDCCLXIV.

12. REDUCED SLIGHTLY. WIDTH OF ORIGINAL 12.9 CM.

HW to the Countess Temple, 28 January 1764: 'I can find no faults but in the longer metre. This I have tried to supply here and there by a syllable, or by little inversions. . . . Your Ladyship will probably improve on my hints, for your own genteel pen is much more likely to strike out proper alterations than I, who work by dull rules, can do. . . . I will hope for further orders as to the impression, which I trust will not be so rigidly confined as you first proposed.'

JPO, p. 13: '9 April 1764. Began to print some little poems of Lady Temple; 100 copies. 23 April. Finished them.'

The MS of HW's prefatory verses was owned (in 1937) by Sir John Murray.

Quarto in half-sheets; approximately 28 x 22 cm. uncut.
Signatures: [A]–H²; I¹.
Pagination: [1] title-page; [2] blank; [3]–4 Verses by HW, dated 26 January 1764; [5]–34 text.

Since I have never seen a blank I₂, I believe that the single leaf I₁ was imposed separately.

STATES AND VARIANTS

In some copies, signature F shows a slight readjustment of the page numbers. The two states can be differentiated as follows: in the first state, '21' is above 'goe' of goes, '22' is above 'pro' of prove, and '23' is above 'ace' of place; in the second and slightly more common state, '21' is above 'th' of health, '22' is above 'ove' of prove, and '23' is above 'lac' of place. It is an unimportant difference, but HW's copy, now WSL, contains what I have called the first state. Since copies presented in 1774 and 1781 (to William Cole and George Grenville) have the second state, I am willing to admit this as a later state. If the change was made at press, early copies containing signature F in the second state could very well have been assembled. It is possible, however, that this signature was reprinted a few days later, after a shortage had been discovered, but before the type had been distributed.

The whole volume was also reset and reprinted many years later, presumably by Kirgate, to produce an edition analogous to that of the thick-paper *Odes* (No. 1 above). This reprint is on wove paper, and the Verses to Lady Charles Spencer (Detached Pieces, No. 13 below) are on p. [35], leaf I₂. Other easily identified differences are the following: 'Finis' on p. 34 is 3.8 cm. in length, whereas in the original the word is in larger type and therefore spreads to about 4.9 cm.; on p. 22, line 9, the original has 'great procession,' but the reprint follows Lady Temple's original MS (now WSL) and MS corrections in several copies to read 'gay procession.'

The following points seem to me important evidence about this reprint: (1) The Verses to Lady Spencer were certainly not printed with the *Poems* originally, since they are on different paper, but they were probably printed only a few weeks later, and are often bound with the *Poems*. Thirty years later, therefore, Kirgate believed that they were intended to go with the *Poems* and printed them in that way, on the last leaf, but he also printed some separate copies to sell as Detached Pieces (see Detached Pieces, No. 13, below). (2) Cole's copy, inscribed 'Wm. Cole 1774,' now WSL, is of the original edition, as is a copy at Yale inscribed 'The Gift of the Honble. Horace Walpole. Jany. 20, 1783. J. B.' The reprint can therefore be assumed to be later than 1783. (3) All the presentation copies are of the original edition, whereas no copy on wove paper has any association record earlier than 1810; in this respect the two editions are strikingly similar to the two editions of Gray's *Odes*. (4) In the sale of Mrs. Damer's library at Hodgson's, 1902, there was a copy (resold at the Anderson Galleries in 1909 and 1911) with a MS note by HW on the wrapper: 'Lady Temple's Poems, the only copy I have left.' Furthermore, a second copy from Mrs. Damer's library is now at Harvard and is the original edition. (5) In February 1798 Kirgate sold a copy to George Baker for 10/6 (his receipted bill now WSL), and at Kirgate's sale in 1810 (Supplement, lots 99–103) twenty-nine copies were sold; the two of these copies that can be identified* are on wove paper. (6) Wove paper is uncommon before 1790, and is used in no other SH production except the Printer's Farewell (1797). (7) The blue-gray wrapper of one copy (now WSL) of the reprint is watermarked '1794.'

From the evidence available, only one conclusion seems to me possible: at some time late in the century, probably after 1794, Kirgate reprinted a considerable number of copies (perhaps fifty). It may be that the thick-paper copies of the *Odes* should be dated somewhat

---

* One copy is in Utterson's collection, now WSL; Utterson bought lot 101. A copy now at Harvard has '99' in the corner, and must therefore have been in lot 99, bought by Heber. The latter copy has several proof corrections, and is inscribed 'Corrected Copy' in Kirgate's hand; but this does not seem to mean that Kirgate wanted to call attention to his work as a spurious reprint. I take it to mean merely that Kirgate had collated this copy with the original as a kind of *ex post facto* proof-reading.

later than 1790, if the two reprints were prepared at about the same time; and since some of the Detached Pieces were apparently reprinted after HW's death, it is possible to believe that both Gray's *Odes* and Lady Temple's *Poems* were also reprinted then. On that hypothesis Kirgate could be accounted an honest printer as long as HW lived.

COPIES

1. HW's copy, with his bookplate and some MS identifications by him. Contemporary calf; Gray's *Odes,* Lady Temple's Verses to Lady Charles Spencer, and a MS poem by Lady Temple, bound in; bookplate of E. G. Hibbert. Offered by T. Thorpe, Catalogue for 1841, lot 2072, £4.14.6; re-offered in Thorpe's Catalogues for 1844 and 1845, £5.15.6; Sotheby's, 10 April 1902 (Hibbert Sale), lot 352, to Quaritch, £60; offered by Quaritch, Catalogue 328 (1914), lot 194, £70; offered by Quaritch, Catalogue 395 (1925), lot 451, £75; sold to Barnet J. Beyer in 1925; offered by Beyer for $1250; sold to Mr. Templeton Crocker; Crocker, December 1939, to WSL, in a collection.

2. With bookplates of HW, Mrs. Damer, and Geoffrey Madan; MS corrections on pp. 22, 33; calf. Geoffrey Madan, 1932, to WSL, £10.

3. Inscribed on title, probably by George Grenville, 'From the Honble. Mr. Walpole Nov. 12, 1781.' Now WSL (see Gray's *Odes,* No. 1 above, copy 7).

4. Inscribed on title-page, 'Wm. Cole 1774'; with Verses to Lady Charles Spencer bound at end. Bound with Cole's copy of Gray's *Odes* and other pieces, described above (No. 1, copy 2). Now WSL.

5. Inscribed on fly-leaf, 'The Gift of the Honble. Horace Walpole. Jany. 20, 1783. J.B.' Half calf; Leavitt, 22 January 1877 (Hastie Sale), lot 2292, to Joseph J. Cooke; bequest of Mr. Cooke, 1883, to Yale.

6. With bookplate of Mr. Horatio Walpole, and with Verses to Lady Charles Spencer at end. Boards, broken, uncut; Dulau, Catalogue 276 (1939), lot 534, to an unknown purchaser, £8.8.0.

7. With Garrick's Verses on Gray's *Odes,* Bentley's Verses to the Press, and the Verses to Lady Charles Spencer; all presumably presented, perhaps at different times, to Thomas Barrett of Lee. Original wrapper, uncut; Sotheby's, 12 July 1859 (Barrett Sale), lot 520, to Boone, 12/–; Anderson, 29 April 1921 (Arbury-Smith Sale), lot 310, $15; now Mr. Frederick Coykendall of New York.

8. Uncut copy; Hodgson's, 30 April 1902 (Damer Sale), lot 136, to Denham, £6.10.0; offered in Denham's Catalogue, 1902, £8.10.0; purchased by Mr. Percival Merritt in New York in 1908, and bound in calf by Sanford; now in the Merritt Collection, Harvard.

9. Original blue wrapper, uncut, with MS note by HW on wrapper, 'Lady Temple's Poems, the only copy I have left.' Hodgson's, 30 April 1902 (Damer Sale), lot 137, to Tregaskis, £6.12.6; offered by Tregaskis, Catalogue 581 (1905), lot 596, £10.10.0; re-offered in Catalogue 593 (1906); Anderson, 9 November

1909 (Buddy Sale), lot 566, $15; Anderson, 7 March 1911 (Xavier Sale), lot 799, to Scribner's, $33.

10–11. Of the twenty-nine copies in Kirgate's Sale in 1810 (Supplement, lots 99–103), two can now be traced; both are reprints, on wove paper. Lot 101, containing six copies, was sold to Utterson for 9/–; one of these is bound in the collection of miscellaneous pieces described above (Gray's *Odes,* copy 9). Lot 99, containing five copies, was sold to Heber for 6/6; one of these, marked '99' on the wrapper, has MS corrections by Kirgate; now at Harvard. Another copy on wove paper, bought by wsl from Quaritch in 1937 for £4.4.0, in original wrapper (watermarked '1794'), uncut, doubtless derives ultimately from Kirgate's collection.

13. HÉNAULT, CORNÉLIE. 1768.

Lowndes 15.

JPO, p. 13: '11 April 1768. Began to print 200 copies of the Président Hénault's Tragedy of *Cornélie.* 11 June. Finished *Cornélie.* Sent 150 copies to Paris.'

HW to George Montagu, 15 April 1768: 'My press is revived, and is printing a French play written by the old Président Hénault. . . . I print it to please the old man, as he was exceedingly kind to me at Paris; but I doubt whether he will live till it is finished. He is to have a hundred copies, and there are to be but an hundred more, of which you shall have one.'

That HW sent 150 copies is shown by Mme. du Deffand to HW, 6 July 1768: 'Votre *Cornélie* est arrivée. . . . Le Président en a eu quatre-vingts exemplaires et moi soixante-dix; nous nous accordons pour la distribution.'

Octavo in half-sheets; approximately 20 x 13 cm. uncut.
Signatures: A²; one leaf, variously placed; B–M⁴; N².
Pagination: Title-page, with verso blank; [iii]–iv Hénault's dedicatory letter to HW; [v] blank; [vi] Acteurs; [1]–91 text; [92] blank.

COPIES

1. HW's copy, with his bookplate and MS note; calf with his arms on sides. SH Sale, iv.163, to Thorpe, 14/–. Now in the Merritt Collection at Harvard.

2. William Cole's copy, presented 29 October 1774; MS note by HW pasted in at end, and copied by Cole on verso of title-page. Red morocco, with cipher of Charles Bedford on spine and his bookplate; a duplicate leaf of *Acteurs* is inserted from another copy. Gift of Cornelia Kennedy Sada to Harvard in 1894.

3. E. V. Utterson's copy, with his bookplate and a copy (in Kirgate's hand) of the inscription in Cole's copy. Calf, by C. Lewis. King and Lochée, 4 December 1810 (Kirgate Sale), to Utterson, £3.4.0 (in a volume of tracts); offered by Sotheran, in various Catalogues (1889–1893), for £1.18.0; now at the University of Texas.

CORNÉLIE,

VESTALE.

TRAGÉDIE.

IMPRIM·ÉE
à STRAWBERRY-HILL.
MDCCLXVIII.
13.

4. A copy with a MS note by HW on title-page, 'Par M. le Président Henault.' Now owned by Mrs. Scott-Murray, Heckfield Place, Basingstoke, Hants.

5. Bound with *The Mysterious Mother,* 1768. Red morocco, with cipher of Charles Bedford on spine and his bookplate. Sotheby's, 25 May 1875 (Benzon Sale), lot 246, to Pickering, £7.12.0; Sotheby's, 12 April 1902 (Hibbert Sale), lot 878, to Pickering, £12.5.0; Parke-Bernet, 4 May 1939 (Spoor Sale), lot 900, to Brick Row for WSL, $40. Both this copy and copy 2 above were sold with Bedford's books at Christie's, 1 March 1861.

6. Inscribed on fly-leaf, 'From Mr. Walpole (written by the President Henaut)'; book-label of Chateau du Tremblay. Green morocco (about 1814) by C. Smith; offered in Longman's General Catalogue (July 1814, lot 1645), in a collection of 41 volumes, £350; Christie's, 1 March 1892 (Property of a gentleman), lot 123, to Nattali, 11/–; Bangs, 29 October 1901 (Miscellaneous Sale), lot 575, $7.50; Anderson, 19 November 1908 (Poor Sale), lot 976, $31; Papantonio, July 1940, to WSL, $40.

14. THE MYSTERIOUS MOTHER. 1768.

Lowndes 16.

'Short Notes,' p. xlix: '15 March 1768. I finished a tragedy called *The Mysterious Mother,* which I had begun 25 December 1766; but I had laid it aside for several months. . . . The two last acts were not now as much finished as I intended.'

HW to George Montagu, 15 April 1768: 'I have finished my tragedy, but as you would not bear the subject, I will say no more of it, but that Mr. Chute, who is not easily pleased, likes it, and Gray, who is still more difficult, approves it. I am not yet intoxicated enough with it to think it would do for the stage, though I wish to see it acted.' There is some evidence that the play might have been produced, in 1778, had not Sir John Hawkins objected to the theme of incest: see W. L. Simmons, 'Sir John Hawkins,' in Ohio State University, *Abstracts of Dissertations,* 1939, pp. 123–124.

HW to H. S. Conway, 16 June 1768: 'Mr. Chute has found the subject of my tragedy, which I thought happened in Tillotson's time, in the Queen of Navarre's Tales.' (See HW's Postscript to the play, p. 3.)

JPO, p. 13: '14 June 1768. Began to print 50 copies of my tragedy of *The Mysterious Mother.* 6 August. Finished them.'

HW was extremely careful in distributing copies: I have records of copies given to Samuel Lysons, Thomas Barrett, Richard Bull, Charles Bedford, Michael Lort, and Lady Diana Beauclerk, only; and most (if not all) of these were presented many years later. No copy was in Mrs. Damer's collection sold at Hodgson's in 1902, and only one in Kirgate's Sale in 1810. George Baker, writing to Francis Annesley, 5 March 1800 (MS now WSL), says that he can procure a copy of *Cornélie* for three guineas, but 'I find *The Mysterious Mother* is not to be had.' In 1779, when HW finally allowed Sir Horace Mann to see a

THE

Mysterious Mother.

A

TRAGEDY.

By Mr. HORACE WALPOLE.

Sit mihi fas audita loqui! VIRGIL.

PRINTED AT STRAWBERRY-HILL:
MDCCLXVIII.

14.

copy, he required Mann to send it back (see Mann to HW, 25 September and 16 October 1779). See Richard Bull's copy below for a similar request. HW's reluctance to give copies away, of course, tended to encourage people to make MS copies of it: at least seven are extant. Three MS copies quote a note from Cole's copy of the first edition, but no record of Cole's copy has been found.

Lady Diana Beauclerk's copy is now at Princeton; her seven drawings to illustrate the play were given a special room at SH. See HW to William Mason, 18 February 1776: 'Lady Di Beauclerk has made seven large drawings in sut-water (her first attempt of the kind) for scenes of my *Mysterious Mother*. Oh, such drawings! . . .' See also HW to Sir Horace Mann, 31 October 1779: 'Lady Di Beauclerk has drawn seven scenes . . . that Salvator Rosa and Guido could not surpass their expression and beauty. I have built a closet on purpose for them here at Strawberry Hill. It is called the *Beauclerk closet;* and whoever sees the drawings, allows that no description comes up to their merit—and then, they do not shock and disgust, like their original, the tragedy.' They were sold in the SH Sale, 1842, xvii.32, to Col. D. Damer, M.P., for thirteen guineas, but their present owner is not known (1940).

Octavo in half-sheets; approximately 19.3 x 12.5 cm. trimmed.
Signatures: Quarter-sheet, unsigned; B–R^4; S^2.
Pagination: [i] title-page; [ii] blank; [iii] Errata; [iv] Persons; [1]–120 text; [1]–10 Postscript; one blank leaf, often missing.

STATES AND VARIANTS

The error on p. 34 (corrected by Errata) is corrected in MS, probably by HW, in many copies; the other correction, on p. 8, is less frequently made in MS.

The following MS note is inserted in a copy of George Baker's Catalogue (1810) at Harvard: 'A copy of the Mysterious Mother, on THICK paper, was sold for *nine pounds* at a sale at Evans's in April 1833. It would have justly excited the indignation of Horace Walpole to find his printer had taken off a copy of his own play, at his own press, superior to any printed for himself.' [Evans, 3 April 1833, lot 118, 'This copy on thick paper is supposed to be unique.' In the Jolley Sale at Sotheby's, 1844, another copy of the *Mysterious Mother* and also a copy of *Fugitive Pieces* are advertised as on thick paper.] Since I have no other knowledge of such a reprint, I suspect this description to be an error; to say 'on thick paper' of a copy on good paper is as natural an error for a bookseller as to say 'large paper' of an untrimmed copy—a frequent error. Kirgate had no copies for sale

[81]

in 1800, and only one copy was in his library when it was sold in 1810; he is therefore not to be suspected of any reprint such as the thick-paper *Odes*. The paper in *Cornélie* and *The Mysterious Mother* is the same in all copies that I have examined, a rather heavy paper with watermark 'crown, lily, L V G' and countermark 'W'. I am inclined to think that this unusually thick paper may have led to the unjust accusation of Kirgate.

OTHER EDITIONS

In 1781, HW arranged to have the tragedy reprinted and published by Dodsley, to forestall unauthorized reprints. After the announcement of the intended publication had prevented the spurious edition, HW decided not to publish his edition. The story is contained in the following letters.

HW to William Mason, 6 May 1781: 'My *Mysterious Mother* has wandered into the hands of booksellers, and has been advertised with my name without my knowledge. Like a legislator I have held out both rewards and punishments to prevent its appearance, but at last have been forced to advertise it myself; but unless the spurious edition appears, I shall keep it back till everybody is gone out of town, and then it will be forgotten by the winter. I intend, too, to abuse it myself in a short advertisement prefixed.'

HW to William Mason, 22 May 1781: 'My publication shall certainly not precede your arrival. I can scarce even call that delay a compliment, having already suspended its appearance. In short, my advertisement prevented the spurious editions, and I flatter myself I am forgotten; at least I have gained time, and at worst will publish in July or August, when all the world is dispersed. . . .'

HW to Conway, 28 May 1781: 'I was going to publish it in my own defence, as a spurious edition was advertised here, besides one in Ireland. My advertisement has overlaid the former for the present, and that tempts me to suppress mine, as I have a thorough aversion to its appearance. Still, I think I shall produce it in the dead of summer. . . . It is printed.'

HW to William Mason, 3 July 1781: 'The whole impression was printed off in a week after it was delivered to Dodsley, as I then thought I should scarce be able to get the start of the spurious edition. . . . It is said to be printing in Ireland.'

HW to Lord Charlemont, from Strawberry Hill, 23 November 1785: 'The new edition of the tragedy . . . shall be at your command as soon as I go to London, as I have not a copy here; but this edition has not the merit of the first impression—I mean, of being printed here, and of being a rarity. I was forced to make Dodsley print in haste a sufficient number for sale, to prevent a spurious edition that was advertised. My advertisement fortunately did stop the other impression, as I had hoped, and, having done so, I never published my own. . . . I omitted the postscript. . . .'

Although the book was never distributed by Dodsley, and so was not 'published,' it was printed, and HW began soon to present copies of this edition to his friends, in lieu of the SH edition. In addition, thirty-one copies of it were in Kirgate's Sale in 1810 and fourteen in the SH Sale in 1842.

In 1791, an edition was published in Dublin: it was undertaken without HW's approval, but after some grumbling he allowed it to be published. (See HW to Lord Charlemont, 17 February 1791. The title-page is a cancel; the original title-page, preserved in a copy at Columbia, is dated 1790.) Copies of this edition also exist with a close imitation of the large SH fleuron or vignette (used in Gray's *Odes*) overprinted on the title-page. This 'forged' fleuron is of more than passing interest: when it is carefully compared with Grignion's original [on the title-page of Gray's *Odes*, No. 1 above], the differences, in every part of the design, are immediately apparent; yet the imitation is sufficiently close to have deceived students and collectors for one hundred and fifty years. Presumably the imitation was prepared about 1792 by somebody in London: the same engraving appears on the title-page of Jonathan Richardson's *Works*, published by a group of booksellers in 1792, and on the title-page of J. Dodsley's new (projected?) edition of HW's *Anecdotes* in 1796. [Both these books are mentioned under *Anecdotes of Painting*, No. 10 above.] We know, therefore, that the plate was available in London, 1792–96, even if we do not yet know who added this engraving to some copies of the Dublin edition of the *Mysterious Mother*. (It may be well to point out that when Kirgate reprinted Gray's *Odes* on thick paper, he used Grignion's original engraving. Bewick's close copy of the smaller SH fleuron, engraved on wood late in the century and reproduced in Hugo's *Bewick Collector*, does not seem to have been used in any book; Mr. Rudolph Ruzicka, who called my attention to it, thinks the copy may have been prepared merely as a sample of workmanship.)

A reprint of the Dublin edition was published in London in 1791, and another edition was published in London in 1796.

COPIES

1. HW's copy, with a long note (signed 'HW') concerning the plot, and on an inserted leaf another long note (signed 'Orford') written about 1791; calf, with his arms on sides. SH Sale, iv.161, to Strong, £4.14.6; Sotheby's, 10 May 1843 (Lord Berwick Sale), lot 2762, to Thorpe, £4.12.0; Sotheby's, 22 May 1848 (Eyton Sale), lot 1453, to Lilly, £2.10.0; Sotheby's, 8 August 1868 (Slade Sale), lot 1050, to Harvey, £4; Sotheby's, 11 July 1901, lot 76, to Stevens and Brown, £16; in the collection of Mr. Clarence S. Bement, with his bookplate; now in the Morgan Library.

2. Inscribed by HW, 'With MSS alterations by Mr. Mason.' Red morocco; Hodgson's, 28 February 1924 (Milnes-Gaskell Sale), lot 97, to Maggs, £29.10.0; owned in 1938 by Mr. Samuel Courtauld of London.

3. Richard Bull's copy. Citron morocco, interleaved. Sotheby's, 29 June 1926 (Burgh Sale), lot 163, to Spencer, £39; now Mrs. James C. Dunn of Washington, D.C. An inserted note (1780?) by HW reads: 'Mr. Walpole has sent to Mr. Bull the only copy he has left of the play, but begs to have it returned . . .'

4. Presentation copy to Thomas Barrett of Lee; uncut. Sotheby's, 12 July 1859 (Barrett Sale), lot 508, to Lilly, £1.8.0; offered by Lilly, in 1863, for £5.5.0.

5. Lady Diana Beauclerk's copy, with her name on title-page. Old tree calf; Sotheby's, 23 July 1888 (Miscellaneous Sale), lot 1004. Bookplate of Junius S. Morgan, Jr.; now in the Morgan Collection at Princeton.

6. Samuel Lysons's copy, inscribed on fly-leaf: 'Given me by the author, Horace Earl of Orford. The MS corrections etc. are in his Ldship's handwriting'; signature of Lysons. Offered by J. Lilly, 1856, £5.5.0. Now bound in red morocco, with Lord Walpole's bookplate; at Wolterton Park, Norwich.

7. Michael Lort's copy, inscribed on fly-leaf: 'M. Lort. A gift of the Author.' Leigh and Sotheby, 20 April 1791 (Lort Sale), lot 3697, to Gough, £4.10.0; Sotheby's, 5 April 1810 (Gough Sale), lot 3883, to Bindley, £1.17.0; Evans, 5 August 1820 (Bindley Sale), lot 865, £1.10.0, to George Hibbert; Evans, 16 March 1829 (Hibbert Sale), lot 8354, £2.3.0. Bound soon afterwards in red morocco, by C. Lewis, with Fitz-Gibbon (Earl of Clare) crest on sides; Sotheby's, 31 January 1881 (Clare Sale), lot 108, to Pearson, £6; Sotheby's, 4 June 1896 (Crampon Sale), lot 473, to Pickering, £2.2.0; offered by Pickering and Chatto, Undated Catalogue (about 1900?), lot 3653, £6.6.0; Sotheby's, 7 May 1904 (Ford Sale), to Pickering, £1.10.0; Samuel Marx, 19 October 1932 (Andreini Sale), lot 1070, to Brick Row, $30; Brick Row, 1933, to WSL (with two letters by HW), $100.

8. Presentation copy, with autograph letter of HW, written in third person, bound in. Blue morocco. Offered by Quaritch, Catalogue 328 (1914), lot 196, for £10.10.0.

9. Bound, probably about 1790, in yellow morocco by Roger Payne; bookplate of Robert Hoe. Sotheby's, 20 December 1823 (Brockett Sale), lot 2943, to Thorpe, £3.6.0; Evans, 20 March 1834 (Hanrott Sale), lot 1024; Sotheby's, 26 March 1868 (Windus Sale), lot 990, to Pickering, £5.15.0; Anderson, 5 May

1911 (Hoe Sale), lot 3406, $600; now in the Huntington Library. Another Hoe copy, in blue morocco by Clarke and Bedford, is now at Harvard.

Of the numerous presentation copies of the London edition of 1781, four may be of special interest.

1. Inscribed on the fly-leaf: 'This book was presented by the Author to Richd. Brinsley Sheridan, as the present proprietor of it was informed, by the Honble. Douglas Kinnaird. The marginal Notes, etc., are in the handwriting of Sheridan.' The notes, in pencil, are numerous, often pointing out sources. Another MS note reads: 'J. Knight—purchas'd at a Chandler's Shop in the Village of Fetcham in Surrey, where, with many other Books, it had been deposited by Richd. Brinsley Sheridan, as a Security for necessaries furnish'd to that unfortunate Gentleman, whilst he resided at Randalls Park, Leatherhead, and the Rectory at Fetcham. . . .' Also inscribed on fly-leaf: 'Leonard Brickell, M. D. Chichester 1867.' Contemporary russia; half-title wanting. Sotheby's, 21 March 1902 (Miscellaneous Sale), lot 1216, to Hatchard, £6; Parke-Bernet, 4 May 1939 (Spoor Sale), lot 792, to Brick Row for WSL, $95.

2. Inscribed on half-title (by HW, according to the sale catalogue), 'From the Author, 1788.' Contemporary vellum; bookplate of Miss Mary Berry. Anderson, 19 November 1908 (Poor Sale), lot 1016, $33; Anderson, 27 April 1916 (Coggeshall Sale), lot 604, $65.

3. Presentation copy to Lord Harcourt; now at Nuneham.

4. Presentation copy to Sylvester Douglas [later Lord Glenbervie], with autograph letter from HW. Red morocco by Kalthoeber. Sotheby's, 27 July 1864 (Daniel Sale), lot 1723, to Harvey, £2.10.0; owned (in 1936) by Mrs. Scott-Murray, Heckfield Place, Hants.

15. HOYLAND'S POEMS, 1769.

Lowndes 17.

HW to William Mason, 5 April 1769: 'I enclose a short advertisement [preface] for Mr. Hoyland's poems. I mean by it to tempt people to a little more charity, and to soften to him, as much as I can, the humiliation of its being asked for him; if you approve it, it shall be prefixed to the edition.'

JPO, p. 13: '10 April 1769. Began to print Mr. Hoyland's poems, to be sold for his benefit. 300 copies. 24 April. Finished them.'

William Mason to HW, 8 May 1769: 'I have just heard from Mr. Stonehewer that the edition of poor Mr. Hoyland's Odes is finished. By the last account I had of him from York, I find his situation is very deplorable, though, when my correspondent wrote, the state of his mind was more sane than it had been.'

HW to William Mason, 11 May 1769: 'When I see Mr. Stonehewer, I will know if he would choose another edition of poor Mr. Hoyland's *Poems*. I doubt *not*, as when he sent for the last twenty, he said he believed he *could* get off them.'

Two of the five poems of this slender volume were reprinted from Hoyland's *Poems*, 1763.

POEMS

BY

THE REVEREND

Mr. HOYLAND.

PRINTED at STRAWBERRY-HILL:
MDCCLXIX.
15.

Octavo in half-sheets; approximately 20 x 12.5 cm. uncut.

Signatures: A²; B–C⁴; D².

Pagination: [i] title-page; [ii] blank; [iii]–iv HW's Advertisement; [1]–19 text; [20] blank.

OTHER EDITIONS

There is another edition, printed on similar paper, with precisely the same collation. It can be identified at once by the imprint on the title-page, which instead of 'Printed at Strawberry Hill: MDCCLXIX' contains only 'Printed in the Year 1769.' It also contains a printer's ornament on p. 7 instead of the parentheses that have been made into a design in the SH edition. I think that this may be an authorized edition, printed in London (or perhaps York) later in the year.

The two editions have always been known, I think, though seldom mentioned. But Sotheby's Catalogue of the Eyton Sale in 1848 specifies two editions.

COPIES

1. HW's copy was sold with other pieces, SH Sale, iv.168, to Thorpe; inasmuch as I have not seen it offered since 1842, I think it may have contained no identifying marks.

2. Presentation copy to Thomas Grenville; now in the Grenville Collection in the British Museum.

3. Four copies were in the Kirgate Sale in 1810; one (together with other small pieces), lot 357, was bought by Utterson for £3.4.0; a copy bound in calf brought five shillings at the Utterson Sale in 1852, lot 88; perhaps the same copy, rebound in half morocco, uncut, with Utterson's bookplate, was in the Geoffrey Madan Collection; it was sold by Quaritch, August 1939, to WSL, £5.

16. WORKS. 1770.

Lowndes 35.

HW to William Cole, 20 August 1768: 'I am going to reprint all my pieces together, and, to my shame be it spoken, find they will at least make two large quartos. You, I know, will be partial enough to give them a place on a shelf; but as I doubt many persons will not be so favorable, I only think of leaving the edition behind me.'

JPO, p. 13: '24 August 1768. Began to print an edition in quarto of all my works. . . . 24 April 1769. Finished [Hoyland's *Poems*]; and the printer returned to the edition of my works.'

'Short Notes,' pp. li–lii: '1773. Wrote *Nature will Prevail,* a moral entertainment in one act. . . . 1774. At the beginning of this year wrote my answer to Mr. Masters's Remarks in the *Archaeologia.*'

HW to John Pinkerton, 29 June 1787 [dated 29 August 1787 in Mrs. Toynbee's edition]: 'I have a mind to complete my account of *Royal and Noble Authors,* for which I have amassed a great number of additions, both of works and omitted writers. . . . I will, if you care to see it, trouble you with a sight of my intended supplement, to which, perhaps, you can contribute some additions, as I think you told me. I am in no haste, for I only intend to leave it behind me, and have actually put all the materials in order, except the article of Lord Elibank [p. 545 of Volume I].'

JPO, p. 20: '6 July 1787. Resumed printing my works in quarto, with additions to *Royal and Noble Authors.* Not continued.'

HW later told Nicol that he undertook the edition of his own works because he had learned that a bookseller had prepared an edition to be published after HW's death; this long letter, to George Nicol, 30 August 1792, is reprinted in the JPO, pp. 51–52.

HW's MS notes concerning the arrangement of the pieces in the *Works* are now in the Morgan Library. These comprise several reworkings of his plans at different dates; probably the earliest (*ca.* 1768–69) is as follows:

> My Works in Quarto.
>
> Vol. 1.
>
> As already printed.
>
> Vol. 2.
>
> Castle of Otranto.
> Account of the Patagonians.
> Historic Doubts on Richard 3d.
> Supplement to the above.
> Aedes Walpolianae.
>
> Vol. 3.
>
> Anecdotes of Painting and Catalogue of Engravers.
>
> Vol. 4.
>
> [A considerable list of political pieces and of miscellaneous prose and verse.]

Another list, written many years later, as the text shows, has the contents of the first volume (*Fugitive Pieces, The Mysterious Mother, Royal and Noble Authors*) in the upper right corner of the page, and then continues:

> Vol. 2d. (already printed).
>
> The Castle of Otranto.
> An Account of the Giants.
> Historic Doubts, &c.

Aedes Walpolianae.
Nature will prevail.

————

(to be added).

Letters on Tragedy.
Thoughts on Comedy.
Parody of Lord Chesterfield's Letters.
On Keeping the Sabbath.
Letter on Chatterton.
Character of Lady Hertford.
Preface to Description of Strawberry Hill.
Detached Thoughts. Strange Occurrences.
Letters.

Third Volume.

Anecdotes of Painting.
Defence of General Conway.
Detection of a late Forgery.
Life of Mr. Baker.
Additional Verses, as by the list.

This list of verses is included, on another leaf of the Morgan MS, as well as an earlier list of prose and a list containing both prose and verse.

From these references and from the bibliographical evidence contained in the *Works,* it is possible to reconstruct the dates of printing with reasonable accuracy. Volume I through p. 528 was printed first, and then Volume II as planned in the MS first quoted, that is, pp. 1–287. Volume I was probably completed early in 1770, and the title-page (dated 1770) printed off. Kirgate, in his copy (now Clark Memorial Library) described below, marks the *Castle of Otranto, Historic Doubts,* and *Aedes Walpolianae* 'printed in 1771'; the second volume, as originally planned, was therefore completed in 1771. Next, in Volume II the *Reply to Dean Milles,* dated 28 August 1770, was probably printed soon afterwards, but this may have been done as late as 1774, with the reply to Mr. Masters. From the entries in 'Short Notes' (quoted above), it seems reasonable to assume that *Nature will Prevail* (pp. 289–304) was printed in 1773 or 1774, and the reply to Mr. Masters in 1774. The last part of Volume I, containing additions to the *Royal and Noble Authors* and the *Postscript* of 1786 (No. 33 below), was printed in 1787 (entries as late as the *Supplement* to Chesterfield's Letters, published in June 1787, are included.

Two volumes, quarto; approximately 30.7 x 24.5 cm. uncut.
Signatures: Vol. I. One leaf; B–3X⁴; 3Y–4B⁴; 4C².
Vol. II. B–Qq⁴; *Ff–*Ii⁴.

[89]

FUGITIVE PIECES

IN

VERSE AND PROSE.

Pereunt et imputantur.

STRAWBERRY HILL:
PRINTED BY THOMAS KIRGATE, MDCCLXX.

16. TITLE-PAGE OF WORKS IN QUARTO, REDUCED. WIDTH
OF ORIGINAL 14.3 cm.

Pagination: Vol. I. Title-page, with verso blank; 1–525 text, includ-ing *Fugitive Pieces in Verse, The Mysterious Mother, Fugitive Pieces in Prose,* and the *Catalogue of Royal and Noble Authors;* [526–528] Index to *Royal and Noble Authors;* [529]–536 Pieces omitted; 537–555 Noble Authors omitted; 556–564 Postscript to *Royal and Noble Authors.* (The fly-title to the *Catalogue,* p. [243], has been cancelled in two copies that have the added title-pages dated 1787.)

Vol. II. [1]–304 text, including *Castle of Otranto, Account of the Giants, Historic Doubts* with Supplement, *Aedes Walpolianae,* and (pp. [289]–304) *Nature will Prevail;* [*221]–*244 Reply to Dean Milles; [*245]–*251 Reply to Mr. Masters; [*252] blank.

It is clear at once that signatures *Ff–*Ii should follow the Supple-ment to *Historic Doubts* at p. 220, between Ff_2 and Ff_3; they are so placed in Kirgate's copy. The title-page (*Fugitive Pieces*) is repeated in Volume II in Kirgate's copy.

The work makes an impressive showing with its sumptuous mar-gins. (The same large paper was used for the *Description of SH* in 1784.) The last half-sheet of Volume I is printed on a different, though similar, paper, thus furnishing additional evidence that this was the last part to be printed. HW purchased from William Caslon a new supply of 'English' type for the printing of the work (see the record in JPO, pp. 95–96), and the relatively clean, unbroken type increases the effectiveness of the pages.

STATES AND VARIANTS

On p. 525 of Volume I, the last page of the text of *Royal and Noble Authors* as it was originally printed, the word 'Finis' is placed at the bottom in one copy (now WSL); in the other three copies that I have examined (WSL, Clark, and Harvard) 'Finis' is replaced by 'End of Volume the First,' although this line has been marked for deletion in the WSL copy because the *Catalogue of Royal and Noble Authors* has been bound in two volumes. I think it likely that 'End of Volume the First' represents a later state: 'Finis' appears at the end of Volume II in the editions of 1758 and 1759, and it is likely that Kirgate merely followed his copy in setting up the page, and then altered the line because this was to be the first volume of a set. It is difficult to be certain, however, about such a small point.

The WSL copy mentioned above, bound in two volumes by Kirgate, has added title-pages for the *Catalogue of Royal and Noble Authors*, with imprint dated 1787. These are similar to the fly-title for the *Catalogue*, p. [243], with the addition of volume number and imprint, but the whole title-page was reset, presumably in 1787 or later. In the second volume of this set, pp. 425–564, Kirgate altered the volume number (on the first leaf of each sheet) by inserting a vertical stroke by hand, to make it read 'Vol. II'; similarly, 'End of Vol. I' has been inserted by hand on p. 424. At the end of the second volume of this special set, he inserted Signature 4C of the edition of 1798, containing the Appendix. One end-paper in this copy is dated 1807, and this is presumably about the time that Kirgate had it bound.

An interesting copy, inscribed on several fly-titles, 'Printed at Strawberry-Hill, by me, Thos. Kirgate, in 1771 ['1770' in first volume, on fly-title of *Mysterious Mother*],' is now in the William Andrews Clark Memorial Library. At the end of the *Catalogue of Royal and Noble Authors* are four extra leaves, pp. 549*–550* (after p. 550), containing an account of Robert Nugent, and pp. 565–570, containing the Appendix. I think that these leaves were copied, by Kirgate or a later owner, from the same leaves in the edition of 1798, for several reasons. (1) Page 550 in that edition completes the account of Irish peers with Lord Clive, so that Lord Nugent can appropriately be inserted on an extra leaf preceding the account of Lady Luxborough on p. 551; but in the SH edition the account of Lord Barrington runs over to the middle of p. 551, and Lord Clive does not appear until p. 553. (2) The running-title on p. 550* is 'Appendix to' in error; this seems a likely error if it was being reprinted hastily with the three leaves of the Appendix from another edition, but in an original cancel such an error would be very unlikely. (3) The paper is smaller than that used in the rest of the book, and has the initials 'S L' (probably Lay). Lay was making paper in this period, but it is difficult to believe that this smaller paper would have been authorized by HW. (4) Typographical peculiarities show that these leaves were not printed at SH: *pursuivant* (p. 565) is printed with a short '*s*,' as if the compositor were more accustomed to that form; the numerals '1789' (p. 570) are modern, with no ascenders or descenders; the italic type on pp. 565 and 566 (unfortunately only a dozen words) is a rounded modern-face type much later than the Caslon italic used at SH; on p. 569 the misprints 'there' for 'their' and 'atchieved' for 'achieved' suggest hasty reprinting without careful correction of the proofs.

Nevertheless, it is not impossible that HW did print an Appendix before his death, and that Miss Berry copied it in 1798. In the SH Sale, iv.165, with the *Catalogue of Royal and Noble Authors* (1758) is a copy of the *Postscript* 'with additions to ditto, very scarce.' (It is possible, but I think unlikely, that this means merely additions to the *Catalogue of Royal and Noble Authors*, not to the *Postscript*.) The same copy (possibly) of the *Royal and Noble Authors* is recorded in Lowndes (Utterson Sale, 1859), described as having an 'enlarged Postscript.* I think that this copy, if it could be found, might contain the original from which Miss Berry printed the Appendix in the *Works* in 1798.

HW's failure to complete the edition of his works may be explained by a MS note in the Grenville copy (now British Museum) of *Historic Doubts:* 'This copy had belonged to Kirgate, Mr. Walpole's printer. Kirgate said that it was originally printed at SH; . . . but after the printing of this part, the whole bundle of the *Historic Doubts* was accidentally destroyed and Mr. Walpole abandoned the printing of the edition—this copy was however preserved by Kirgate, who considered it accordingly as rare and valuable.' At least one copy of the first volume was used as part of the first volume of the *Works* in 1798 (see copy 10 below), and additional copies of the first volume may lurk in other sets of the published *Works*. The watermark in the

* The entry in Lowndes (p. 2818, under *Royal and Noble Authors*) is puzzling: 'Utterson in 1859, with the Postscript, £1.12.0, and with an "enlarged Postscript," £3.4.0.' In the first place, I have no other record of an Utterson Sale in 1859; can the date be a misprint for 1852 or 1857? In 1852 a single copy of *Royal and Noble Authors*, sold for £1.12.0, is listed. But in 1857 an uncut copy with the Postscript, bound 3 volumes in 2 in half green morocco, sold for £3.4.0; the preceding item, Waller's *Poems*, sold for £1.12.0, according to the priced copy of the sale catalogue at Yale. Since £3.4.0 would be an extraordinarily high price for a good copy with the usual Postscript, it seems possible that the presence of the 'enlarged Postscript' was announced at the sale. In that case the record in Lowndes could be explained as follows: 1859 is a misprint for 1857; and the two adjacent prices in a marked catalogue have been misinterpreted to refer to two copies of *Royal and Noble Authors*.

SH edition (lily, Strasburg bend, L V G) differentiates it at once from the paper of the edition, including the copies on large paper, printed in 1798.

COPIES

The rarity of this incomplete work perhaps justifies a tentative census of copies at this time.

1. Harvard (Merritt Collection), Volumes I and II, uncut. This may have been the copy that Kirgate sold to Baker in 1798 for £2.12.6 (MS bill now WSL); Sotheby's, 8 June 1825 (Baker Sale), lot 786, to Cruden, 10/6; Cruden's collection was acquired by J. W. K. Eyton; Sotheby's, 22 May 1848 (Eyton Sale), lot 1476, 7/6.

2. Two volumes bound in three, with the title-pages of 1787 added, and with four extra leaves probably reprinted from the edition of 1798; inscriptions by Kirgate; bookplates of Sir Henry Hope Edwardes, O. L. Merriam, and W. A. Clark, Jr.; crimson morocco by F. Bedford. This may have been King and Lochée, 14 December 1810 (Kirgate Sale), lot 128, to Baker, 17/–; Sotheby's, 8 June 1825 (Baker Sale), lot 828, to Cruden, 10/6; Christie's, 23 May 1901 (Edwardes Sale), lot 601, to Maggs, £10; Anderson, 12 June 1920 (Merriam Sale), lot 669, to G. D. Smith for W. A. Clark, Jr., $120. It is now in the Clark Memorial Library at Los Angeles.

3. *Catalogue of Royal and Noble Authors* only; bound in two volumes by Kirgate, and illustrated by Harding's *Portraits* (1803); half russia; armorial book-stamp of Blake family. This was almost certainly King and Lochée, 4 December 1810 (Kirgate Sale), lot 419, to Denley, £4.10.0; offered by Elkin Mathews, Catalogue 19 (1928), lot 223, £150; Elkin Mathews, June 1928, to WSL, £120.

4. *Catalogue of Royal and Noble Authors* only; in two volumes. This was lot 418 in Kirgate's Sale, bought by Bindley, £1.13.0; Evans, 5 August 1820 (Bindley Sale), lot 839, to Taylor, 9/6. I have no later record of this copy.

5. *Catalogue of Royal and Noble Authors* only. This was lot 127 in the Supplement to Kirgate's Sale (14 December), bought by Alexander for three shillings. I have no later record of this copy.

6. Volume I only (to p. 528), uncut; now bound in half red morocco. This may have been lot 400 in Kirgate's Sale, to Unwin, £1; it was purchased by WSL in December 1939 with the Gaskill Collection.

7. Volume I, pp. 245–528 only; sewed, uncut. Hodgson's, 30 April 1902 (Damer Sale), lot 158, to Tregaskis, 18/–; offered by Tregaskis, 1902–1905, for £2.2.0; Anderson, 9 November 1909 (Buddy Sale), lot 570, $30; Anderson, 25 May 1911 (Bishop Sale), lot 482, $17.50.

8. Two volumes, but lacking *Royal and Noble Authors;* bookplates of E. V. Utterson and Lord Carlingford. Evans, 21 March 1834 (Hanrott Sale), lot 1371; Sotheby's, 27 March 1857 (Utterson Sale), lot 1787, £4; now owned by Lord Strachie.

9. *Historic Doubts* and additions only. From Kirgate; now in the Grenville Collection, British Museum.

10. Volume I, pp. 1–520 only. In a set of *Works,* 1798, now WSL.

11. One half-sheet (pp. 27–30 of Volume I). Bought by WSL at Sotheby's, 1932, with a Kirgate letter; sold by a descendant of Grosvenor Bedford.

12. Title-page only of *Royal and Noble Authors* (p. [243]). In a volume of Detached Pieces, now WSL, from the Holford Collection.

13. One leaf, Pp₁ of Volume II, with MS alterations by HW. Bound in Percy Morris's set of HW's *Correspondence,* sold at Sotheby's, 19 December 1927, lot 366; now WSL.

17. REPLY TO DEAN MILLES. Written in 1770.

Lowndes 18.

Note by Kirgate in the Cruden-Eyton copy: 'Not more than six copies were printed in this manner at Strawberry Hill, at which place there is but one copy left.'

'Short Notes,' p. li: '1770. In the summer of this year wrote an answer to Dr. Milles's Remarks on my *Richard the Third.*'

HW to William Cole, 10 January 1771: 'Mr. Gray will show you my answer to Dr. Milles.' (This refers, I judge, to the MS of his answer.)

Although the *Reply* is dated 28 August 1770, it appears to have been printed (as an offprint of the quarto *Works*) somewhat later, perhaps as late as 1774.

Quarto; approximately 30.7 x 24.5 cm. uncut (Princeton copy).
Signatures: A–C⁴.
Pagination: [1]–24 text.

This was printed on the same paper, and from the same setting of type, as the text in the quarto *Works,* described above; the pagination and signatures are of course different.

COPIES

Of the copies printed, only the following partial census is possible.

1. HW's copy, with a long MS note in his hand on pp. 14–15, gray wrapper; this is probably the single copy that Kirgate said was still at SH; Hodgson's, 30 April 1902 (Damer Sale), lot 141, to Sotheran, £45; now in the Morgan Collection at Princeton.

2. A copy with MS note (quoted above) by Kirgate. Sotheby's, 8 June 1825 (Baker Sale), lot 812, to Cruden, 11/–; Cruden's collection was acquired by J. W. K. Eyton; Sotheby's, 22 May 1848 (Eyton Sale), lot 1457, to W. Stewart, 8/6. This copy has not been traced since 1848.

3. An uncut copy in original wrapper, with a similar MS note by Kirgate. King and Lochée, 14 December 1810 (Supplement to Kirgate Sale), lot 139, to

Baker, 7/–; Sotheby's, 8 June 1825 (Baker Sale), lot 815, in a collection of loose pieces, to Upcott, £3.5.0. This collection was sold at Evans's, 18 June 1846 (Upcott Sale), lot 1075; Sotheby's, 31 July 1867 (George Smith Sale), lot 7600, to Fortescue, £46; now at Chewton Priory (Lord Waldegrave).

18. MÉMOIRES DU COMTE DE GRAMMONT. 1772.

Lowndes 19.

HW to George Montagu, 22 July 1751: 'You must hear how busy I have been upon Grammont. You know I have long had a purpose of a new edition with notes and cuts.'

Mme. du Deffand made some corrections in the introduction, and asked HW to omit her name in the dedication: see her letters to him, 12 and 14 April 1772. She also suggested some corrections after she received her copy, in her letter of 25 January 1773.

JPO, p. 16: '29 April 1771. Began to print 100 copies of the *Mémoires de Grammont*. . . . May 1772. At the end of this month finished the *Mémoires de Grammont,* which had been delayed by various accidents.'

HW to William Cole, 8 January 1773: 'I want to send you . . . a Grammont, of which I have printed only an hundred copies, and which will be extremely scarce, for twenty-five copies [the list in the *Description of SH* says thirty] are gone to France.'

Quarto in half-sheets; approximately 22.5 x 18 cm. (trimmed).
Signatures: Half-sheet, unsigned; b–f²; A–4D²; one leaf.
Pagination: [i] title-page; [ii] blank; [iii] Dedication; [iv] Avis de l'Editeur; [v]–vi Avertissement; [vii]–xxi Epitre; [xxii]–xxiii Table; [xxiv] Errata; [1]–290 text; [291–293] Index; [294] blank.
    Three plates: the frontispiece, and opposite pp. vii and 92.

Three WSL copies contain HW's bookplate: a copy presented to the Duchess of Bedford, a copy presented to Richard Bull, and a copy with the bookplates of H. F. and R. C. Hornby. I think it possible that in this particular work HW inserted his bookplate to serve as a presentation inscription. HW's own copy, now WSL, has no bookplate, but has his arms on the sides.

Nine copies, a considerable remainder, were in Kirgate's Sale (1810).

OTHER EDITIONS

HW's edition was reprinted and published by Dodsley in 1783;

MEMOIRES

DU COMTE

DE

GRAMMONT,

Par Monſieur le Comte

ANTOINE HAMILTON.

NOUVELLE EDITION,

Augmentée de Notes & d'Eclaircissemens neceſſaires,

Par M. HORACE WALPOLE.

Des gens qui écrivent pour le Comte de Grammont, peuvent compter ſur quelque indulgence.

V. l'Epitre prelim. p. xviii.

IMPRIMÉE à STRAWBERRY-HILL.
M. DCC. LXXII.

18.

Mme. du Deffand, who had died in 1780, was named in the dedication of this edition. The work has of course been frequently reprinted, but not specifically as a reprint of the SH edition.

COPIES

1. HW's copy, with his MS notes, a pen-and-ink sketch, and additional prints. Calf, rebacked, with HW's arms on sides. SH Sale, iv.144, to Strong, £16.5.6; Sotheby's, 22 May 1848 (Eyton Sale), lot 1459, to Cunningham, £1.19.0; offered by Sotheran, December 1879, lot 382, for £12.12.0; Sotheby's, 20 December 1929 (Miscellaneous Sale), lot 870, to Tregaskis, £50; Tregaskis, August 1931, to WSL, £70.

2. Presentation copy in 1781 to Richard Bull, inscribed by him, with his bookplate and cipher; pages ruled in red, many MS notes, extra-illustrated; two letters from HW to Bull (now removed) were laid in. Red morocco; bookplate of HW on dedication leaf. Bought by Elkin Mathews from one of Bull's descendants in Ireland, 1928; Elkin Mathews, 1931, to WSL, £35.

3. With signature of Anne Seymour Damer on fly-leaf. Tree calf. Brick Row, 1934, to WSL, $26.

4. Presentation copy in 1772 to the Duchess of Bedford; bookplate of HW inside cover; unfinished proof of Powle's engraving of Mme. de Grammont inserted. Calf, rebacked. American Art Association, 10 April 1917 (Purdy Sale), lot 360, $17.50; G. D. Smith, 1926, to WSL, $80.

5. Presentation copy to James Bindley, with his bookplate. Contemporary calf. Evans, 21 January 1819 (Bindley Sale), lot 2115, to Cuthell, £2.12.6; Sotheby's, 20 December 1823 (Brockett Sale), lot 2975, to Rowntree, £4.14.6; Sotheby's, 24 July 1906 (Miscellaneous Sale), lot 447, to Quaritch, £10.10.0.

6. Presentation copy to Rachel Lloyd [housekeeper at Kensington Palace]. Sotheby's, 2 November 1915 (Crockett Sale), lot 1117, to Howard, £2.18.0.

7. With additional portraits of Nell Gwyn, Duchess of Cleveland, Miss Jennings, Miss Price, and Miss Stewart, inserted. (Probably) King and Lochée, 4 December 1810 (Kirgate Sale), lot 383, 'with some additional plates,' to Southgate, £1.11.6; bound (about 1814) in green morocco by C. Smith. Offered in Longman's General Catalogue (July 1814, lot 1645), in a collection of 41 volumes, £350; Christie's, 1 March 1892 (Property of a gentleman), lot 125, to Nattali, £2.10.0; now in the Morgan Collection at Princeton.

8. With numerous MS notes in an eighteenth-century hand, and inscription on fly-leaf, 'This book cost me £5.5.0'; MS notes, in a later hand, transcribed from HW's copy of the edition of 1746. Bookplate of Arthur Galton, and a presentation inscription to him, signed by Lord and Lady Ancaster, dated Christmas, 1915. Morocco by Rivière. (Probably) Sotheby's, 4 February 1913 (Miscellaneous Sale), lot 437, to Young, £6; purchased by T. Thorp at the sale of the library of Mrs. Holbrooke, Bladon Castle, Burton-on-Trent; Thorp, 1939, to WSL, £12.12.0.

HW's copy of the edition printed at Paris, 1746, with his notes and MS index, was in the Phillipps Collection; sold at Sotheby's, 10 June 1899; Sotheby's, 13 May 1902 (Ford Sale), lot 291, to Denham, £53.

Of the edition of 1783, printed at London, a copy with the bookplate and signature of Thomas Walpole and the Conyers bookplate was bought by WSL from T. Thorp, 1938, for £1.10.0. Richard Bull's copy of this edition, enlarged to 4 volumes, folio, was sold at Sotheby's, 24 April 1934, to Seymour, for £63.

19. LETTERS OF EDWARD VI. 1772.

Lowndes 20.

HW to William Cole, 29 May 1771: '[I send] seven letters of Edward the Sixth to Barnaby Fitzpatrick. Lord Ossory, to whom they belong, has lent them to me to print, but to facilitate that, and to prevent their being rubbed or hurt by the printer, I must entreat your exactness to copy them, and return them with the copies.'

William Cole to HW, 16 June 1771: 'I herewith return your seven original letters of King Edward VI to Mr. Barnaby Fitzpatrick, together with my copies of them.' In addition to transcribing the letters, Cole added some notes.

HW to Lord Ossory, 23 June 1771: 'I have got your letters again, and the copies. . . . I must ask your Lordship in what manner you would have me print them; I mean, whether for publication, or a smaller number only to give away. I submit to you whether the latter is not the preferable way, for as there are so very few they will barely make a sixpenny pamphlet, and not being all new, people might not think them quite important enough for sale. On the contrary, a smaller number will keep them a curiosity, and yet be sufficient to preserve them. . . . You see I have learnt the mysteries of my trade.'

'Short Notes,' p. li: 'End of September [1771], wrote the Advertisement to the *Letters of King Edward the Sixth.*'

JPO, p. 17: '1 June 1772. Began to print 200 copies of the Letters of Edward VI to Barnaby Fitzpatrick; half for Lord Ossory, to whom the original letters belonged, half for myself. 13 June. Finished them.'

HW to William Cole, 17 June 1772: '*King Edward's Letters* are printed; shall I keep them for you, or send them, and how? I intend you four copies; shall you want more? Lord Ossory takes an hundred, and I have as many; but none will be sold.'

William Cole to HW, 22 June 1772: 'If it would not be impertinent in me after so bountiful a present, I would beg one for the present Vice-Chancellor, Dr. Browne.'

HW to William Cole, 28 June 1772: 'I have sent you six copies.'

HW to William Mason, 6 July 1772: 'I have printed *King Edward's Letters,* and will bring you a copy.'

The original MSS are now in the Royal Library at Windsor.

Quarto in half-sheets; approximately 24 x 19 cm., uncut.

COPIES

OF SEVEN

ORIGINAL LETTERS

FROM

KING EDWARD VI.

TO

BARNABY FITZ-PATRICK.

STRAWBERRY-HILL:

PRINTED IN THE YEAR M.DCC.LXXII.

19.

Signatures: Half-sheet, unsigned; b²; A–C²; D¹.

Pagination: Title-page, with verso blank; [iii]–viii Advertisement by HW; [1]–14 text.

STATES AND VARIANTS

One WSL copy, uncut in original wrapper, has '116' on the cover; this was therefore lot 116 in Kirgate's Sale (Supplement) in 1810, bought by Heber. This copy is on a somewhat cheaper paper, without watermark, whereas all other copies examined have a watermark 'crown, post horn, G R' and countermark 'J W.' Perhaps HW decided to print a few on cheaper paper; or it is possible that Kirgate, who owned seven copies when he died, was beginning as early as 1772 to lay up treasures for himself without informing his employer.

OTHER EDITIONS

The letters were reprinted from the originals in 1856, and again (in the Roxburghe Club's *Literary Remains of Edward VI*) in 1857. They were also printed, with HW's Advertisement, in the *Dublin University Magazine* for November 1854.

COPIES

1. HW's copy, with signature and MS notes; bound with *Miscellaneous Antiquities;* prints and drawings inserted; calf, with his arms on sides. SH Sale, iv.146, to Thorpe, £3.10.0; Sotheby's, 27 March 1857 (Utterson Sale), lot 1788, to Leyton, £3.10.0; now Lord Waldegrave, Chewton Priory.

2. Presentation copy, 29 June 1788, from Lord Ossory to Rev. J. Elderton, with presentation letter bound in; also a letter from HW to Elderton (removed by WSL); three portraits inserted. Calf. Hodgson's, 21 October 1937 (Markham Sale), lot 473, to Maggs for WSL, £11.

3. Richard Bull's copy, with his bookplate; red morocco, extra-illustrated. Sotheby's, 29 June 1926 (Burgh Sale), lot 218, to Pickering, £14.10.0; offered by Pickering and Chatto, Catalogue 240 (1927), lot 9620, for £21; Pickering and Chatto, 1932, to WSL, £14.10.0.

4. Presentation copy, probably to George Grenville; inscribed 'From the Honble. Mr. Walpole Nov. 12, 1781.' See Gray's *Odes* above, copy 7.

5. Extra-illustrated by 13 portraits of Edward VI and 2 of Edward Seymour; probably one of Kirgate's copies. Bound in green morocco (about 1814) by C. Smith. Offered in Longman's General Catalogue (July 1814, lot 1645), in a collection of 41 volumes, £350; Christie's, 1 March 1892 (Property of a gentleman), lot 126, to Nattali, £3.10.0; offered by Maggs, Catalogue 208 (1905), lot 883, for £2.12.6; from the Gaskill Collection, December 1939, to WSL.

MISCELLANEOUS
ANTIQUITIES;

O R,

A COLLECTION OF

CURIOUS PAPERS:

Either republifhed from SCARCE TRACTS, or now
firft printed from ORIGINAL MSS.

NUMBER I.

TO BE CONTINUED OCCASIONALLY.

Invenies illic et fefta domeftica vobis.
Sæpe tibi Pater eft, fæpe legendus Avus.

OVID. Faft. lib. **1.**

STRAWBERRY-HILL:
PRINTED BY THOMAS KIRGATE, M.DCC.LXXII.
20.

20. MISCELLANEOUS ANTIQUITIES, Nos. 1 and 2. 1772.

Lowndes 21.

HW to William Cole, 17 June 1772: 'I am out of materials for my press. I am thinking of printing some numbers of miscellaneous MSS from my own and Mr. Gray's collections. . . . Among Gray's are letters of Sir Thomas Wyatt the elder. I am sure you must have a thousand hints about him.'

'Short Notes,' p. li: '1772. In July wrote the *Life of Sir Thomas Wyatt*, No. 2 of my edition of *Miscellaneous Antiquities*.' Gray had made the transcript of Wyatt's papers: see Gray to HW, 2 September 1760. Cole also responded to HW's letter of 17 June 1772 by sending numerous useful notes: see his letter to HW, 22 June 1772.

JPO, p. 17: '22 June 1772. Began to print No. I of *Miscellaneous Antiquities*, 500 copies on commoner paper for sale, and 25 copies on writing paper for presents. Finished 28 June. July and August, nothing printed. 21 September. Began to print No. II of *Miscellaneous Antiquities*. 10 December. Finished it, after many interruptions from illness.'

HW to William Mason, 6 July 1772: 'I have . . . begun a kind of *Desiderata Curiosa*, and intend to publish it in numbers, as I get materials.'

HW to William Cole, 8 January 1773: 'Not being able to return to SH, where all my books and papers are, and my printer lying fallow, I want some short bits to print. Have you anything you wish printed? I can either print a few to amuse ourselves, or if very curious and not too dry, could make a third number of *Miscellaneous Antiquities*.'

HW to William Cole, 18 February 1773: 'The continuation of the *Miscellaneous Antiquities* is uncertain. I thought the affectation of loving veteran anecdotes was so vigorous, that I ventured to print 500 copies. 130 only are sold—I cannot afford to make the town perpetual presents, though I find people exceedingly eager to obtain them when I do: and if they will not buy them, it is a sign of such indifference, that I shall neither bestow my time or my cost to no purpose. All I desire is to pay the expenses, which I can afford much less than my idle moments.'

HW to William Mason, 2 March 1773: 'The *Miscellaneous Antiquities* have not sold above a fifth of them; so there will be no more.'

Perhaps both the shortage of materials and the disappointing sales of the first two numbers deterred HW from further ventures in this series.

Quarto in half-sheets; approximately 24 x 19.5 cm. uncut. Each number was priced at two shillings, and sold by Bell.

Signatures: No. I. [A]–N².

No. II. [A]–P²; Q¹.

Pagination: No. I. Title-page, with verso blank; [iii]–iv Advertisement by HW; [1]–48 text.

No. II. Title-page, with verso blank; [3]–54 text; 55–62 Appendix.

STATES AND VARIANTS

Most copies (500 in JPO) are on a thin, cheap paper with vertical chain-lines. These are the copies that HW has in mind when he complains of the slow sale. He did begin to use some copies for presents, but a good many were left on his hands: three copies in original wrappers were in Mrs. Damer's collection, sold in 1902; six copies were in Kirgate's Sale in 1810; and twelve parts were among the remainders in the SH Sale in 1842 (v.206).

The few copies on writing paper (25 in JPO) are to-day very rare; I have seen only one set of the two numbers (now WSL. In General Fitzwilliam's copy and in a presentation copy bound with Cole's copy of Gray's *Odes,* both now WSL, the first number only is on writing paper; the second number only is on writing paper in a set now in the Clark Memorial Library.) The paper in the first number is the same as that used in *Letters of Edward VI,* printed two weeks earlier; the paper in the second number is the same as that used in the *Description of SH,* the work that followed *Miscellaneous Antiquities.*

COPIES

1. HW's copy; see *Letters of Edward VI,* copy 1.

2. Proof sheets of both numbers, with MS corrections by HW and Kirgate. Offered by T. Thorpe, General Catalogue for 1845, lot 1942, for 12/–.

3. Presentation copy, probably to George Grenville; inscribed, 'From Mr. H. Walpole Jan. 11, 1782.' See Gray's *Odes* above, copy 7.

4. Original wrappers, uncut; formerly owned by Mrs. Erskine, a grandniece of Grosvenor Charles Bedford, from whom she presumably inherited these copies; Sotheby's, 15 November 1932 (Erskine Sale), lot 476 (with *Letters of Edward VI* and other pieces), to Maggs for WSL.

5. General Fitzwilliam's copy, with his bookplate (he died in 1789); some MS notes. The first number is on letter paper. With six other SH pieces; offered by Quaritch for £10.10.0 in 1909, 1914, and 1920; a copy of Gray's *Odes,* included in this volume in General Fitzwilliam's MS Catalogue in 1787, has since been removed. Contemporary calf, rebacked; from the Geoffrey Madan Collection; Quaritch, August 1939, to WSL, £8.

6. With inscription on title-page of each part, 'From the Hon. Mr. Walpole,' in an unidentified hand; MS note by HW on p. 6 of second number; the first number is on letter paper. Bound (about 1820) with William Cole's copy of the *Odes* and other pieces; see Gray's *Odes* above, copy 2.

7. Extra-illustrated (about 1795) with numerous plates; bound with *Letters of Edward VI*. Red morocco; bookplate of Edward Astley (probably the third son of Sir Philip Astley, died 1739), and an unidentified bookplate; name (Boyce?) partly erased from title-page; offered in Longman's Catalogue, 1813, for £18.18.0; Sotheby's, 20 December 1823 (Brockett Sale), lot 2977, to Rowntree, £15.10.0; (probably) offered by Sotheran, Catalogue 504, 1891, for £9.9.0; Spencer, 1925, to WSL, £40.

8. Original wrappers, uncut; both numbers are on writing paper. Bookplate of Holland House; possibly presented by HW to Henry Fox, 1st Baron Holland; offered by Tregaskis, December 1927, £10; Tregaskis, 1936, to WSL, £5.10.0.

21. DESCRIPTION OF THE VILLA.

Lowndes 22.

Since I have seen no copy of the shorter *Description*, I record it from Mr. Toynbee's notes in the JPO, p. 61. Lowndes dates this 1772, and Mr. Toynbee says it 'was printed apparently in 1774.' I find no reference to it in HW's letters, at least nothing that can be separated from the edition of 1774, except perhaps the following remark in a letter to William Cole, 30 November 1780: 'Now I have certainly printed but one edition for which the prints are designed.' Possibly by inference this means that he had printed an earlier edition for which the prints were not designed. But Cole did not so interpret it, for in his MS copy of HW's letter, a comma is inserted after the word 'edition.'

COPIES

Two copies are recorded, as follows:

1. In Lord Waldegrave's collection at Chewton Priory, a copy formerly owned by Lord Harcourt; on the fly-leaf is a note by Lord Harcourt, saying that this copy was given to him by Mrs. Damer in 1801.

2. In the Storer Collection at Eton College, inscribed in Kirgate's hand, 'Catalogue for Shewing the House. Little better than Waste Paper.' Another inscription in HW's hand reads, 'Very imperfect for many additions and alterations since this was printed.' (JPO, p. 61.) Despite a ticket bearing Mrs. Damer's name in Kirgate's hand, this copy was apparently never given to her; its auction record can be traced as follows:

King and Lochée, 4 December 1810 (Kirgate Sale), lot 410, to Baker, 10/–.
Sotheby's, 8 June 1825 (Baker Sale), lot 791, to Cruden, 3/–.
Sold privately by Mr. Cruden to J. W. K. Eyton.
Sotheby's, 22 May 1848 (Eyton Sale), lot 1464, to Lilly, 3/–.
Sotheby's, 7 May 1904 (Ford Sale), lot 643, to Sotheran, £3.5.0.

It is clear that this copy has been included among Storer's books only since 1904.

A

DESCRIPTION

OF THE

VILLA

OF

HORACE WALPOLE,

Youngeſt Son of Sir Robert Walpole Earl of Orford,

A T

Strawberry-Hill, near Twickenham.

With an INVENTORY of the

FURNITURE, PICTURES, CURIOSITIES, &c.

STRAWBERRY-HILL:
PRINTED by THOMAS KIRGATE, M.DCC.LXXIV.
22.

22. DESCRIPTION OF THE VILLA. 1774.

Lowndes 23.

HW to William Cole, 20 August 1768: 'When the round tower is finished [it was not finished until June 1771], I propose to draw up a description and catalogue of the whole house and collection.'

HW to Cole, 23 October 1771: 'After next summer, by which time my castle and collection will be complete . . . I propose to form the catalogue and description.'

JPO, p. 17: '5 July 1773. After interruption; began to print 100 copies of Description of Strawberry Hill. The printer hurt his hand, which made another long interruption.'

HW to William Mason, 29 July 1773: 'I am printing the Catalogue.'

HW to Mme du Deffand, 11 September 1773: 'Je viens de l'imprimer [i.e., Mme. de Sévigné's letter on pp. 93–94 of Description] dans un catalogue raisonné que j'ai fait de ma collection.'

JPO, p. 17: '1774. The Description of Strawberry Hill was finished this year. The printer was employed in making catalogues of my portrait-prints and other ways.'

HW to William Cole, 21 July 1774: 'I have finished the catalogue of my collection, but you shall never have it without fetching. [HW gave Cole one of the six copies on large paper when Cole was at SH, 29 October 1774.] . . . I propose in time to have plates of my house added to the catalogue, yet I cannot afford them unless by degrees. Engravers are grown so much dearer without my growing richer, that I must have patience.'

HW to the Earl of Hardwicke [ca. 1775–77]: 'I printed a very few [catalogues] as a sample, intending to have prints to it.'

The plates (27 in all) were prepared at intervals during the next few years, as HW's letters show. They were inserted by HW in some copies of the 1774 edition, and new impressions of them were included in the 1784 edition (No. 30 below).

HW to William Cole, 10 December 1775: 'My plates for Strawberry advance leisurely.' 30 November 1780: 'He [Mr. Gough] has learnt, I suppose, from my engravers, that I have had some views of Strawberry Hill engraved. . . . He says they are engraved for a second edition of my Catalogue. Now I have certainly printed but one edition for which the prints are designed. He says truly, that I printed but a few for use.' 19 December 1780: 'I intend next summer to set about completing my plan of the Catalogue and its prints.' 16 June 1781: 'I am now setting about the completion of my Aedes Strawberrianae. A painter [Edwards] is to come hither on Monday to make a drawing of the Tribune and finish T. Sandby's fine view of the Gallery, to which I could never get him to put the last hand. They will then be engraved with a few of the chimney pieces, which will complete the plates.'

HW to William Mason, 16 August 1781: 'I . . . have a painter [Edwards] making drawings for the description of my house and collection.'

Two floor plans at the end are dated 1781. The plates inserted in his own copy (now wSL) by HW are on the paper that was used for the Appendix, and hence like the Appendix they were probably printed in 1781; the last two plates, containing the architect's sketches of the offices erected in 1790, are on different paper, and were probably printed about 1790. One copy (now wSL) has a new impression of the plates, on paper watermarked 'J Whatman 1822.'

A complete set of proofs (27 plates) is in the British Museum (118.D.27).

Quarto in half-sheets; approximately 23.8 x 19 cm. uncut.
Signatures: Two leaves, not conjugate; B–Hh².
Pagination: Half-title with vignette, verso blank; title-page, with verso blank; [1]–119 text; [120] blank.

STATES AND VARIANTS

HW's copy, lacking the two preliminary leaves, formerly owned by Lord Carlingford and now wSL, contains many MS additions and HW has also inserted 'the prices of such pieces as I can recollect.' This copy has an earlier state of some leaves: (1) on p. 14, the last line begins with a new sentence, whereas in other copies the preceding line ends with a colon; (2) the inscription on p. 69 has been corrected in MS, whereas in other copies the type has been corrected and reset; (3) the last paragraph on p. 73 has been corrected and reset in other copies; (4) 'Jervas' on p. 79 has been corrected in MS, whereas in other copies the type has been corrected to 'Jarvis'; (5) on p. 93, 'Sévigné' is spelled with a grave accent over the final 'e,' whereas in other copies this has been corrected. It seems probable from these differences (and there may be more) that this copy is made up at least in part of revised proofs, from which these alterations were made before the hundred copies were printed.

In a copy in the Clark Memorial Library, 119 pages unbound, these leaves have been corrected, but leaf Z_1 (see next paragraph) survives in uncancelled state.

Leaf Z_1 is a cancel in all copies (including those on large paper) except the two copies described above. The original, preserved in those copies, shows that the cancellation was made to change the description (p. 85) of a portrait: 'Maria Skerret lady Walpole, whole length, and very fine; the attitude copied by Zincke from a picture of Annibal Caracci.' The revised description reads: 'A naked Venus, whole length, and very fine; copied by Zincke from a picture of Annibal

Caracci.' Kirgate, in a MS note in a copy of the *Description* of 1784, also explains that the naked Venus was a portrait of Maria Skerret, Sir Robert's mistress and later his wife.

Six copies only were printed on large paper, according to HW's list in the Appendix. HW's copy and the copy he presented to Cole are now (1940) owned by Lord Waldegrave. Mrs. Damer's copy, uncut, is now WSL. The Hoe copy was wrongly described as on large paper; it is now in the Huntington Library—unbound in sheets, but on the normal post paper.

APPENDIX AND ADDITIONS (included in most copies)

In writing to William Cole, 16 June 1781, HW says: 'I must add an appendix of curiosities purchased or acquired since the *Catalogue* was printed. This will be awkward, but I cannot afford to throw away an hundred copies.' Both the watermark and the dates in the text indicate that the Appendix was printed soon afterwards. It consists of Signatures Ii–Pp²; pp. [121]–145 Appendix; [146–147] List of the books printed at SH; [148] blank.

Thereafter two additional sections were printed; by their differing watermarks and by the dates in the text, these can be dated approximately as follows:

Additions since the Appendix, Qq², pp. [149]–152; summer of 1784.

More Additions, Rr² and Ss¹, pp. [153]–158; summer of 1786.

COPIES

1. HW's copy, with MS notes and insertions by HW and Kirgate; with the plates prepared in the next few years to illustrate the catalogue. Calf, with HW's arms on sides, and with his bookplate as Earl of Orford. SH Sale, iv.151, to Bohn for Beckford, £18.10.0; Sotheby's, 3 July 1883 (Beckford or Hamilton Palace Sale), lot 256, to Quaritch, for B. Currie, £29; bookplate of Laurence Currie; Maggs, 1933, to WSL (with Vertue's Harleian Collection), £200.

2. HW's copy, 116 pages only, with no half-title or title-page; HW's MS notes of 'the prices of such pieces as I can recollect' and his MS additions. Half-calf, uncut, with bookplate of Lord Carlingford. Sotheby's, 30 July 1920 (Miscellaneous Sale), lot 1097, to Sellar, £10; Quaritch, 1937, to WSL, £50.

3. HW's copy, with MS additions and notes, over 60 drawings at end; frontispiece (on vellum) with arms of Sir Robert Walpole and ancestry of Catherine Shorter. Red morocco, by Clarke and Bedford; with Avery bookplate. SH Sale, iv.152, to Thorpe, £11.0.6; offered in Thorpe's General Catalogue, 1844, lot

1799, £21; Anderson, 12 November 1919 (Avery Sale), lot 961, $375, to George D. Smith for the New York Public Library.

4. With MS notes by T. Kirgate (three copies were sold with Kirgate's library); now in the Murdock Collection at Harvard.

5. HW's copy, on large paper, boards. SH Sale, iv.153, to 'Money,' £5.5.0; now in Lord Waldegrave's Collection, Chewton Priory.

6. William Cole's copy, with his MS notes; presented 29 October 1774, when Cole visited HW at SH; large paper, uncut. Sotheby's, 12 July 1859 (Barrett Sale), lot 523, to Boone, £1.19.0; now in Lord Waldegrave's Collection, Chewton Priory. This copy caused some annoyance to HW by passing into the hands of a dealer after Cole's death; see HW to Lady Ossory, 15 September 1787.

7. Boards, rebacked, uncut; inscribed (probably by Mrs. Damer): 'Large paper to the small Edn. 1774'; Hodgson's, 30 April 1902 (Damer Sale), lot 147, to Denham, £8.17.6; Anderson, 17 April 1903 (Miscellaneous Sale), lot 561, $21; Parke-Bernet, 4 May 1939 (Spoor Sale), lot 904, to Brick Row for WSL, $7.50.

23. PICTURES, CURIOSITIES, &c. IN THE CABINET OF ENAMELS AND MINIATURES. [1773.]

Not in Lowndes.

The title (not reproduced) appears only on the blue-gray wrapper.

This pamphlet and No. 24, *Curiosities in the Glass Closet,* seem to have remained unrecorded until 1902, when the collection bequeathed to Mrs. Damer was sold at Hodgson's. HW never considered them to be separate pieces, apparently, and a careful examination indicates that they are in fact merely offprints (with some alterations) of certain pages of the *Description* of 1774. Perhaps copies were kept where they could be consulted by visitors.

Quarto in half-sheets; printed on the same paper that was used for the *Description.*

Four half-sheets and one leaf, without signatures; pp. 1–18.

The evidence that this is an offprint and not an earlier or a later edition follows. On pp. 1–7 and 16–18 the type is identical with pp. 78–84, 95–97 of the *Description;* one cross-reference on p. 5, to p. 75 of the *Description,* has been removed. The third item on p. 8, 'Maria Skerret lady Walpole' agrees with the uncancelled Z_1 (p. 85) of the *Description* and is printed from the same setting of type. After this item in the *Description* is a list of 'Other pictures and curiosities in the same room,' extending to the middle of p. 86; this list has of course been removed from the offprint, since it does not belong with the description of the Cabinet of Enamels. The rest of p. 8 is printed from the same setting of type as the uncancelled Z_1 (bottom of p. 86) of the *Description*, but the type of the cancel has been reset: this fact indicates that the offprints were prepared as soon as the corresponding parts of the *Description* had been printed, in the autumn of 1773, and that HW's decision to suppress Maria Skerret's name was made later, probably in the spring of 1774. Pages 9–15, despite some readjustments and differing page divisions, are printed from the same type as the *Description*. The long footnote in the *Description* (pp. 93–94), in which HW printed the supposed letter from Mme. de Sévigné, has been removed, so that the last three pages agree exactly with pp. 95–97 of the *Description*. Finally, two small textual points prove that this pamphlet follows the *Description* instead of preceding it: on p. 2 'Jarvis' and on p. 15 'Sévigné' (with an acute accent) agree with the corrected *Description*, whereas the proofs in the Carlingford copy read 'Jervas' and 'Sévignè,' respectively.

COPIES

The following copies, all in original wrappers and untrimmed, are recorded:

1. Hodgson's, 30 April 1902 (Damer Sale), lot 129, to Robson, £1.10.0; Sotheby's, 28 July 1933 (Mount-Stephen Sale), lot 619, to Maggs for WSL, £10 (with copy 2 and five other pieces).

2. Hodgson's, 30 April 1902 (Damer Sale), lot 130, to Tregaskis, £1.10.0; offered by Tregaskis, 1902–1905, for £3.3.0; Sotheby's, 28 July 1933 (Mount-Stephen Sale), lot 619, to Maggs for WSL. Presented by WSL to Seymour de Ricci; offered (probably the same copy) by Quaritch, Catalogue 530 (1937), lot 1070, for £4.

3. Purchased by WSL, December 1939, in the Gaskill Collection. Probably this is the copy that was sold at Anderson's, 9 November 1909 (Buddy Sale), lot 588, $9.50.

4. Harvard (Merritt Collection).

5. A copy (probably not one of the four listed above) offered by Edwards, Catalogue 330 (1913), lot 498, 10/–; original wrapper, uncut, with engraving of the Cabinet; bought by Lewis Buddy III.

24. CURIOSITIES IN THE GLASS CLOSET. [1773.]

Not in Lowndes.
The heading on the first page is repeated as a title on the blue-gray wrapper.
For the history of this pamphlet, see No. 23. This is likewise an offprint, from the same setting of type, of pp. 107–110 of the *Description*.

Quarto, one half-sheet, pp. 1–4; printed on the same paper that was used for the *Description*.

COPIES

The following copies are recorded:

1. Bound with Lord Harcourt's copy of the short *Description,* No. 21 above. Now Lord Waldegrave; see JPO, p. 61.

2. Purchased by WSL, December 1939, in the Gaskill Collection; in original wrapper, untrimmed. Probably this is the copy that was sold at Anderson's, 9 November 1909 (Buddy Sale), lot 586, $11.

3. Harvard (Merritt Collection); in original wrapper, untrimmed. Either this copy or copy 2 was sold at Hodgson's, 30 April 1902 (Mrs. Damer's Sale), lot 128, to Robson, £1.16.0.

25. DORINDA, A TOWN ECLOGUE. 1775.

Lowndes 26.

JPO, p. 18: 'June 1775. In this month printed 300 copies of Dorinda, a Town Eclogue, by the Honorable Richard Fitzpatrick, only brother of John Earl of Ossory; and the next week, a loose sheet, added to it, of Charles Fox's verses to Mrs. Crewe.' (For the verses to Mrs. Crewe, see the Detached Pieces, No. 28 below.)

HW to William Mason, 12 June 1775: 'I shall send you soon Fitzpatrick's *Town Eclogue,* from my own furnace. The verses are charmingly smooth and easy. . . . P. S. Here is the *Eclogue.*'

According to G. O. Trevelyan's *Early History of Charles James Fox* (Second ed., 1880, p. 326), Dorinda was Mrs. Crewe. The poem was probably written near the end of May, since HW wrote to Mason, 27 May 1775: 'I am to have a longer copy [he had just transcribed Charles Fox's Verses to Mrs. Crewe] of verses by Fitzpatrick, which I expect to like much, since he writes as easily as his friend, and is a more genuine poet.'

Quarto in half-sheets; approximately 24 x 19 cm. uncut.
Signatures: A–B².
Pagination: [1] title-page; [2] blank; [3]–8 text.

STATES AND VARIANTS

In the eighth line of p. 3, an 's,' omitted by the printer at the end of the word 'Summer,' has been added by hand in most copies. In only one copy have I seen the error corrected at press: this copy, now WSL, is trimmed to octavo size and bound in Percy Morris's extra-illustrated set of the *Letters to Lady Ossory.*

DORINDA,

A

TOWN ECLOGUE.

STRAWBERRY-HILL:
PRINTED BY THOMAS KIRGATE, M.DCC.LXXV.

25.

OTHER EDITIONS

A second edition was published by Ridley in 1775. *Dorinda* was also included in the first volume of the *New Foundling Hospital for Wit*, 1784.

COPIES

1. HW's copy, with his MS notes, bound in calf with other SH pamphlets; bookplates of E. V. Utterson and Lord Carlingford. SH Sale, iv.149, to Thorpe, £1.15.0; this is probably the copy sold at Sotheby's, 27 March 1857 (Utterson Sale), lot 1792, to Leyton, £4; now (1939) Lord Strachie, Sutton Court.

2. A copy inscribed 'From the Author'; now in the Morgan Library, inserted in the fourth volume of HW's copy of *Anecdotes of Painting*.

3. Richard Bull's copy, with his bookplate and MS notes; bound (about 1781) with three MS poems by Fitzpatrick, copied by Bull, and Bull's *Lines sent to Lady Miller's Vase*, 1781; red morocco, interleaved. Sotheby's, 29 June 1926 (Burgh Sale), lot 220, to Maggs for Huntington Library, £21.

4. Red morocco by Jenkins and Cecil; with the verses to Mrs. Crewe and *The Muse Recalled*. Bookplates of Frank Grant, Sir T. Dawson Brodie, and F. A. Gaskill. Sotheby's, 25 February 1875 (Benzon Sale), lot 244, to Harvey, £1.11.0; Sotheby's, 8 March 1904 (Brodie Sale), lot 1288, to Tregaskis, £1.15.0; offered by Tregaskis for £5.5.0; from the Gaskill Collection, December 1939, to WSL.

5. With the verses to Mrs. Crewe, and letters of General Fitzpatrick and Charles James Fox; a letter from HW, probably to Lady Browne, removed by WSL; calf by Rivière. Offered by Tregaskis, Catalogue 827 (1920), lot 347, £7.17.6; Sotheby's, 28 July 1933 (Mount-Stephen Sale), lot 627, to Maggs for WSL, £10.

26. THE SLEEP-WALKER. 1778.

Lowndes 27.

JPO, pp. 18–19: '24 June 1778. Resumed the Press. Began to print the Sleep-Walker, a translation of the Somnambule of M. de Pondeveylt [Pont-de-Veyle], by and for Lady Craven, who acted it at her house at Benham-place, Bucks. 30 August. Finished the Sleep-Walker, 75 copies.'

HW to William Cole, 22 August 1778: 'I shall be in town in a few days, and will send you . . . a translation of a French play that I have just printed here. It is not for your reading, but as one of the Strawberry editions, and one of the rarest, for I have printed but 75 copies.'

Note by Cole in his copy: 'Sent to me by the Hon. Horace Walpole, 27 August 1778.'

Octavo in half-sheets; approximately 19.6 x 12.2 cm. uncut.
Signatures: [A]–H⁴.

THE

SLEEP-WALKER,

A

COMEDY:

In TWO ACTS.

TRANSLATED from the FRENCH,
In MARCH, M.DCC.LXXVIII.

Strawberry-Hill:
Printed by T. Kirgate, m.dcc.lxxviii.
26.

Pagination: [i] title-page; [ii] Verses by HW to Lady Craven; [iii–iv] Prologue; [v–vi] Epilogue; [vii]–viii Persons; [1]–56 text.

COPIES

1. Cole's copy was offered for sale after his death by B. White (1784), lot 6665. Richard Bull acquired it and had it bound in red morocco. It was sold at Sotheby's, 29 June 1926 (Burgh Sale), lot 164, to Edwards, £21; offered by Edwards, Catalogue 608 (1937), lot 393, for £5.

2. HW's copy, with *Hieroglyphic Tales* and other pieces, was in the SH Sale, iv.168, sold to Thorpe, £7.7.0. Another copy, uncut, was in HW's collection of plays called the *Theatre of George 3*, 58 volumes. This collection was sold at Sotheby's, 10 June 1914 (Miscellaneous Sale), lot 551, to Maggs, £210. The *Sleep-Walker,* bound by HW in the appropriate volume, was removed by Maggs Brothers and sold separately to Mr. Gaskill in November 1914; it was bound in red morocco for Mr. Gaskill by Dr. Charles L. Nichols. Bought by WSL, December 1939, in the Gaskill Collection, it has now been returned to its place in the collected *Theatre of George 3*.

3. Hodgson's, 30 April 1902 (Damer Sale), lot 148, to Dobell, £19.5.0. This copy was in original wrapper, untrimmed; a MS note by Kirgate on cover: 'But few of these, Kergate.'

Eight copies were included in the sale of Kirgate's library in 1810.

27. LETTER TO THE EDITOR OF THE MISCELLANIES OF THOMAS CHATTERTON. 1779.

Lowndes 28.

HW to William Mason, 24 July 1778: 'Two months ago I did draw up an account [in his letter to Bewley] of my share in that affair. That narrative and an answer to this insult [in Broughton's edition of Chatterton's works] which I wrote last night I will publish, signed with my name, but not advertised by it.' 10 August 1778: 'I have lengthened my Chattertonian pamphlet, and now think shall not publish it.'

HW to William Cole, 15 August 1778: 'My defense amounts to thirty pages of the size of this paper.'

'Short Notes,' p. lii: '1778. At the end of July wrote my answer to the editor of Chatterton's Works. 1779. In the preceding autumn had written a defense of myself against the unjust aspersions in the Preface to the Miscellanies of Chatterton. Printed 200 copies at Strawberry Hill this January, and gave them away. It was much enlarged from what I had written in July.'

JPO, p. 19: '1779. In January printed 200 copies of my pamphlet on Chatterton.'

HW to William Cole, 15 January 1779: 'I am actually printing my justification about Chatterton, but only 200 copies to give away. . . . You shall have a copy as soon as ever it is finished, which my printer says will be in three weeks.

A

L E T T E R

TO THE

Editor of the Miſcellanies

OF

THOMAS CHATTERTON.

STRAWBERRY-HILL :
PRINTED BY T. KIRGATE, M.DCC.LXXIX.
27.

You know my printer is my secretary too.' 28 January 1779: 'You shall see Chatterton soon.' 18 February 1779: 'I sent you my Chattertoniad last week.'

Mason to HW, 10 March 1782: 'I read your unpublished letter . . . over again, and am still more sorry than ever that it is not in general hands.'

HW to Mason, 14 March 1782: 'I did not publish my letter on Chatterton, because I am sick of most things, and especially of being the subject of talk.'

Octavo in half-sheets; approximately 23 x 15 cm. uncut; printed on somewhat cheaper paper than that used in most of the SH books.
Signatures: One quarter-sheet; B–H⁴.
Pagination: Half-title and title-page, with versos blank; [1]–55 text; [56] blank.

STATES AND VARIANTS

In his own copy and in seven other copies that I have seen, HW corrected the misprint on p. 22 ('elequence' for 'elegance') by hand.

The book was never 'published' by HW, I think, and a considerable number remained undisposed of for many years: seventeen copies were included in Kirgate's Sale (1810), and seven in the SH Sale (1842). An unopened copy, now wSL, is printed, except for the preliminary leaves, on a different paper, with horizontal chain-lines: it is obviously a left-over copy—perhaps Kirgate prepared some extras beyond the authorized 200.

OTHER EDITIONS

The *Letter* was reprinted serially in the *Gentleman's Magazine* for 1782; according to the editor's note, this was done with HW's consent.

COPIES

1. HW's copy, with his MS notes, with Tyrwhitt's edition of the *Poems* and Broughton's edition of the *Miscellanies,* bound in calf with HW's arms on sides, was in a collection of eighteen volumes on Chatterton in the SH Sale, vii.49 (London Sale, viii.1040*–1042); purchased by Strong for £4.10.0. Sixteen pamphlets from this collection, including the *Letter,* bound in four volumes, can be traced as follows: in *Catalogue Raisonné* of the library of Mr. A. A. Smets, 1860; Leavitt, 25 May 1868 (Smets Sale), lot 446; purchased by wSL from the New York Mercantile Library in 1934 for $600.

2. Another copy with notes and corrections by HW, bound in morocco by Rivière, was sold at Sotheby's, 28 June 1912 (A. C. Drummond Sale), lot 404, to Sabin, £5.

3. Another copy is in volume 39 of HW's *Tracts of George 3*, now WSL.

4. Another copy with MS notes, inscribed by HW, 'For Miss Berry,' was offered in a collection of twenty items by White in 1850, for £3.13.6; it is now (1939) in the library of Major E. C. Shirley, Ettington Park, Warwick.

5. Cole's copy, inscribed on verso of title, 'Sent to me by Mr. Walpole Febr. 14, 1779. Wm. Cole,' bearing also the signature of George Steevens and the bookplate of T. Gosden, cannot be traced with certainty in early sales; probably it was included in a group of tracts on Chatterton in White's Catalogue (of Cole's library) in 1784 and in the sale of Steevens's library in 1800. Some MS notes by Cole; half-title wanting; bound by Gosden. It was purchased by WSL from Goodspeed in 1934 (with 28 other tracts on Chatterton) for $125.

6. Richard Bull's copy, with his bookplate, and a letter from HW inserted, interleaved and bound in red morocco; Sotheby's, 29 April 1880 (Bull Sale), lot 732, to Harvey, £2.13.0; Sotheby's, 12 July 1910 (G. F. Smith Sale), lot 119, to Dobell, £2.4.0.

7. A copy with Kirgate's proof-corrections was owned in 1834 by Cruden (Martin, p. 504). It was offered by Thomas Thorpe in his General Catalogue for 1845, lot 1946, for 10/6. Presumably the same copy was offered by Hardcastle of Newcastle, 2 November 1860 (Thomas Bell library), lot 4511.

8. Presentation copy to the Duchess of Portland; autograph slip by HW pasted on verso of title-page, 'To Her Grace the Duchess Dowager of Portland with Mr. Walpole's most respectfull compliments.' Bound in red morocco with Rowley *Poems*. Syston Park bookplate. Sold by Quaritch in 1923 for £7.10.0; Davis and Orioli, December 1941, to WSL, £21.

9. Inscribed (probably by William Seward): 'From the Hon. Horace Walpole, now Earl of Orford'; bound with Dr. Jortin's *Remarks on Spenser's Poems* in green morocco by Rivière and Son; note from HW (in Kirgate's hand) to Seward inlaid. Now in Huntington Library.

28. WILLIAM JONES, THE MUSE RECALLED. 1781.

Lowndes 30.

JPO, p. 19: '11 August 1781. Finished 250 copies of Mr. Jones's Ode on the marriage of Lord Althorp and Miss Bingham, eldest Daughter of Lord Lucan. Mr. W. Jones of Queen's Oxford was the Translator of some Eastern Poetry.'

HW to Earl of Strafford, 31 August 1781: 'As your Lordship has honored all the productions of my press with your acceptance, I venture to enclose the last, which I printed to oblige the Lucans.'

Quarto in half-sheets; approximately 24 x 19.5 cm. uncut.
Signatures: [A]–B²; C¹.
Pagination: Title-page, with verso blank; [1]–8 text.

OTHER EDITIONS

The poem was reprinted in Paris, for private distribution, in 1782.

THE
MUSE RECALLED,
AN ODE,

OCCASIONED BY

THE NUPTIALS OF

LORD VISCOUNT ALTHORP

AND

MISS LAVINIA BINGHAM,

Eldeſt Daughter of CHARLES Lord LUCAN,

MARCH VI, M.DCC.LXXXI.

By WILLIAM JONES, Esq.

STRAWBERRY-HILL:
PRINTED BY THOMAS KIRGATE, M.DCC.LXXXI.
28.

COPIES

1. HW's copy, bound with other SH pieces, was in the SH Sale, iv.149. Probably this copy, separated from the other pieces, is the one offered in T. Thorpe's Catalogue for 1846, lot 1951, 10/6.

2. Richard Bull's copy, in red morocco, is now in the Central Public Library of Northampton.

3. The copy presented by HW to George Grenville is described above, under Gray's *Odes*, copy 7, now WSL.

Six copies were in Kirgate's Sale in 1810, three bought by Heber and three by Baker; and fifty-nine copies were offered in the SH Sale, v.199, purchased by Thorpe for one guinea. From this remainder, uncut and unbound copies have continued to circulate since 1842; four are now WSL.

29. LETTER FROM THOMAS WALPOLE. 1781.

Lowndes 31.

Concerning this book, I know very little. It is not mentioned in contemporary letters, so far as I know, nor does HW refer to it in the JPO. Nevertheless, there can be no doubt that the book was printed at SH: HW included it in the list at the end of his *Description of SH*, 1784. Since the letter is dated 'Paris, October 20, 1781,' it was presumably printed in the late autumn.

According to HW's list in the *Description of SH*, 120 copies were printed; a MS list, now in the Huntington Library, given by HW to Richard Bull, also has 120 copies. Bull's own MS list gives 200 copies, but HW's number is more likely to be correct.

Quarto in half-sheets; approximately 24 x 18.5 cm. uncut.
Signatures: One leaf; B–E².
Pagination: Title-page, with verso blank; [1]–15 text; [16] blank.

COPIES

Perhaps because of its limited interest or perhaps because only a few of the 120 copies were circulated by Thomas Walpole, the *Letter* is one of the rarer SH pieces. Kirgate sold a copy to Baker in 1798, for 10/6, and to Annesley in 1800, for £1.1.0; these transactions are recorded in Kirgate's bills, now WSL. Whether he disposed of other copies in similar fashion, I do not know. Only two copies remained in his library to be sold in 1810. No copy was offered in the sale of Mrs. Damer's books in 1902.

1. HW's copy, bound with Lady Temple's *Poems* and other pieces, was in the SH Sale, iv.149, to Thorpe, £1.15.0. Apparently Thorpe broke up the volume, inasmuch as his Catalogue for 1846 offered HW's copy of the *Letter*, with autograph note by HW, uncut, lot 1953, £1.11.6.

2. Thomas Walpole's copy, with his initials, bound in a volume of printed and MS pieces concerning the lawsuit. Chamonal of Paris to Mr. Lathrop C. Harper; Mr. Harper, May 1925, to the John Carter Brown Library.

A LETTER

FROM

THE HONORABLE

THOMAS WALPOLE,

TO THE

GOVERNOR and COMMITTEE

OF THE

Treaſury of the Bank of England.

STRAWBERRY-HILL:

PRINTED BY THOMAS KIRGATE, M.DCC.LXXXI.

29.

3. Richard Bull's copy is at Heckfield Place, Basingstoke, Hants (Mrs. Scott-Murray).

Of the three copies now at Farmington, one is from the Holford Collection (Annesley's copy) and one from the Gaskill Collection. Other copies are at Harvard and Princeton; the Merriam copy is now at the Clark Memorial Library.

30. DESCRIPTION OF THE VILLA. 1784.

Lowndes 24.

JPO, p. 19: '1784. Printed 200 copies of the Description of Strawberry Hill on larger paper for the cuts, and appendixes to that and the former small edition which had no cuts.'

HW to Mrs. Fenn, 7 July 1784: 'I have long begun a description of my collection, and a very imperfect list was printed several years ago, but was suppressed. I have not yet completed it, but whenever it shall be ready to appear, a copy shall certainly be at Mr. Fenn's command.'

HW to Lady Ossory, 15 September 1787: '. . . though printed, I have entirely kept it up [i.e., held it back], and mean to do so while I live, for very sound reasons.'

In 1784 or soon afterwards, HW drew up a list (a copy is inserted in T. Crofton Croker's extra-illustrated copy of the SH *Sale Catalogue,* now WSL) of eighty people to whom he desired to bequeath copies; shortly before his own death he revised this list by placing the word 'Dead' opposite the names of people who had died since he had first compiled the list. Many of these copies, inscribed by HW or the recipient, have survived, as have (probably) most of the other copies printed. Despite his reluctance, HW also distributed some copies before his death.

Quarto; approximately 30.5 x 24.5 cm. uncut.

Signatures: 1 leaf; A (half-sheet); B–M⁴; N (half-sheet); O (2 single leaves).

Pagination: Title-page with verso blank; [i]–iv Preface, with ornamental headpiece and engraved tailpiece; [1]–86 text; 87–88 List of books printed at SH; 88 Errata and Directions to binder; 89–92 Appendix; 93–94 Curiosities added; 95–96 More additions.

There are 27 plates, the first 25 of which are listed on p. 88; the last two (Offices and Ground plan of offices) were prepared later, as the watermarks show, probably about 1790. The preparation of plates to be inserted in some copies of the small quarto edition of 1774 [No. 22 above] was something of an afterthought. The first mention of them seems to be in HW's letter to Cole, 21 July 1774, after the hundred

A

DESCRIPTION

OF THE

VILLA

OF

Mr. HORACE WALPOLE,

YOUNGEST SON OF SIR ROBERT WALPOLE EARL OF ORFORD,

A T

Strawberry-Hill near Twickenham, Middlefex.

WITH AN INVENTORY OF THE

FURNITURE, PICTURES, CURIOSITIES, &c.

STRAWBERRY-HILL:
PRINTED BY THOMAS KIRGATE, MDCCLXXXIV.
30. REDUCED. WIDTH OF ORIGINAL 15 cm.

copies had been printed: 'I propose in time to have plates of my house added to the catalogue.' And in the JPO (quoted above) HW is specific: 'Printed 200 copies . . . on larger paper for the cuts, and appendixes to that and the former small edition, which had no cuts.' The different plates were designed and engraved by various artists.

STATES AND VARIANTS

As originally planned and printed in 1784, the book contained 88 pages plus the preliminary leaves. But since only a few copies were distributed before HW's death, the several additions are usually present, as follows:

> Appendix, pp. 89–92, printed in the summer of 1786.
> Curiosities added, pp. 93–94 (O_1), printed about 1789.
> More additions, pp. 95–96 (O_2), printed about 1791.

On a slip cut from a wrapper, HW wrote, 'This Copy has some few Additions and is intended for the next Edition. H. W. 1788.' I have no doubt that the slip (now WSL) was cut from the wrapper of a copy of the *Description*.

A set of proof-sheets, with corrections by HW and Kirgate (now WSL), has a single leaf, N (pp. 89–90), containing an earlier state of the Appendix. The final form of the Appendix, pp. 89–92, is also present, but O_1 and O_2 are lacking. Probably no copies of the book as finally approved by HW contain this first state of the Appendix.

A copy of the work (now WSL), inscribed on the title-page, 'Given me by Mr. Walpole in 1788,' lacks the last two plates (*ca.* 1790), but it has all the textual additions including O_2 which cannot be earlier than 1791. It also contains an earlier state of O_2 with the heading 'Added in MDCCXC.' The second and usual O_2 contains the same entries as this first state, except for one that was perhaps inadvertently omitted, and it adds on p. 96 ten newly acquired items.

In some copies, the title-page (usually an added leaf preceding the regular title) is printed in two (or three) colors. Some copies of the title-page in colors also exist as separate leaves. (See the Detached Pieces, No. 58 below.)

Lowndes, followed by booksellers and by Dr. Toynbee in his notes to the JPO, says that twelve copies were printed on large paper, and Dr. Toynbee (JPO, p. 67) described Charles Bedford's copy, now

Lord Waldegrave, as large paper, with measurements somewhat different (taller and narrower) from those of the ordinary issue. In the JPO itself (and also in the Catalogue of Kirgate's Sale) the edition of 1784 is described as large paper merely to differentiate it from the edition of 1774. It is perhaps significant that the edition on large paper does not appear in Martin or in the first edition of Lowndes (Martin even refers specifically to Bedford's copy, then owned by a descendant), being first recorded in Bohn's edition of Lowndes in 1864—three years after Bedford's copy, described as on large paper, was sold at Christie's. HW was careful to specify in his list that six copies of the small quarto edition (1774) were on large paper, and he records in the JPO the 25 special copies of *Miscellaneous Antiquities;* it therefore seems to me significant that when he recorded the number of copies of the edition of 1784, he made no mention of copies on large paper. Furthermore, in Bull's list (now Huntington Library), which was corrected by Kirgate, 100 copies of the edition of 1774 are recorded, with 6 on large paper; the edition of 1784 is recorded as royal quarto, 200 copies, with no mention of large paper; surely this would have been the place for Kirgate to mention the fact if he had really printed any on large paper. I shall therefore remain somewhat skeptical about copies on large paper, at least until I have been able to examine Bedford's copy.

On the other hand, twelve sets of the plates were printed on French paper (possibly by Kirgate on his own initiative). Lord Harcourt wrote in his copy, given to him by Mrs. Damer in 1801: 'The impressions of the plates in this book are on French paper, upon which twelve sets only were struck off.' (This copy is now owned by Mr. S. A. Courtauld; see Dr. Toynbee's *SH Accounts*, p. 99.) Kirgate sold to Baker, 4 February 1798, 'A set of French paper cuts to Catal. of Strawb.' for four guineas, according to his bill, now WSL. In one WSL copy, containing the bookplates of William Alexander and R. E. Gathorne-Hardy, the plates are on French paper. Since these special plates do not seem to be matched with the so-called large-paper copies, and since HW seems to have made no arrangement about any special copies, I suggest the following explanation as a working hypothesis: the plates on French paper were Kirgate's private venture; there were no copies on large paper; the number 12 (correctly asso-

ciated with the special plates) was applied mistakenly to some untrimmed copies. But this explanation remains only a guess.

OTHER EDITIONS

The *Description* was reprinted in 1842 by W. Strange, and of
course in HW's *Works,* 1798.

COPIES

1. HW's copy, with proof plates and MS notes; calf, with HW's arms on
sides. (Probably) SH Sale, iv.154, to H. Bohn, £16; Sotheby's, 3 July 1883
(Beckford Sale), lot 257, to Bain, £16.5.0.

2. HW's copy, bound with *Aedes Walpolianae* 1747; now Lord Waldegrave.

3. Extra-illustrated with drawings, some with MS notes by HW purchased
at SH Sale; half morocco, uncut. (Probably) King and Lochée, 4 December
1810 (Kirgate Sale), lot 411, to Utterson, £1.18.0; Sotheby's, 27 March 1857
(Utterson Sale), lot 1789, to Lilly, £27; offered by Lilly in 1868, £31.10.0; in
Catalogue of Mr. Henry Probasco of Cincinnati, 1873.

4. Charles Bedford's copy, with inscription by HW inserted, 'Description of
Strawberry Hill, for Charles Bedford, Esq. my deputy'; beneath is written,
'Mrs. Damer and Lord Frederick Campbell have great pleasure in executing
the directions of the late Earl of Orford. Grosvenor Square June 14, 1797.'
Extra-illustrated by Bedford, with a MS index; morocco. Christie's, 1 March
1861, lot 21, £53.11.0; now Lord Waldegrave.

5. Uncut copy, inscribed by HW, 'For Anthony Storer, Esq.' Now Eton College Library.

6. Pinkerton's copy, inscribed on fly-leaf, 'J. Pinkerton, left to me by the
Will of Horace Walpole, Earl of Orford.' Russia. Sotheby's, 20 December 1823
(Brockett Sale), lot 2979, to Cuthell, £1.10.0; offered in Longman's Catalogue,
1829, lot 4019, £4.4.0; offered in Lilly's Catalogue, 1843, £2.2.0.

7. Udney's copy, inscribed on wrapper, 'For Mr. Udney, Teddington'; beneath is written, 'Mrs. Damer and Lord Frederick Campbell have great pleasure in executing the directions of the late Earl of Orford. Grosvenor Square
June 12, 1797'; also a note by Udney. Now in the Morgan Collection at
Princeton.

8. A copy bequeathed to Sir William Musgrave (died 1800), with similar inscriptions; some MS notes; Barnsley bookplate. (Barnsley was the seat of Musgrave's cousin, who succeeded to the Baronetcy.) Red morocco. Sotheby's, 3
July 1935 (Musgrave Sale), lot 462, to Maggs for Lord Rothschild, £9.15.0;
presented by Lord Rothschild in July 1935 to WSL.

9. A copy bequeathed to Mary Dickenson; numerous notes by Miss Anne
Clark. Half calf. Frank Woore of Derby, April 1934, to Pickering and Chatto;
Pickering and Chatto, April 1934, to WSL, £7.7.0.

10. Extra-illustrated with numerous plates and SH Detached Pieces, and
original drawings by Harding and Carter; MS notes by HW and Kirgate;

name, perhaps S. Boyce, partly erased on title-page; probably from Kirgate's library. Russia by C. Lewis, rebacked. Sotheby's, 12 June 1933 (Miscellaneous Sale), lot 365, to Maggs, £42; Maggs, August 1933, to WSL, £62.

11. Extra-illustrated with 100 original drawings, chiefly by S. Harding, and numerous engravings; formerly owned by Kirgate's friend, William Bawtree (1744–1824), engraver; copy of *The Disaster* inserted, with MS account (written in 1871 by Bawtree's grandson) of the occasion for the poem. Inlaid to folio; russia, rebacked. Sotheby's, 14 July 1924 (Miscellaneous Sale), lot 183, to Spencer, £46; Spencer, June 1933, to WSL, £100.

12. Extra-illustrated with numerous prints and drawings; MS notes and additions by HW and Kirgate. Inlaid to folio, russia, rebacked, with arms of HW on sides. It was probably to illustrate this volume that HW cut up a volume of prints from pictures, antiquities, and curiosities at Strawberry Hill, opposite which (in another copy of the *Description*) Kirgate wrote in the margin, 'Cut up to illustrate a description of SH.' SH Sale (London, 21 June 1842), viii.1123, to William Knight, £22.11.6; Sabin, August 1927, to WSL, £600.

13. Richard Bull's copy, extra-illustrated with prints, drawings by John Carter, and Detached Pieces; autograph memoranda by HW inserted; coat of arms of Richard Bull painted inside cover. Inlaid to folio (probably about 1790); formerly bound in russia, now in green morocco. Sold at Sotheby's in 1880 to Ellis, £110; Mrs. Curtis, of Langford Hall, Newark, August 1937, to WSL, £225 (with Kirgate's copy of *Fugitive Pieces,* 1758, and HW's copy of Webster's *Arithmetic,* 1730).

14. Proof-sheets, some with numerous corrections by HW and Kirgate; pp. 25–32 and all plates wanting. Page 84 is in an early state, without the 'Additions' prepared in the summer of 1784; page 88 is in an early state, without 'Errata' and 'Directions to Binder'; leaf N (89–90) contains an early state of the Appendix; O_1 and O_2 wanting. Uncut, now bound in half red morocco; MS note by Peter Cunningham; bookplate of William Frederick, 9th Earl Waldegrave, and book-label of F. W. Goudy. Offered by T. Thorpe in his General Catalogue, 1845, lot 1949, £2.2.0; Sotheby's, 22 May 1848 (Eyton Sale), lot 1471, to Cunningham, 2/–; Anderson, 29 April 1921 (Arbury-Smith Sale), lot 361, $10.50; F. W. Goudy, June 1938, to WSL, $150.

15. A copy inscribed on title-page, 'Given me by Mr. Walpole in 1788'; with leaf O_2 in an early state, 'Added in MDCCXC.' The last two plates, prepared about 1790, are wanting, but the revised O_2 (printed in 1791) is present. Half morocco; Edwards, April 1928, to WSL, £4 (with several prints).

16. Bound in green morocco (about 1814) by C. Smith; added title-page in red, blue, and black; extra-illustrated by 14 views and 56 portraits, including 6 in water color, 4 in sepia, and 2 in pencil. Bookplate of Robert Hoe. Offered in Longman's General Catalogue (July 1814, lot 1645), in a collection of 41 volumes, for £350; Christie's, 1 March 1892 (Property of a gentleman), lot 129, to Nattali, £10.10.0; Sotheby's, 21 May 1909 (Property of a gentleman), lot 410, to B. F. Stevens for Mr. Hoe, £20; Anderson, 19 January 1912 (Hoe Sale), lot 3418, $325; now in Huntington Library.

[128]

17. Inlaid to folio, extra-illustrated by and bound with John Carter's *Drawings and Sketches,* 1788; MS notes by Carter, including a priced list of drawings, and by HW; russia, rebacked. Bookplates of Sir William Augustus Fraser and Robert Hoe; large SH fleuron inserted. Sotheby's, 30 April 1901 (Fraser Sale), lot 1786, to Harvey, £74; Sotheby's, 7 May 1904 (Ford Sale), lot 683, to Simpson, £58; Anderson, 26 April 1912 (Hoe Sale), lot 3359, $310; now in Huntington Library.

31. ESSAY ON MODERN GARDENING. 1785.

Lowndes 32.

JPO, p. 20: '5 July 1785. Began to print the translation by the Duc de Nivernois of my Essay of Modern Gardening. 20 August. Paid an assistant to Kirgate for printing it. In the last week of the month finished it—400 copies; sent 200 to the Duke at Paris; kept the rest myself for presents.' The assistant, Edward Yardley, worked from 12 July to 20 August 1785; in his bill is a charge of sixpence 'to the Letter Founder for 100 acute é' needed to print the French text. (JPO, pp. 68, 88.)

HW to Lady Ossory, 17 September 1785: 'I ask how I may send you a new book printed here. . . . It is the translation of my *Essay on Modern Gardens.*'

HW to William Parsons, *ca.* 1790: '. . . of which he has but two more copies left.'

HW, in writing to the Duke, 6 January and 1 February 1785, promised to correct proofs himself, since Kirgate knew no French; but not all the errors were eliminated by HW.

In the Merritt Collection at Harvard is HW's list of people to whom he intended to present copies: a facsimile was included in the illustrated American issue of the JPO in 1923.

Quarto in half-sheets; approximately 24 x 19.5 cm. uncut.
Signatures: 1 leaf; A–Aa².
Pagination: English title-page, with recto blank; French title-page; [1]–94 text, beginning with first page of English text on verso (signed 'A₂') of A₁; [95] blank. English text printed to face the French translation.

The first leaf is frequently so bound as to bring the title-page on the recto. Large SH fleuron on English title-page; ornamental headpieces and tailpieces.

OTHER EDITIONS

The puzzling French reprint, *ca.* 1790, is a small octavo.

ESSAI SUR L'ART

DES

JARDINS MODERNES,

Par M. HORACE WALPOLE,

TRADUIT EN FRANÇOIS

Par M. LE DUC DE NIVERNOIS,

En MDCCLXXXIV.

IMPRIMÉ à STRAWBERRY-HILL, par T. KIRGATE, MDCCLXXXV.

Signatures: A–I⁸.

Pagination: English title-page with recto blank; [2] French title-page; [3]–142 text; [143] blank.

Very little is known of this rare book, and I can merely record the results of my study of two copies. It is a cheap reprint of the Strawberry Hill edition, on French paper. (I can distinguish in the watermark the word 'Fin' and the date '1788.') The type, according to Mr. C. P. Rollins of the Yale Press, is Fournier, a French face; and the page with its signature marks at the side looks distinctly non-English.

A careful study of the text shows that nearly all the changes in the French text are corrections of Kirgate's errors; on the other hand, I have listed upwards of sixty serious errors that have been introduced into the English text: 'which' is spelled 'wich,' important words are frequently omitted, words are divided queerly at the ends of lines (pref/erred), and miscellaneous typographical errors are very common. In short, the French is at least more accurate than Kirgate's text (no very high praise), whereas the English text is so disgracefully bad as to be almost unreadable. I think there can be no doubt that the compositor was a Frenchman.

Besides this bibliographical or typographical evidence, HW's failure to refer to this edition suggests that copies were not known in London. My conclusion is that this edition was printed (probably surreptitiously) in Paris, *ca.* 1788–90.

Mr. Lewis included a brief discussion of this edition in the bibliographical note appended to his edition of *Modern Gardening* (1931), pp. 78–80.

The *Essay* was first printed in the *Anecdotes,* Vol. IV, 1771 (reprinted 1782, 1786, 1827, and later editions); and it appears in the second volume of HW's *Works,* 1798. In 1904, Lewis Buddy printed a type-facsimile of the edition of 1785, with facsimiles of HW's letters (in Kirgate's hand; now Princeton) to the Duke concerning the translation, and an introduction by Alice Morse Earle. In 1931, WSL printed the English text alone (from *Anecdotes,* 1782), with preface and bibliographical note.

COPIES

1. Presentation copy, about 1790, to William Parsons, with his inscription and bookplate; MS note by HW pasted in, 'Mr. Walpole has the pleasure of

sending Mr. Parsons the book he promised him, of which he has but two more copies left.' With two letters from Nivernois to HW (removed by WSL); half calf, rebacked. Sotheby's, 9 May 1922 (Miscellaneous Sale), lot 526, to Dobell, £2.12.0; from the Geoffrey Madan Collection; Quaritch, Catalogue 415 (1928), in a collection; Quaritch, August 1936, to WSL.

2. Inscribed on fly-leaf, probably by Lord Dacre's son: 'This Book was sent by Mr. Horace Walpole to Lord Dacre with a polite note, the day before my Lord's death; they had been from their youth great Friends, & were endeared to each other by a sincere regard, & a mutual love and taste for literature & the fine Arts—Thos. Barrett Lennard.' Contemporary calf, with Dacre bookplate inside front cover; two prints inserted. Sotheby's, 7 November 1938 (Barrett-Lennard Sale), lot 36, to Maggs for WSL, £1.10.0.

3. Richard Bull's copy, with his bookplate, extra-illustrated; with a letter from Duc de Nivernois, 9 October 1786, to Chevalier Charles Jerningham (died 1814), sending the book to him to be given to Lady Clarges; note from Lady Clarges, who gave the book to Bull; also MS music by Nivernois. Red morocco; Sotheby's, 29 June 1926 (Burgh Sale), lot 219, to Quaritch, £28; Quaritch, April 1928, to WSL, £39.

4. With two pages of MS additions by HW. Morocco; Sotheby's, 21 May 1909 (Miscellaneous Sale), lot 411, to Edwards, £14.

5. HW's copy, with prints and MS notes. Calf, with HW's arms on sides; SH Sale, iv.145, to H. Bohn, £2.5.0; Sotheby's, 3 July 1883 (Beckford Sale), lot 258, to B. F. Stevens, £4.12.0; Anderson, 13 February 1923 (Joyce Sale), lot 858, $80.

6. Presentation copy to Thomas Barrett of Lee in Kent; uncut. Sotheby's, 12 July 1859 (Barrett Sale), lot 514, to Bumstead, 3/–; now Mr. Robert Hartshorne, Highlands, New Jersey.

7. With two letters from HW (in Kirgate's hand) to Nivernois. Uncut; half green morocco; bookplate of T. A. Swinburne (died 1893). King and Lochée, 4 December 1810 (Kirgate Sale), lot 392, to Bindley, 15/–; Evans, 20 February 1819 (Bindley Sale), lot 967, to Cuthell, 17/–; Sotheby's, 20 December 1823 (Brockett Sale), lot 2983, to Rowntree, £1.13.0; now in the Morgan Collection, Princeton.

32. HIEROGLYPHIC TALES. 1785.

Lowndes 33.

'Short Notes,' p. li: '1772. This year, the last, and some time before, wrote some *Hieroglyphic Tales*. There are only five.'

HW to William Cole, 28 January 1779: 'I have some strange things in my drawer, even wilder than the *Castle of Otranto,* and called *Hieroglyphic Tales* —but they were not written lately. . . .'

JPO, p. 20: '27 September 1785. Began to print my *Hieroglyphic Tales,* only six copies, besides the revised copy. 5 November. Finished the *Hieroglyphic Tales.*'

HIEROGLYPHIC

TALES.

Schah Baham ne comprenoit jamais bien que les choses absurdes & hors de toute vraisemblance.

Le Sopha, p. 5.

STRAWBERRY-HILL:
PRINTED BY T. KIRGATE, MDCCLXXXV.

only six copies printed.

32.

The original MS was apparently bequeathed to Miss Berry, and passed from her to Richard Bentley; it is now WSL.

Octavo in half-sheets; approximately 19.2 x 11.5 cm. (Bull's copy).
Signatures: One leaf; A–G⁴; H².
Pagination: Title-page, with verso blank; [iii]–ix Preface; [x] blank; [1]–50 text; [51] Postscript; [52] blank.

Apparently the book was printed without a half-title: Bull's copy at Princeton (the only copy I have been able to examine) has no half-title, and Toynbee's collation (JPO, p. 69) of the Dyce copy makes no mention of a half-title.

OTHER EDITIONS

The Tales were included in the fourth volume of the *Works*, 1798; a separate edition was printed at Newcastle by Emerson Charnley, in 1822; and a new edition was published by Elkin Mathews, in 1926.

COPIES

1. A set of proofs, with MS notes of identification (reprinted in JPO, p. 70) by HW; title-page and last three pages in MS. Cruden owned this copy in 1834, according to Martin, p. 505; Sotheby's, 27 March 1857 (Utterson Sale), lot 1701, £11.5.0; now in the British Museum.

2. HW's copy, bound with *The Sleep-Walker* and other pieces; SH Sale, iv.168, to Thorpe, £7.7.0.

3. A copy inscribed by HW, 'Only six copies of this were printed, besides the revised copy [i.e., the proofs listed above]'; also inscribed, 'This copy cost me £7. A. Dyce.' Now in the Dyce Collection in the South Kensington Museum. This may well be copy 2, separated from the other pieces.

4. An uncut copy. King and Lochée, 4 December 1810 (Kirgate Sale), lot 380, to Baker, £16; Sotheby's, 8 June 1825 (Baker Sale), lot 764, to Cruden, £3.5.0; sold privately by Cruden to J. W. K. Eyton; Sotheby's, 22 May 1848 (Eyton Sale), lot 1473, to W. Stewart, £2.2.0.

5. Presentation copy to Barrett, inscribed, 'A Strawberry Edition to be delivered on my death to Thomas Barrett Esq. of Lee, in Kent. H. W.' Original wrapper. Sotheby's, 12 July 1859 (Barrett Sale), lot 513, to Boone, £5.5.0; in Lord Carlingford's library; Sotheby's, 20 May 1903 (Strachey Sale), lot 685, to A. Jackson, £11.10.0; now Mr. Robert Hartshorne, Highlands, New Jersey.

6. Presentation copy to Richard Bull, with a similar inscription. Red morocco by Roger Payne, interleaved. Sotheby's, 29 April 1880 (Bull Sale), lot 733, to Harvey, £9; Sotheby's, 11 June 1895 (Lord Orford Sale), lot 325, to Toovey, £37; now in the Morgan Collection, Princeton.

33. POSTSCRIPT TO ROYAL AND NOBLE AUTHORS. 1786.

Lowndes 9.

JPO, p. 20: 'November, 1786. Printed 40 copies of Christina, or Supplement to noble Authors.' [HW used both terms freely in referring to the *Postscript*.]

HW to Lady Ossory, 15 September 1787: 'I printed only forty copies. . . . A Mr. Ireland [i.e., Samuel Ireland], a collector (I believe with interested views), bribed my engraver to sell him a print of the frontispiece, has etched it himself, and I have heard has reprinted the piece—and I suppose will sell some copies as part of the forty.'

Octavo in half-sheets; approximately 19.5 x 12.5 cm. uncut.

Signatures: Folded plate; 1 leaf; A–B⁴; C¹.

Pagination: Frontispiece; title-page, with verso blank; [1]–18 text.

The title-page and leaf C₁ were printed together.

STATES AND VARIANTS

Despite the rumor that HW reported to Lady Ossory, no spurious printing of the *Postscript* has ever been identified. Furthermore, I think it probable that HW intended to refer only to the frontispiece: this may very well have been duplicated, since HW reported as fact and not as rumor that Ireland had copied the engraving. As a dealer in prints, Ireland would have been more interested in this engraving than in HW's text.

In the SH Sale (iv.165) a copy of the *Postscript* 'with additions to ditto' was bought by Bohn. Since I have not been able to see this copy, my explanation must be tentative: this description seems most likely to appy to the six-page Appendix that follows the *Postscript* in the *Works* of 1798, an Appendix that HW prepared some years before his death. Possibly Kirgate printed only a single copy as a kind of revised proof; from this copy, Miss Berry could have secured her text without difficulty in 1798.

There is, to be sure, a second possible explanation. The next entry in the JPO, p. 20, is dated 6 July 1787: 'Resumed printing my *Works* in quarto, with additions to *Royal and Noble Authors*. Not continued.' This entry, it seems to me, must refer to the supplementary lives, pp. [529]–555, and the *Postscript*, pp. 556–564, in the first volume of the quarto *Works*. (See the discussion of the printing of the *Works*, No. 16 above.) It would then have been no great matter to

POSTSCRIPT

TO THE

ROYAL AND NOBLE

AUTHORS.

PRINTED AT STRAWBERRY-HILL,
MDCCLXXXVI.

33.

print a copy of these supplementary lives, perhaps in smaller format, to be preserved with HW's copy of the octavo *Postscript* printed eight months earlier. But these pages (of authors and pieces omitted in the *Catalogue*) are hardly additions to the *Postscript;* the auctioneer's description in 1842 seems to fit the other explanation, the Appendix, and that explanation is therefore more likely.

COPIES

1. HW's copy of the *Postscript,* 'with additions to ditto,' was sold as a separate volume accompanying the *Catalogue of Royal and Noble Authors:* SH Sale, iv.165, to Bohn, £3.3.0.

2. Presentation copy to Richard Bull, with his bookplate, with an accompanying note from HW (10 January 1787) pasted in; portrait of Earl of Salisbury inserted. Green morocco, interleaved. Sotheby's, 29 June 1926 (Burgh Sale), lot 165, to Maggs for WSL, £20.

3. In a contemporary floral wrapper, uncut; portrait of Earl of Salisbury inserted. Hodgson's, 30 April 1902 (Damer Sale), lot 123, to Dobell, £5.5.0; Puttick and Simpson, 13 November 1913 (Miscellaneous Sale), lot 198, to Hornstein, 17/–; Parke-Bernet, 14 May 1939 (Spoor Sale), lot 911, to Brick Row for WSL, $7.50.

4. Inlaid in Sir John Fenn's set of *Anecdotes;* title-page inscribed: 'From the Honble. Horace Walpole to John Fenn. 1787, Feby. 3.' Now WSL.

If the edition was strictly limited to forty copies, it would seem that nearly all have survived; perhaps this is not unexpected, for they were doubtless given in nearly every case to friends who already had copies of the *Catalogue* of 1758. With considerable frequency, in fact, copies of the *Postscript* are bound with the second volume of the *Catalogue.* I have records of copies now extant as follows: two in the British Museum; two at Chewton Priory (Lord Waldegrave); two at Harvard; one at Knowsley (Lord Derby); one in the Clark Memorial Library (Merriam copy); one at Princeton (Gaisford copy); and two, in addition to those described above, at Farmington (Holford copy and Kirgate copy); other copies are doubtless preserved in public or private collections. Four copies were in the sale of Kirgate's library in 1810.

In Quaritch's Supplement for 1875–1877 to his General Catalogue, 1877, p. 571, a MS of the *Postscript,* eighteen pages, *ca.* 1790, was offered; it was described as small octavo, red morocco.

34. HANNAH MORE, BISHOP BONNER'S GHOST. 1789.

Lowndes 34.

HW to Hannah More, 23 June 1789: 'I will forgive all your enormities if you will let me print your poem [which she had just written]. . . . I will be content with printing only two hundred copies, of which you shall have half, and I half.'

BISHOP BONNER's

GHOST.

STRAWBERRY-HILL:
PRINTED BY THOMAS KIRGATE, MDCCLXXXIX.

HW to Lady Ossory, 18 July 1789: 'I have been disappointed of the completion of *Bonner's Ghost,* by my rolling press being out of order, and was forced to send the whole impression to town to have the copperplate [on the title-page] taken off [i.e., printed]. . . . *At night.* Kirgate has brought the whole impression, and I shall have the pleasure of sending your Ladyship this with a *Bonner's Ghost* tomorrow morning.'

JPO, p. 21: '1789. In July printed *Bonner's Ghost* written by Miss Hannah More, 200 copies. She had only 70 copies, the Bishop of London 30, and I, 100.'

Although HW's letter to Hannah More may sound a little importunate, his desire to print her poem seems a gracious response to the honor she had done him by dedicating her poem, *Florio,* to him in 1786.

Lowndes computes the number of copies printed at only 96. The error is perhaps derived from the figures given by HW in his letter to Hannah More, 20 July 1789: 'This morning I carried his thirty to the Bishop of London [Porteus]. . . . Tomorrow departs for London . . . a parcel containing sixty-four *Ghosts,* one of which is printed on brown for your own eating. There is but one more such, so you may preserve it like a relic. I know these two are not so good as the white: but, as rarities, a collector would give ten times more for them; and *uniquity* will make them valued more than the charming poetry.'

Quarto in half-sheets; approximately 24 x 19.5 cm. uncut.
Signatures: [A]–B².
Pagination: [i] title-page; [ii] blank; [iii] The Argument; [iv] blank; [1]–4 text.

STATES AND VARIANTS

Of the two copies on brown paper, I have seen neither. Hannah More's copy has not been reported, I think, since July 1789. HW's copy, inscribed by him, was in the SH Sale, vi.111 (with other pieces), to Thorpe, £5.15.6; Sotheby's, 22 May 1848 (Eyton Sale), lot 1475, to Nightingale, 3/–; it has not reappeared since 1848. Among the copies on white paper, I have observed no significant differences.

COPIES

1. HW's copy, unbound, with two MS notes in his hand; now at Chewton Priory (Lord Waldegrave).

2. Another copy at Chewton Priory has MS notes by Kirgate, including the

following explanation: '. . . Miss Moore [sic] was exceedingly anxious for the success of the Bill for the abolition of the Slave Trade, brought into [Parliament] by Mr. Wilberforce, for which the Bishop was solicitous too.'

Seven copies are now at Farmington: one is from the Holford Collection (Annesley's copy), one from the Gable Collection, and one from the Gaskill Collection; the others have no pedigree. I believe that the scarcity of association copies is to be explained by the fact that neither HW nor Hannah More put more than a few copies into circulation. Eleven copies were included in the sale of Kirgate's library, and at the SH Sale in 1842 Thorpe paid £1.10.0 for twenty-six copies. Thorpe gradually disposed of his supply during the next few years, and most of the clean, uncut copies that have been offered in recent years are doubtless from this remainder.

APPENDIX A

Eight pieces are here grouped together at the end of the numbered series, out of chronological order, with no particular justification beyond that of bibliographical convenience. The first two may well be genuine productions of the Press, but I have not been able to see copies; the other six were not printed at SH, I think, despite occasional listing as SH imprints.

35. RULES AND ORDERS for the Government of a Friendly Society commenced in January 28th, 1760, and held at the House of Richard Matthews, the Red Lion, Twickenham. 1774.

Lowndes 25.

Concerning this piece I have no information beyond this entry in Lowndes. It is not recorded in Martin, and there was no copy in the collections of George Baker or J. W. K. Eyton, two of the most persistent collectors in the early nineteenth century. Lowndes lists it as octavo, but whether it was a few pages or a considerable pamphlet, I do not know. (It is perhaps worth remarking that the titular hero of *Cockey's New Year's Address,* described below in Detached Piece No. 43, belonged to Mr. Matthews.)

36. LAWS, RULES AND ORDERS belonging to the Amicable and Fraternal Society held at Mr. Wm. Young's, the Black Dog, in Twickenham, begun June 25th, 1779.

Lowndes 29, 107.

This piece seems to be similar to No. 35 above. It seems to me probable that Kirgate printed these without HW's knowledge; perhaps he was paid for the work, or perhaps he did it to please his friends at the Red Lion and the Black Dog, respectively. To many a sodality of this sort, the desire to see a set of rules in print is almost irresistible.

Under the Detached Pieces, Lowndes unknowingly makes a second entry of the same pamphlet; it is there called 'A Book of Club Orders. 8vo. Pp. 15. Begun June 25, 1779,' an entry that seems to have been copied verbatim from Martin (1834). A copy was sold at Sotheby's, 8 June 1825 (Baker Sale), lot 774, to Cruden, 1/6; Cruden's collection was purchased by Mr. Eyton; no doubt it was the same copy, therefore, that was sold at Sotheby's, 22 May 1848 (Eyton Sale), lot 1477, to Nightingale, 2/–. I have no later record of the pamphlet. The description in the Eyton Catalogue reads: 'Strawberry Hill, printed by Thos. Kirgate, this last line in the printer's autograph, stitched, uncut, octavo.'

Yet, if Kirgate did print these two pieces, it is rather strange that he should keep no copy of either one, and that George Baker, his earliest bibliographer, should have possessed a copy of the second one only. The presence of No. 36 in the Baker Sale does not force us to accept it as a genuine SH product, inasmuch as other books that were certainly not printed at SH are included in the same section of the Baker Sale; the heading is very general: 'Works privately printed at Strawberry Hill, and relative to Lord Orford.' Martin and Lowndes, I suppose, relied chiefly on the Baker copy for their evidence.

The MS note in Kirgate's hand, then, is the best evidence, sufficiently strong, perhaps, to outweigh any objections. Both pieces could have been prepared for HW, but it is perhaps more likely, as I have suggested above, that Kirgate undertook them on his own responsibility; Baker's *Catalogue* in 1810 also marks this piece 'not printed for Mr. Walpole.' There is now at Farmington a MS (in Kirgate's hand) dated 1785, containing a number of 'Resolutions' that are essentially the regulations to govern a social gathering; the existence of this MS suggests to me that Kirgate may have had a fondness for such half-serious regularizing of the social or convivial gatherings he attended.

37. J. H. MÜNTZ, ENCAUSTIC: OR, COUNT CAYLUS'S METHOD OF PAINTING. 1760.

Lowndes 81.

'Short Notes,' p. xlv: '29 October 1759. I began the account of a new discovery of painting upon wax; it was invented at Paris by the Comte de Caylus, and was improved here by Mr. Müntz. 12 November. I dismissed Mr. Müntz; and, upon his leaving me, laid aside the intention of publishing the account of the new encaustic.'

JPO, p. 9: '7 November 1759. Began to print the account of the new encaustic. Lucan was postponed. But Mr. Müntz my painter being turned away soon after, from whose discoveries and improvements the account was drawn up, I laid aside the Encaustic entirely, and resumed Lucan. He afterwards published another account of the Encaustic himself.'

This book is placed in the Appendix principally because I have never seen the SH fragment. Baker's *Catalogue* of 1810, followed by Martin and Lowndes, describes it as follows: octavo, title-page and dedication (to Mary, Lady Hervey), printed by Thomas Farmer, 7 pages. If a copy was in Kirgate's Sale, it was not separately listed, and I have found no other records of copies.

The book as Müntz published it in London, in 1760, is dedicated to Lord Edgcumbe. George Montagu's copy is now at Farmington.

38. LORD CORNBURY, THE MISTAKES. 1758.

Lowndes 6.

Because in Baker's *Biographia Dramatica* this play is said to have been printed at SH, it finds a place in the SH list in Lowndes. But at the end of this entry, Lowndes refers the reader to p. 524 where, under Lord Cornbury, the facts are correctly established: 'The advertisement was written by Horace Walpole, Earl of Orford [misprinted Oxford]. Some have erroneously supposed it was printed at Strawberry Hill.' The book belongs in a Walpolian bibliography because of the advertisement, reprinted in his *Works;* but not in a bibliography of Strawberry Hill.

APPENDIX A

39. THE HISTORY OF ALCIDALIS AND ZELIDA [TRANSLATED FROM VOITURE]. 1789.

Lowndes 36.

In the main entry, under the title, Lowndes says: 'Some copies have a fictitious title, purporting to have been printed at Strawberry-hill, MDCCLXXXIX., and have produced considerable prices.' I think that Lowndes is correct in listing the book as a fictitious imprint: one can readily believe that numerous pamphlets were printed without HW's knowledge (e.g., Nos. 35 and 36 above), but Kirgate could hardly have been unaware of any such printing; yet no copy was in Kirgate's Sale. To be sure, Kirgate had no copy of No. 35 or No. 36, but those very ephemeral pamphlets are not exactly analogous.

What happened, I think, can be explained by the bibliographical evidence. The book is a slender octavo, printed on unwatermarked paper; the text is set in a non-Caslon, probably Fry, type (and is therefore eliminated from consideration as a product of the SH Press). The title-page with SH imprint, in a somewhat mixed type, is a cancel. It seems not unlikely, therefore, that new title-pages were prepared for a few copies. What is probably the original title-page (not examined) has the London imprint of J. Barker. Still another issue (not examined, and not recorded by Lowndes, but see British Museum *Catalogue*) has the SH imprint, but is dated 1763: Goldsmid's copy was of this issue.

A MS note in the WSL copy, from the Gaskill Collection, quotes a note from the Goldsmid Catalogue (Evans, 13 December 1815): 'Surreptitiously printed at SH: it is said [that] no more than 10 copies were printed.' There are still (1940) at least three copies in England: in the British Museum, in the Dyce Collection at South Kensington, and at Chewton Priory (Lord Waldegrave). There was no copy in the Baker Sale (1825) or in the SH Sale (1842).

Eyton's copy (sold at Sotheby's in 1848) came from Lord Berwick's Sale in 1843. T. Thorpe offered another copy in 1844, with the following note: 'The above volume was printed at SH, of which press some copies bear the imprint. The present was Kirgate's copy.' Evidently Kirgate did own a copy, even if it was not included in his sale; Thorpe's note seems to imply that this copy had the Barker imprint, although it seems somewhat strange that Kirgate should have lacked the SH imprint.

40. ELEGY ON THE DEATH OF MISS CAROLINE CAMPBELL. [1789?]

Not in Lowndes.

This six-page pamphlet is often advertised as a product of the SH Press, but the only justification for the attribution seems to be the fact that Miss Campbell was a member of the Walpolian circle. She died in January 1789, according to the *Gentleman's Magazine,* and the verses were presumably composed and printed at that time. I have found no reference to the piece in HW's letters, and the printing does not greatly resemble Kirgate's work; the paper was made by Portal and Company, a maker not represented in genuine SH productions. I do not accept this piece.

41. HASTY PRODUCTIONS BY LORD ORFORD. Norwich 1791.

Lowndes, p. 2822.

This work needs no consideration as an imprint of the SH Press, but because Lowndes included it under HW's works, it is perhaps worth listing and rejecting here. The author was HW's nephew George, the third Earl.

42. THE IMPENETRABLE SECRET.

Lowndes, p. 2822.

This pleasant little game, played with ten cards, was first ascribed to HW, to the best of my knowledge, by W. Strong, the bookseller of Bristol, in 1843. The attribution has been accepted ever since, I think, and Mr. Lewis described the game as 'probably invented by HW' when he reprinted it in 1939.

In rejecting this as a Walpolian or SH piece, therefore, I am breaking with a tradition of passive acceptance or toleration that has been established for nearly one hundred years. But I do reject it, even though no single piece of evidence that I can adduce is stronger than mild probability. The only copy extant, so far as I know, is now in the British Museum; this is the copy from which Mr. Lewis's reprint was made. The description of it I owe to Mr. A. J. Watson: there are ten engraved cards, with maxims on both sides, and a printed leaf of Explanation, in a wooden case which is bound in brown calf; HW's bookplate is on the inside cover of the box. The chain-lines (in the leaf of Explanation) are vertical, and the small portion of watermark at the top of the leaf is not identifiable. This was among the books in the Glass Closet, in the SH Sale, vi.28, bought by Strong; Strong offered it in his Catalogue, 1843, lot 1443, for £2.2.0; a note identified it as 'from the SH collection' and it was described as 'unique, probably invented by HW . . . the "Explanation of the secret" printed at SH.' The game was acquired by E. A. Crowninshield, and then sold at Puttick and Simpson's, 12 July 1860 (Crowninshield Sale), lot 348, to Messrs. T. and W. Boone; it was purchased from the Boones by the British Museum, 2 July 1861.

HW's failure to mention *The Impenetrable Secret* in his letters is, it seems to me, a significant point. It is not difficult to believe that HW could have invented the game (the instructions are rather more complicated than the game itself), but it is extremely difficult to believe that he could have refrained from telling anyone about it or from sending copies to his friends. But there are also other objections.

The advertisements are distinctly troublesome if we are to think of this game as invented by HW and printed only for his own amusement. In the *London Chronicle*, 24 April 1760, there is an advertisement by R. Withy for 'The New Impenetrable Secret,' and two advertisements above it is one by T. Kinnersly in St. Paul's Churchyard, 'Where may be had . . . The Impenetrable Secret.' (Quoted in Mr. Lewis's edition, pp. 13–15.) In the *St. James's Chronicle*, 10 January 1769, there is an advertisement for the sixth edition of 'The

Impenetrable Secret; or, Young Gentlemen and Ladies pleasing in-structor . . . [with] maxims from the most celebrated authors. Printed for W. Nicoll.' Furthermore, a much earlier advertisement of the game is probably extant: Hildeburn's list of Philadelphia imprints (copied by Evans) refers to an advertisement of *The Impenetrable Secret*, presumably but of course not necessarily the same work, in *The Pennsylvania Gazette*, 11 May 1749, 'just published' by Franklin and Hall; but some error seems to have crept into Hildeburn's notes, since Dr. Reitzel of The Historical Society of Pennsylvania writes me that there is no trace of the advertisement in any number of the *Gazette* for May 1749. I suspect that the maxims interested Franklin ('Poor Richard') and that he reprinted the game in Philadelphia. Another edition was advertised in 1775 by Story and Humphreys of Philadelphia, 'just published and printed with types, paper and ink manufactured in this Province.' But the record of London editions is more important; I think it unlikely that a game invented by HW could have been reprinted so steadily in London without stirring him to some comment or protest.

The bibliographical evidence is also against the piece. The type of the leaf of 'Explanation' seems to be Caslon, to be sure, but that was the most widely used type in the middle of the century. The ornamental border is wholly unlike any acknowledged SH printing; the use of 'hath' (twice) is unlike HW who seems to have used 'has' consistently, even in his *Mysterious Mother*. The style of the 'Explanation' is altogether too stilted and awkward to be accepted as Walpolian, I think: HW was a fluent and elegant writer, but these two paragraphs are so crabbed as to be almost unintelligible.

Finally, the position of this game in HW's library is puzzling. It was sold with the duodecimos from the Glass Closet, the repository of the books that were of particular interest to HW. In the Glass Closet, according to the *Description of SH*, was a complete set of the books printed at SH, but *The Impenetrable Secret* was not put with the SH books in the 1842 sale.

The evidence in favor of *The Impenetrable Secret* as a Walpolian production seems to be limited to Strong's enthusiastic cataloguing. The evidence against it seems stronger to me, and I therefore reject the piece.

A game of twenty cards, called 'The Magical Cards, or Le Secret Impénétrable, by T. Molineux,' was printed at Manchester in 1821. (G. H. Last, Catalogue 247, December 1939.) Whether this was an entirely separate game or merely an enlargement of the old one, I do not know; I have not seen a copy.

BIBLIOGRAPHY OF THE STRAWBERRY HILL PRESS

DETACHED PIECES

Vers sur cette expreſsion ordinaire, *Tuér le tems*:

C'est le Tems qui parle:

Lorsque, pour s'amuser, ſans ceſse ils s'evertuent,
Ces Meſsieurs les humains ,ils diſents qu'ils me tuent:
Moi, je ne me vante de rien;
Mais, ma foi, je m'en vange bien.

Imitated:

To Chloe.

In vain with deadly trifles arm'd
To murder Time you try;
Your toil derides the Foe unharm'd,
Tho he affects to fly.

A thouſand Lilly hands, like yours,
The ſelfsame plot we ſee in;
They may indeed abridge his hours,
But cannot touch his Being:

Tremble, dear Nymph, at ſuch a foe,
Who if he ſtays or flies,
Enſures revenge or ſwift, or ſlow;
Shall dim or cloſe thoſe eyes·

1.

1. VERS SUR CETTE EXPRESSION ORDINAIRE, Tuer le tems. 1757.

Lowndes 63; Martin, p. 509.

JPO, p. 3: '18 August 1757. Mr. Müntz printed for his first essay a sonnet written that evening by Mr. Walpole on killing time; the thought from a French epigram.'

Kirgate's MS note on a copy now WSL: 'Printed by Muntz, the Swiss Painter, who knew nothing of Printing.'

The French epigram was written by René Boudier de la Jousselinière. HW possessed a copy of *Le Porte-feuille trouvé, ou Tablettes d'un Curieux* (Genève, 1757), which contains a number of Boudier de la Jousselinière's fugitive verses.

The verses are printed on one side of a quarto leaf measuring approximately 23 x 18.8 cm. trimmed.

STATES AND VARIANTS

The copy illustrated here is the only edition found. There is evidence, however, that this setting may be a reprint: the paper of one copy at Farmington seems to be identical with that used for the *Disaster* (1797) and the late printing of Pentycross's Verses (Nos. 18 and 45 below), though it bears no watermark. Bull's copy (Huntington) does show part of this watermark. The second copy at Farmington is on a thinner paper, with a watermark (crown, post horn) that seems identical in design with paper used in 1795. Kirgate seems, therefore, to have reprinted the verses. Both WSL copies derive from him: one, with MS note in his hand, is in a collection of Detached Pieces bought by E. V. Utterson at the sale of Kirgate's library in 1810; and the other is in a collection of pieces sold by Kirgate to Francis Annesley in 1800. Lord Waldegrave's copy is also in a collection formed by Kirgate, and the bibliographical evidence suggests that Bull's copy came from Kirgate.

The text agrees in arrangement, capitalization, and spelling (except for a few slight variations), with HW's MS in the JPO, and it would have been a simple matter for Kirgate to set up the piece from that source.

The finished presswork of these copies also makes me unwilling to accept them as original. Kirgate points out that Müntz knew nothing of printing, and the queer undotted 'j' (from a different fount?) seems indeed to bear out Kirgate's accusation; but the presswork, on the whole, is good—very different from Müntz's work on Bentley's *Verses*, No. 4 below.

It is not impossible to believe that four copies of a fugitive piece printed in 1757 could survive; but I find it very difficult to believe that Kirgate, who first came to the Press years afterwards, could have had available for distribution after HW's death three or more copies of so slight a piece. The sum of the evidence, I grant, is inconclusive; but I think it likely that HW's copy, when it is recovered, will be found to belong to an earlier edition.

COPIES

Huntington (Bull); Lord Waldegrave; WSL (2 copies); Eyton Collection (sold 1848).

2. THE PRESS SPEAKS, TO LADY TOWNSHEND, 'FROM ME WITS AND POETS THEIR GLORY OBTAIN.' 1757.

Lowndes 87; Martin, p. 511.
JPO, p. 4: '19 August 1757. Lucy Young, Countess of Rochford, Ethelreda Viscountess Townshend, Miss Bland, and James Earl Waldegrave dining at Strawberry hill, were carried to see the printing-office, where the following lines being ready prepared were taken off [here follow the lines to Lady Townshend].'
HW to George Montagu, 25 August 1757: 'T'other day my Lady Rochford, Lady Townshend [etc.] . . . dined here, and were carried into the printing-office, and were to see the man print. There were some lines ready placed, which he took off; I gave them to my Lady Townshend; here they are . . .'

The verses are printed on one side of a leaf measuring 22 x 27 cm., with vertical chain-lines. The nineteenth-century reprint discussed below measures 25.5 x 19.7 cm.

STATES AND VARIANTS

A copy of the verses (now WSL) bought in a collection at the sale of the library of John A. Spoor, Parke-Bernet Galleries, 4 May 1939, lot

The PRESS Speaks:

FROM ME Wits and Poets their Glory obtain ;

Without ME their Wit and their Verſes were vain.

Stop, TOWNSHEND ! and let ME but Print what you ſay ;

You the Fame I on others beſtow,　will　repay.

2.　THE PRESS SPEAKS, TO LADY TOWNSHEND. ORIGINAL EDITION.

888, is clearly original; I have seen no other copy of this printing. It is almost certainly the copy sold with Mrs. Damer's books, Hodgson's, 30 April 1902, lot 163, to Denham, £8.10.0. It is set in a large, bold type which seems to be Two Lines English, Caslon, and every noun is capitalized; perhaps the large type was used to enable Lady Townshend, who was then fifty-four years old, to read it more easily. The punctuation of this copy agrees closely with HW's MS transcription in the JPO, while that of the reprint does not.

The reprint is set in Fry type; the punctuation and capitalization are entirely different, and the third line reads 'paint' instead of 'print.' This text was necessarily set up from the *Letters to George Montagu,* first published in 1818, or from a later edition; in the *Letters* the punctuation and capitalization are the same, and the third line reads 'paint'—an error that seems to have remained uncorrected until Mrs. Toynbee edited the *Letters.* Both the paper and the type prove that this reprint belongs with the group of forgeries that can most usefully be described at this point.*

Ten Detached Pieces, reprinted in the nineteenth century, must be discussed together. These are: I. To Lady Townshend (No. 2); II. To Lady Rochford (No. 3); III. Garrick's Verses to Mr. Gray (No. 7); IV. Verses to Lady Charles Spencer (No. 13); V. 'There was a little man' (No. 14); VI. The Magpie and her Brood (No. 17); VII. Verses to Mrs. Crewe (No. 28); VIII. To Miss Mary and Miss Agnes Berry (No. 36); IX. Rules for seeing the House: 'Lord Orford is very ready to oblige' (No. 90); and X. The Printer's Farewell (No. 48). Copies of all ten are in an extra-illustrated set of Eliot Warburton's *Memoirs of Horace Walpole,* 1851–52; this set, now WSL, has been enlarged by the insertion of 312 prints and eleven (only *The Muse Recalled* is original) SH pieces; the four title-pages, 'printed expressly for this copy,' have the imprint of Colburn and Co., 1852. It is entirely possible that the title-pages were prepared at a later date, but I think not much later: no prints later than 1851 are included, so far as I can tell, and the binding (red morocco, elaborately gilt-tooled, by Rivière) appears to fit this period. The set was sold at Sotheby's, 29 April 1937 (Property of the late Arthur Potts, Esq. of Hoole Hall, Cheshire, sold

* I have also included a summary of the evidence in an article in *Print,* Summer 1941.

THE PRESS SPEAKS:

From me wits and poets their glory obtain;

Without me their wit and their verſes were vain.

Stop, Townſhend, and let me but paint what you ſay ·

You, the fame I on others beſtow, will repay.

2. THE PRESS SPEAKS, TO LADY TOWNSHEND.
NINETEENTH-CENTURY REPRINT.

by order of his grandchildren), lot 753, to Dulau, £14; sold by Dulau to WSL, August 1938, for nineteen guineas. The date of the binding is important, since it supplies a terminal date before which these forgeries must have been printed; but I can certainly establish merely that the binding was executed before 1880, since in that year the name of the firm was altered to Rivière and Son. The forgeries were therefore perpetrated before 1880 and probably before 1852. A slightly earlier date is suggested by the presence of three of the forgeries (Nos. I, II, and IV) in the collection (now WSL) of Detached Pieces bound, probably for Robert Holford, by Lewis in red morocco; this binding may have been executed as early as 1840, and the three forgeries appear to have been included when the volume was bound.

To establish an initial date after which the forgeries must have been printed is the next problem.

Paper. Five of the pieces, numbered I, II, III, V, and X above, are printed on trimmed pieces of foolscap paper with the Dutch Garden of Holland (Pro Patria) watermark, or the initials L V G as countermark. This uniformity of paper, in pieces ostensibly printed in 1757, 1764, and 1797, is the strongest evidence that all the forgeries were prepared at one time. But since this paper can be dated accurately by its use in books printed in 1762–65, we know only that the anonymous forger procured a packet of old paper. No. IV is printed on wove paper, in obvious imitation of the Kirgate reprint described under the Verses to Lady Charles Spencer (No. 13 below). Nos. VI and VII are on laid paper, without visible watermark in the copies I have examined. In Nos. VIII and IX the top of a crown watermark is visible; the copy of No. VIII at Harvard has the countermark IPING, a name that also appears in the paper used for the facsimile (about 1814?) of T. F. Dibdin's *Lincoln Nosegay*.

Type. The typographical evidence does not divide in exactly the same manner, fortunately, so that all ten pieces can be linked despite the apparent differences in paper. Nos. I, II, and VI, so far as I can tell, are printed entirely in Fry type; they can thus be dated 'not earlier than 1764,' when the Fry foundry was established in Bristol, and the pieces ostensibly printed in 1757 are at once convicted as forgeries. Nos. IV, V, VII, VIII, IX, and X are printed in Wilson type, and hence cannot be earlier than 1770. Furthermore, two (Nos. V and IX) of these six pieces have a wrong-fount, modern-face 'y' that was not cast until considerably later. Finally, No. III (To Mr. Gray) is set in Wilson roman and Fry italic.

At first glance, this mixture of obviously non-Caslon types seems absurd for an attempted forgery. But the explanation is a simple one, I think: to the nineteenth-century forger, accustomed to the modern fat-face types of his time, all the old-style types (Caslon, Baskerville, Wilson, Fry) looked alike because all differed in about the same way from the modern-face types. An eye trained to one style, in other words, does not readily detect differences within a completely differ-ent style; we who are accustomed to twentieth-century home furnish-ings, for instance, are likely to think that all late-Victorian parlors looked alike. (With the recent revival of old-style types, of course, amateurs are again learning to recognize the differences between Cas-lon and the transitional types of the late eighteenth century.)

The first and most important conclusion that I establish from a de-tailed study of the paper and the type, then, is that all ten forgeries must be considered as a unit, the work of one man (or group) at one time; it is also clear that an attempt was made to deceive by the use of old paper and old type.

Now if all ten forgeries are considered as a unit, they must be later than 1797, when No. X was first printed; and in any case they must be after HW's death in 1797, since he would have recognized them as forgeries. Secondly, I absolve Kirgate of any blame, since he would certainly have known the difference between Caslon type and Fry or Wilson, however uninterested he may have been in the fine art of typography. (A Fry specimen book was in his library in 1810, lot 137.) Furthermore, in Mr. Holford's collection of Detached Pieces (now WSL), every piece is listed in Kirgate's bills to Annesley, except for the three nineteenth-century forgeries now in the volume; it looks as if somebody, probably Mr. Holford, had added these three to An-nesley's set (largely of Kirgate reprints) before the volume was bound by Lewis. The forgeries must therefore be later than 1810, the date of Kirgate's death. (Another forger might have made an attempt be-fore Kirgate's death, but this seems unlikely.) The text of the Verses to Lady Townshend can only come from an edition of the *Letters,*

1818 or later, as I have pointed out above. The date is therefore established as between 1818 and 1880, probably before 1852, and (on the partial evidence of the Holford volume) probably before 1840.

Whether more than ten pieces were reprinted, I do not know. The presence of all ten in a single set of Warburton's *Memoirs* makes me think that no others were attempted. The presence of ten in that volume, of three (Nos. VIII, IX, and X) in a copy (now WSL) of L. B. Seeley's *Horace Walpole and his World,* elaborately extra-illustrated in 1884–1890, and of three in the Holford volume, suggests that copies may have been distributed to collectors in some quantity.

COPIES (of Verses to Lady Townshend)

Original edition: WSL (Damer copy).

Nineteenth-century reprint: WSL (3 copies).

Other copies (not seen, and therefore not differentiated as to edition): Victoria and Albert (Dyce); Mr. G. P. Winship (see JPO, p. 27; probably the reprint, to judge from measurements); offered by Quaritch in Catalogue 530 (1937); Eyton Collection (sold 1848). These last three may be the same copy.

This is one of the rarest of the Detached Pieces, and Dr. Toynbee did not see a copy for his description of it in the JPO.

3. THE PRESS SPEAKS, TO LADY ROCHFORD, 'IN VAIN FROM YOUR PROPEREST NAME YOU HAVE FLOWN.' 1757.

Lowndes 88; Martin, p. 511.

JPO, p. 4: '19 August 1757. Lady Rochford desiring to see the manner of composing for the press, four lines from a play [*The Fair Penitent*] were given to the Printer, which he set, but while the company was kept in discourse, he privately changed them, and printed the following which had been prepared too [here follow the lines to Lady Rochford].'

HW to George Montagu, 25 August 1757: '. . . I gave him [the printer] four lines out of *The Fair Penitent,* which he set; but while he went to place them in the press, I made them [the ladies] look at something else without their observing; and in an instant he whipped away what he had just set, and to their great surprise, when they expected to see *Were ye, ye fair,* he presented to My Lady Rochford the following lines. . . . You may imagine, whatever the poetry was, that the gallantry of it succeeded.'

The verses are printed on one side of a leaf measuring 13.8 x 22 cm., with horizontal chain-lines. The nineteenth-century reprint measures 25.5 x 19.7 cm.

The PRESS Speaks:

IN vain from your propereſt Name you have flown,
And exchang'd lovely CUPID's for HYMEN's dull Throne;
By my Art ſhall your Beauties be conſtantly Sung,
And in ſpite of yourſelf you ſhall ever be YOUNG!

THE PRESS SPEAKS:

In vain from your propereſt name you have flown,

And exchanged lovely Cupid's for Hymen's dull throne;

By my art ſhall your beauties be conſtantly ſung,

And in ſpite of yourſelf you ſhall ever be *young*.

3. THE PRESS SPEAKS, TO LADY ROCHFORD.
Original edition above; reprint below.

STATES AND VARIANTS

A copy of the verses (now WSL) bought in a collection of Detached Pieces at the sale of the library of John A. Spoor, Parke-Bernet Galleries, 4 May 1939, lot 894, is clearly original; I have seen no other copy of this printing. It is almost certainly the copy sold with Mrs. Damer's books, Hodgson's, 30 April 1902, lot 164, to Denham, £3.3.0. Both this and No. 2 above are printed, I think, on the same paper as Gray's *Odes*. The text of this piece is set in Great Primer Roman, Caslon Old Style; in capitalization and spelling it agrees with HW's transcription of the verses in the JPO.

The text of the reprint, like that of No. 2 above, was set up from the letter to Montagu. This nineteenth-century reprint is fully discussed under Verses to Lady Townshend, No. 2 above.

COPIES

Original edition: WSL (Damer copy).
Nineteenth-century reprint: WSL (3 copies).
Other copies (not seen, and therefore not differentiated as to edition): Victoria and Albert (Dyce); Mr. G. P. Winship (see JPO, p. 28; probably the reprint, to judge from measurements); offered by Quaritch in Catalogue 530 (1937); Eyton Collection (sold 1848). These last three may be the same copy.
It seems likely that neither Lowndes nor Martin saw the original printing of this or of the Verses to Lady Townshend, since both are listed by Martin (followed by Lowndes) as octavo.

4. TO THE PRINTING-PRESS AT STRAWBERRY HILL. 1757.

Lowndes 57; Martin, p. 509.
JPO, p. 4: '19 August 1757. Mr. Bentley came to Strawberry Hill and while Mr. Walpole was abroad, gave Mr. Müntz a sonnet which he set; and when Mr. W. came home, they printed it off, without his knowing what was composed, as he had done for Lady Rochford.'
But the date on WSL's copy, in HW's hand, is 25 August. HW wrote to Montagu, 25 August 1757: 'Poor Mr. Bentley has been at the extremity with a fever . . . but is so well recovered that Mr. Müntz is gone to fetch him hither to-day.' HW's dates are often untrustworthy, and the verses were certainly printed later than the Verses to Lady Rochford (No. 3 above) of 19 August. The likelier date for the printing of this piece is therefore 25 August 1757, or a few days later.
HW sent a copy of the verses to George Montagu, 8 September 1757.

TO THE
PRINTING-PRESS
AT
STRAWBERRY-HILL.

written by Mr Bentley
Aug. 25th 1757.

OF German brain ingenious Birth
    Where Gun-powder had Nurture.
How your Black-arts have fill'd the Earth
    Brim-full of Books and Murder

To *That* is no difcernment giv'n
    Of brave or coward Blood:
Thou fhed'ft thy fable dews, as Heav'n,
    Alike on bad or good.

Yet here fhalt thou let Dullnefs flow
    On the blank Page no more,
But, like Preferment, Senfe beftow.
    Where there was none before.

The verses are printed on both sides of a quarto leaf, measuring approximately 27.5 x 21.7 cm. (Mr. Coykendall's copy); no watermark is visible, but the paper is similar to, or perhaps identical with, that used in Gray's *Odes*. The unsatisfactory presswork seems to me another proof of the genuineness of this printing.

COPIES

Eton College (Storer); Princeton (Morgan—possibly the copy sold with Mrs. Damer's books in 1902); Mr. Frederick Coykendall (Thomas Barrett's copy); WSL (in Utterson's Collection, but with MS note by HW).

5. VERS QUE LOUIS XV. TROUVA. 1757.

Lowndes 92; Martin, p. 511.

T. Kirgate (on the copy at Chewton): 'This was an attempt at printing by Mr. Müntz, a Swiss Painter, who then lived with Mr. Walpole, 1757.' On a copy at Farmington, Kirgate notes: 'Printed by Müntz, a Swiss, Domestic Painter to Mr. Walpole'; to this another hand, probably Francis Annesley's, has appended: 'who did not understand Printing or French.'

This piece was another experiment by Müntz, so that despite the lack of external evidence it should doubtless be dated in August or September 1757, at about the same time as Nos. 1 and 4 above.

The verses are printed on one side of the leaf; Lord Waldegrave's copy, with vertical chain-lines, measures 18.6 x 22.9 cm. The two WSL copies are on smaller slips, with horizontal chain-lines.

STATES AND VARIANTS

It seems probable that the copies examined are all reprints by Kirgate, and that the original printing is still to seek, but the copy illustrated is the only setting that we have recovered. (In the second WSL copy some readjustment of the type can be detected, but no resetting.)

The evidence that this is a late printing follows. It is printed on a paper first used at the SH Press for the quarto edition of HW's *Works,* begun in 1768. The use of this paper renders the genuineness of these copies doubtful; they look like reprintings by Kirgate after 1768, and probably after 1790, at the same time that Kirgate reprinted Garrick's 'To Mr. Gray, on his Odes' (see No. 7 below) upon the same paper. One WSL copy and the copy at Chewton can be traced

Vers, que L O U I S XV. trouva sous fon afsiette, en 1751

    Protecteur ingenu, d'une fidéle Race:
L O U I S! il faut optér, il ni â plus de milieu.
    Ou, range toi du cotes de la Grace,
Ou ne dis plus Louis par la grace de Dieu.

to Kirgate, for both bear notes in his hand; the second WSL copy is in Utterson's collection, and therefore came from the Kirgate Sale; and the bibliographical evidence suggests that Bull's copy came from Kirgate.

The rarity of the piece is not presumptive evidence that it was not reprinted, for Kirgate must have been aware that Müntz printed only a few copies for his own amusement. As in the case of No. 1 above, the evidence is inconclusive; HW's copy is needed to resolve our uncertainty.

COPIES

Bodleian; Harvard (Widener); Huntington (Bull); Lord Waldegrave; WSL (2 copies).

6. EPITAPH ON THEODORE, KING OF CORSICA. 1757.

Lowndes 58; Martin, p. 509.
JPO, p. 5: '29 September 1757. Printed the Epitaph on King Theodore. Only two dozen.'
The tablet erected in the churchyard, in memory of Theodore, Baron Neuhoff, still (1939) bears HW's epitaph. HW transcribed it into his letter to Sir Horace Mann, 29 September 1757.

The epitaph is printed on one side of a quarto leaf, measuring approximately 24.4 x 19.4 cm. (Harvard copy). The three copies in America are all printed on good paper without visible watermark.

OTHER EDITIONS

The epitaph was reprinted in the *London Chronicle,* 4 October 1757, and in HW's *Works* (1798), i.158. Dr. Toynbee transcribes an Italian translation preserved in the Waller Collection (*Letters of HW,* ed. Toynbee, Supplement, ii.102–103).

COPIES

Bodleian (2 copies); Eton College (Storer); Harvard (Merritt—possibly the copy sold with Mrs. Damer's books in 1902); Huntington (Bull); WSL.

7. TO MR. GRAY, ON HIS ODES. 1757.

Lowndes 53; Martin, p. 508.
Garrick's complimentary verses were first printed, 'very inaccurately and they were thrust into the most obscure corner of the paper,' in the *London*

EPITAPH

In the Church-Yard of St. ANNE, S O H O.

Near this PLACE is Interred

'HEODORE King of CORSICA,

Who died in this PARISH, DECEMBER 11th, 1756.

Immediately after leaving the KING's-BENCH-PRISON

By the Benefit of the ACT OF INSOLVENCY;

In Confequence of which HE Regiftered

His Kingdom of CORSICA

For the USE of His CREDITORS.

The GRAVE, great Teacher, to a level brings
HEROES and BEGGARS, GALLEY-SLAVES and KINGS.
But THEODORE this Moral learn'd, e'er dead;
FATE pour'd it's Leffons on his *living* Head,
Beftow'd a KINGDOM, and denied him BREAD.

6.

TO
Mr. GRAY,
ON HIS
ODES.

I.

REPINE not, GRAY, that our weak dazzled Eyes
　　Thy daring heights and brightneſs ſhun,
How few can track the Eagle to the ſkies,
　　Or like Him,　gaze upon the Sun !

II.

The gentle Reader loves the gentle Muſe,
　　That little dares, and little means,
Who humbly ſips her Learning from *Reviews*,
　　Or flutters in the *Magazines*.

III.

No longer now from Learning's ſacred Store
　　Our Minds their health and vigor draw;
HOMER, and PINDAR are rever'd no more,
　　No more the *Stagyrite is Law.*

　　　　　　　　　　　　　　　　　　　　　　IV.

Chronicle, 1 October 1757. The full text of Garrick's letter of 6 October 1757, offering the verses to HW for the SH Press, is reprinted in the JPO, p. 29.

JPO, pp. 5–6: '17 October 1757. Printed two dozen copies of Mr. Garrick's stanzas to Mr. Gray, occasioned by his odes being but moderately well received by the public: here they follow. . . . 26 October. Printed three dozen more of Mr. Garrick's verses to Gray.'

Gray to HW [21 October 1757]: 'I have looked with all my eyes, and can not discover one error, which is the greatest misfortune, that can befall a critick.'

T. F. Dibdin seems to have been the first to mislead numerous booksellers and collectors by asserting in his *Bibliomania* (Second edition, 1811, pp. 715–16) that only six copies of these verses were printed at the SH Press. Apparently Dibdin saw the verses in a copy of Gray's *Odes* then in the library of the Marquis of Bute at Luton. Because of their presumed rarity, Dibdin reprinted the text. The next year John Major, in offering a copy for sale in his *Catalogue of Rare Books and Tracts printed at Strawberry Hill* [1812], notes that only six copies were printed and refers the reader to the reprint of the poem in *Bibliomania*. The *Catalogue of Books and Tracts printed at the Private Press of the Hon. Horace Walpole,* printed by J. McCreery in 1813, likewise says of Garrick's Verses, 'Only 6 copies printed.' Martin accepts the figure: 'Six copies only are said to have been printed'; and, despite Upcott's denial as quoted by Lowndes, many auctioneers and dealers have continued to advertise their copies by suggesting that only six copies were printed. Since the publication of the JPO in 1923, however, it has been known that sixty copies in all were printed.

The verses are printed on both sides of a quarto leaf measuring 27.5 x 22 cm. (Mr. Coykendall's copy). They were reprinted by Kirgate, probably after 1790; of this edition Mr. Lewis Buddy printed a facsimile in 1904. They were also reprinted in the nineteenth century.

STATES AND VARIANTS

If HW had the type distributed (it may have been kept standing) between 17 October and 26 October (he began to print the *Catalogue of Royal and Noble Authors* on 17 October), then there must be two legitimate SH printings for 1757, but I have not been able to discriminate them: the copies printed in 1757 that have been examined (Mr. Coykendall, two in the Huntington Library, and WSL) are all from the same setting of type. The paper of this edition is the same as that used for Gray's *Odes.* The next edition, common enough as Detached Pieces go, was printed on a paper which was first used at

TO
Mr. GRAY,
ON HIS
ODES.

I.

REPINE not, GRAY, that our weak dazzled Eyes
    Thy daring heights and brightneſs ſhun,
How few can track the Eagle to the ſkies,
    Or like Him, gaze upon the Sun!

II.

The gentle Reader loves, the gentle Muſe,
    That little dares, and little means,
Who humbly ſips her Learning from *Reviews,*
    Or flutters in the *Magazines.*

III.

No longer now from Learning's ſacred Store
    Our Minds their health and vigor draw;
HOMER, and PINDAR are rever'd no more,
    No more the *Stagyrite is Law.*

IV.

7. KIRGATE'S REPRINT.

TO
Mr. GRAY,
ON HIS
ODES.

I.

REPINE not, GRAY, that our weak dazzled Eyes
    Thy daring heights and brightneſs ſhun,
How few can track the Eagle to the ſkies,
    Or like Him, gaze upon the Sun!

II.

The gentle Reader loves the gentle Muſe,
    That little dares, and little means,
Who humbly ſips her Learning from *Reviews,*
    Or flutters in the *Magazines.*

III.

No longer now from Learning's ſacred Store
    Our Minds their health and vigor draw;
HOMER, and PINDAR are rever'd no more,
    No more the *Stagyrite is Law.*   **IV.**

SH for the quarto edition of HW's *Works* (*Bibliography*, No. 16 above), begun in 1768. (The original edition of 1764 of the Verses to Lady Charles Spencer, described in *Detached Pieces*, No. 13 below, is an isolated earlier appearance of this paper.) These copies regularly have parts of the watermark (lily, Strasburg bend, LVG) or the countermark (IV) of this paper. To say categorically that this edition was printed in a particular year is impossible; I think it was certainly not printed in 1757—copies are too numerous, for one thing—and there is sufficient cumulative evidence against Kirgate to induce me to class this with all his other reprints shortly before or just after HW's death.

The nineteenth-century reprint, interesting because of its combination of Fry italic type with Wilson roman, is discussed in connection with the Verses to Lady Townshend (No. 2 above).

COPIES

Original edition: Huntington (two copies: one in Bull's collection, and one in a volume of SH pieces bound late in the eighteenth century); Lord Rothschild (not seen, but this copy is bound with HW's copy of Gray's *Odes*); Mr. Frederick Coykendall (Thomas Barrett's copy); Mr. W. M. Elkins (Pinkerton's copy); WSL (Arbury-Smith Sale at Anderson Galleries, 1921; Scribner's, December 1924, to WSL). Also undoubtedly original was a copy sold in Gray's library, Sotheby's, 8 August 1854, lot 239.

Kirgate's reprint: Harvard (2 copies: Merritt, Widener); Princeton (Morgan: 2 copies, one bound with a copy of Gray's *Odes* on thick paper, from Kirgate's library); Yale; Lord Rothschild; WSL (2 copies: in collections of Detached Pieces formed by Utterson and Holford, respectively); Spoor Collection.

Nineteenth-century reprint: Clark Memorial Library (from Robinson); the late Mr. Leonard Whibley; WSL (2 copies).

Other copies (not seen and therefore not differentiated as to edition): Bodleian; British Museum (Grenville); Eton College (Storer); Victoria and Albert (Dyce); Lord Derby; Lord Strachie; Lord Waldegrave; a copy offered by Quaritch in Catalogue 530 (1937).

8. COPY OF A GENERAL ORDER OF THE COURT OF EXCHEQUER, FOR THE FUTURE MORE REGULAR ISSUING OF SUMMONS OF THE PIPE, &C. 1758.

Lowndes 37; Martin, p. 507.

JPO, p. 7: '30 September 1758. 120 copies printed of an Order of the Court of Exchequer, for regulating the issuing of Summons of the pipe.'

AMONG *the* ORDERS *of* TRINITY-TERM *in the Thirty-first Year of the Reign of his Majesty King* GEORGE *the* Second, *in the Book of Orders of the Court of Exchequer, in the Lord Treasurer's Remembrancer's Office, there is contained as follows:*

SERJEANTS-INN HALL Chancery-Lane,

WEDNESDAY, the Twenty-first Day of JUNE, 1758.

WHEREAS by the Statutes of 13th and 14th of Charles the Second, It is enacted that no Sheriff or Sheriffs, for the Year 1661, nor any Sheriff or Sheriffs to be thereafter made or appointed within the Kingdom of England, should be charged in Account to Answer any illeviable Seizure, Farm, Rent or Debt, or other Seizure, Farm, Rent, Debt, Matter or Thing whatsoever, which was not writ in Process to him or them to be Seized, wherein the Persons of whom, or the Lands and Tenements out of which, together with the Cause for which the same should be so Seized, should be plainly and particularly expressed, but should be thereof wholly discharged without Petition, Plea, or other Trouble or Charge whatsoever, by force whereof the several Seizures, Farms, Rents, Debts, Matters and Things, standing in Charge upon the Great or Annual Roll of this Court, ought to be written in the Process, called, *The* SUMMONS *of the* PIPE, Issuing at two stated Times in every Year, to the several Sheriffs within England, for the levying thereof: And in the said Process the Persons of whom, or the Lands and Tenements out of which, together with the Cause for which the same shall be so levied, ought to be plainly and particularly Expressed. NOW THIS COURT, taking Notice that for diverse Years past, the said Process and Summons of the Pipe hath Issued to the several Sheriffs of England, not expressing the several particulars in the said Act mentioned; but instead thereof charging only and describing certain Sums as the Amount of diverse Rents, in certain several Townships and Parishes, or certain Hundreds, and such like general Charges, contrary to the true Intent and Meaning of the said Act of Parliament, to the Trouble and Vexation of the several Sheriffs of England, and to the endangering the Diminution, if not the whole Loss of the King's Majesty's antient Revenues, standing charged in the said Great or Annual Roll.

THIS COURT doth therefore think fit and ORDER, that the Clerk and Comptroller of the Pipe, the Secondaries and other Sworn Clerks of their said Offices in their several Assignments, do before the Issuing of the Summons of Pipe in Hillary-Term next, make diligent Search and Inspection among the Annual or Great Rolls of this Court, and particularly into such of the said Great Rolls as are immediately subsequent to the making the said Act, that they may be thereby enabled to Issue the said Process conformable to the true intent of the said Act. AND this Court doth further ORDER, that upon the Issuing of the said Summons of the Pipe in Hillary-Term next, the said Clerk and Comptroller of the Pipe, the Secondaries and other Sworn Clerks of their said Offices in their several Assignments, do take special Care that the several Seizures, Farms, Rents, Debts, Matters and Things, which ought by the Course of the Exchequer to be written in the said Process of the Summons of the Pipe, to the several Sheriffs of England, to be by them severally Levied, be accordingly so written in the said Process at the Issuing thereof in Hillary-Term next, to every of the said Sheriffs: And that in the said Process so to be Issued to every of the said Sheriffs, the Persons of whom, or the Lands and Tenements out of which, together with the Cause for which the same is to be so Levied, be plainly and particularly Expressed in manner as the same severally appear to stand Expressed in the said Great or Annual Roll, and particularly in such of them as are immediately subsequent to the making of the said Act.

AND

8. REDUCED. WIDTH OF ORIGINAL 17.5 cm.

Martin doubted whether this piece was printed at SH (probably because he misunderstood a note in Baker's *Catalogue*, 1810), but the paper is the same as that used for SH books, 1757–58, and the Caslon type is unexceptionable. HW's entry in the JPO vindicates the piece completely.

Two leaves, folio; approximately 38.5 x 24 cm. uncut. The text of sixty-four lines is printed on the first two pages, with the printed endorsement on p. [4].

COPIES

Bodleian; Eton College (Storer); Harvard (Merritt); Huntington (Bull); Princeton (Morgan); WSL (2 copies).

One of the two copies now at Farmington was sold by Kirgate to Francis Annesley in 1800 for 10/6 (Kirgate's bill, now WSL). But it is unlikely that many of the 120 copies were left at SH after HW's death; there is no copy in the set of Detached Pieces formed by Kirgate that is now at Chewton Priory.

9. [QUESTIONS PROPOSED TO THE SOCIETY OF ANTI-QUARIES], 'PAINTING IN OIL WAS DISCOVERED BY JOHN AB EYCK.' 1760.

Not in Lowndes or Martin, but see No. 10 below.

This piece is not recorded in the JPO. In his *Anecdotes of Painting* (1762), i.24–25, HW says that he proposed to the Society of Antiquaries the question of what the painters used for mixing their colors before the discovery of oil painting. Since the text of this piece concerns that problem, HW probably printed it when he was seeking information on the problem. Although no correspondence between HW and the Society of Antiquaries has been preserved, the question was doubtless put to the Society by HW before he began to print the *Anecdotes* in November 1760.

These 'Questions' are a shorter version of the full text (No. 10 below), and probably represent an earlier, rejected form of No. 10. The copy in Austin Dobson's extra-illustrated *Horace Walpole* (now in the Widener Collection at Harvard) has a note in Kirgate's hand, 'This was not used.' I suppose a few rejected or proof copies may have been laid aside and kept until Kirgate came to the Press.

The best evidence of the authenticity of both No. 9 and No. 10 is perhaps the presence of both in the Storer Collection at Eton College. The copies of No. 9 and No. 10 in Mrs. Damer's collection, sold at Hodgson's in 1902, are probably the copies now at Harvard in the Merritt Collection.

The text is printed on one side of the leaf; one WSL copy measures approximately 25 x 21 cm., but other copies are much cut down: Bull's copy (Huntington) is 7.8 x 9.6 cm. No watermark is visible in

PAINTING in Oil was difcovered by JOHN AB EYCK, who died in 1441. But there are a few Pictures ftill preferved, and painted on Board, before that Time, or before the Secret probably arrived in *England*; as of EDWARD III at *Windfor*, of WILLIAM of *Wickham* at *Oxford*; Two of RICHARD II, (the one at *Weftminfter-*Abbey has indeed been repaired more than once) the other is at *Wilton*; One of HENRY IV at *Hampton-Court* in *Herefordfhire*: more than One of CHAUCER, and of HENRY V. There are alfo feveral in *Italy* of the Old Mafters, before Oil-painting was known there. I afk, With what were they painted ? If it is anfwered, in Water-colours ; I afk, How it came that the Varnifh which JOHN AB EYCK was fearching for when he difco-vered the Ufe of Oil-colours, did not efface the Water-Colours ?

9.

QUESTIONS propoſed to the SOCIETY of ANTIQUARIES.

PAINTING in Oil was diſcovered by JOHN AB EYCK, in 1410. But there are ſome Pictures ſtill preſerved, and painted on Board, before that Time, or before the Secret probably arrived in *England*; as of EDWARD III at *Windſor*, of WILLIAM of *Wickham* at *Oxford*; Two of RICHARD II, (the one at *Weſtminſter*-Abbey has indeed been repaired more than once) the other is at *Wilton*; One of HENRY IV at *Hampton-Court* in *Herefordſhire*: more than One of CHAUCER, and of HENRY V. who (the lateſt of this Number) died in 1422. *With what were theſe Pictures painted?* The old Painters, when they painted on Walls, uſed Size, or what was called Diſtemper; but it is not ſuppoſed that they painted on Board in the ſame manner.

If it is anſwered that They painted in Water-colours, I aſk if They could varniſh Water-colours? JOHN AB EYCK diſcovered the Method of Painting in Oil, as he was ſearching for a Varniſh.

It might be ſaid that the Pictures I have mentioned, were painted after the Uſe of Oil was diſcovered; but it is ſcarce probable that *all* the Pictures I have mentioned were drawn after the Perſons they repreſent were dead. On the curious Picture of RICHARD II and his Patron Saints at *Wilton*, which was engraved by HOLLAR, it is ſaid that That Picture was painted before the Invention of Oil-painting in 1410. I dont know whether that is meant to imply that This Picture was painted in Oil before that Secret was found out by JOHN AB EYCK; as if ſome other Painter had known the ſame Art; or whether it means that This Picture is painted in Water-colours, as I ſhould rather ſuppoſe, by the Gold-ground, and the brightneſs of the Colours, which reſemble ancient illuminated MSS. It has a Glaſs before it, and is finely preſerved, which corroborates the latter Suppoſition.

It is ſubmitted to the Society to reſolve this difficult Queſtion,

With what the Old Painters mixed their Colours?

the three copies examined, but the paper resembles that used for the edition of Lucan in 1760.

COPIES

Eton College (Storer); Harvard (2 copies: Merritt, Widener); Huntington (Bull); Lord Derby; WSL (2 copies).

10. QUESTIONS PROPOSED TO THE SOCIETY OF ANTI-QUARIES. 1760.

Lowndes 99; Martin, p. 512.
Lowndes and Martin record only one version.
These 'Questions' were doubtless printed by HW before November 1760 for presentation to the Society of Antiquaries (see No. 9 above). HW printed the shorter version first, but presumably discarded it after printing some copies that he did not use. This enlarged version was obviously more carefully prepared and written.

The text is printed on one side of a quarto leaf, approximately 24.5 x 15 cm.

COPIES

Eton College (Storer); Harvard (Merritt).

11. PORTRAIT OF JOHN EARL GRANVILLE. 1763.

Lowndes 56; Martin, p. 508.
JPO, p. 10: '10 January 1763. Printed about 30 copies of the portrait of Lord Granville.'
The verses were written 23 December (probably 1762), but were not printed until after the death of Lord Granville, 2 January 1763. The date when the verses were written is confused by HW's conflicting references. In *Works* (1770), i.31, the subtitle is: 'Written immediately after his death in 1763.' In a letter to Mann, 28 January 1763, HW speaks of 'the enclosed lines on Lord Granville, which I wrote last year.' (This can mean either 'last month' or 'about twelve months ago.') In his 'Short Notes,' p. xlvi, HW says under 23 December 1761: 'Wrote a portrait of Lord Granville in verse, to serve as an epitaph for him.' It seems likely, however, that HW, writing long after the event, made the entry in 'Short Notes' under the wrong year, inasmuch as he wrote to Montagu: 'Past midnight, 23 December 1761. I am this minute come home. . . . Shall I fill up the rest of my paper with some extempore lines, that I wrote t'other night on Lady Mary Coke.' Here would have been the chance to quote the Portrait of Lord Granville if he had just composed it earlier in

PORTRAIT

OF

JOHN EARL GRANVILLE.

COmmanding Beauty, smooth'd by chearful grace,
 Sat on each open feature of his face:
Bold was his language, rapid, glowing, strong;
And Science flow'd spontaneous from his tongue:
A Genius, seizing systems, slighting rules;
And void of gall, with boundless scorn of Fools.
Ambition dealt her flambeau to his hand,
And Bacchus sprinkled fuel on the brand.
His wish --- to counsel monarchs, or controul;
His means? --- th'impetuous ardour of his soul;
For while his views outstrip'd a mortal's span,
Nor Prudence drew, nor Craft pursued the plan.
Swift fell the scaffold of his airy . pride,
But, slightly-built, diffus'd no ruin wide:
Unhurt, undaunted, undisturb'd he fell;
Could laugh the same, and the same stories tell:
And more a Sage, than he, who bad await
His Revels, till his conquests were compleat,
Our jovial Statesman either sail unfurl'd,
And drank his bottle, tho' he miss'd the World.

11. ORIGINAL EDITION.

PORTRAIT

OF

JOHN EARL GRANVILLE.

COMMANDING Beauty, ſmooth'd by chearful Grace,
  Sat on each open Feature of his Face.
Bold was his Language, rapid, glowing, ſtrong;
And Science flow'd ſpontaneous from his Tongue.
A Genius, ſeizing Syſtems, ſlighting Rules;
And void of Gall, with boundleſs ſcorn of Fools.
Ambition dealt her Flambeau to his Hand,
And Bacchus ſprinkled Fuel on the Brand.
His Wiſh to counſel Monarchs, or controul;
His Means----th' impetuous Ardour of his Soul:
For, while his Views out-ſtript a Mortal's Span,
Nor Prudence drew, nor Craft purſu'd the Plan.
Swift fell the Scaffold of his airy Pride,
But, ſlightly buïlt, diffus'd no Ruin wide.
Unhurt, undaunted, undiſturb'd he fell;
Cou'd laugh the ſame, and the ſame Stories tell:
And more a Sage than * he, who bade await
His Revels, till his Conqueſts were compleat,
Our jovial Stateſman either Sail unfurl'd,
And drank his Bottle, tho' he miſs'd the World.

                                        H. W.

          * Pyrrhus.

          11. KIRGATE'S REPRINT.

the day. But 23 December 1762, when Granville's death was imminent, seems a very natural date.

HW probably sent the verses to Gray for correction in December 1762, or else just after the death of Lord Granville. Gray returned his corrected version of sixteen lines, omitting four of HW's, in a letter probably written *ca.* 5 January 1763. But although HW adopted some of Gray's changes, a comparison of the draft of the poem in HW's hand (now in the possession of Sir W. A. Waller, Bt.) with the printed version shows that in substance HW retained his own phrasing. (For HW's draft, see *Correspondence of Gray, Walpole, West, and Ashton,* ed. Toynbee, Oxford 1915, ii.214, note 3.)

On the copy at Chewton, Kirgate has corrected the punctuation and has written, 'Printed before I came to Strawberry Hill, which was in 1768.'

The verses are printed on one side of a quarto leaf measuring approximately 17.9 x 14.6 cm. trimmed (Bull); Kirgate's reprint measures 24 x 18.4 cm.

STATES AND VARIANTS

Lowndes mentions an impression in English and French. This note was probably added by Bohn (it is not in Martin) because a copy so described was sold at Sotheby's, 22 May 1848 (Eyton Sale), lot 1479. No such copy has been seen, however, and I venture to suggest that it may have been a leaf from the quarto *Works* of 1770 (where a French translation is printed on the verso), but this is only a guess.

Messrs. Quaritch offered a copy signed 'W. H.' in 1928 (Catalogue 415) and again in 1937 (Catalogue 530). This may have been a typographical error in cataloguing, or it may represent an unrecorded variant or edition.

The copy in Bull's collection (see illustration) is undoubtedly original: it is printed on paper first used in the *Catalogue of Engravers* during the winter of 1762–63. The paper of the reprint appears to be identical with that used in a number of Kirgate's reprints: 'There was a little man' (No. 14), the Pentycross Verses (No. 18), and others. All these are assigned with varying degrees of assurance to 1797; they are discussed more fully under the Pentycross Verses.

The punctuation (but not the capitalization) of the reprint was obviously taken by Kirgate from the text in the *Works* of 1770, and the note explaining line 17 comes from the same source. It is worth adding that both WSL copies derive from Kirgate, as do the Dyce and Lord Waldegrave copies.

OTHER EDITIONS

The verses were reprinted in the *Gentleman's Magazine* for January 1763 (xxxiii.38); in the *Annual Register* for 1762 (printed in 1763), p. 223; in the *London Magazine* for January 1763 (xxxii.39); and also in the *Works* of 1770 and 1798, and (in the review of the *Works*) in the *Monthly Review* for September 1798.

COPIES

Original edition: Huntington (Bull).

Kirgate's reprint: WSL (2 copies).

Other copies (not seen and therefore not differentiated as to edition): Victoria and Albert (Dyce); Lord Derby; Lord Waldegrave.

12. VERSES TO MADAME DE BOUFFLERS AND MADAME DUSSON. 1763.

Lowndes 76, 89; Martin, p. 511.

JPO, p. 11: '17 May 1763. Mesdames de Boufflers and Dusson, two French Ladies who came to England this year, breakfasted at Strawberry Hill, and were carried to see the Printinghouse; where desiring to see something printed, the following lines which had been set ready, were taken off [here follow the verses].'

On the following day, 18 May 1763, at Esher (see HW to George Montagu, 17–19 May 1763), the Duc de Nivernois translated the verses into French ('A Madame de Boufflers,' 11 lines, and 'A Madame D'Usson,' 9 lines), and HW transcribed them into the JPO.

On a copy of the verses, now at Chewton, Kirgate notes who these ladies were and when they came to SH.

On another copy, in the possession of the Duke of Northumberland at Alnwick Castle, there is the following MS note: 'The undermentioned Ladies making a visit to Mr. Walpole at Strawberry Hill to see his printing Press and the manner of printing upon which the following lines were immediately printed off and presented to them.' Perhaps HW gave a copy of the verses to the Duchess of Northumberland.

The verses are printed on one side of a quarto leaf measuring approximately 24 x 19.6 cm.

STATES AND VARIANTS

George Baker, in his *Catalogue of the . . . Press at Strawberry Hill* [1810], lists this piece, but he also lists two others: 'French Verses to Madame de Boufflers, 11 lines' and 'French Verses to Madame

The PRESS speaks,

For Madame de BOUFFLERS.

THE gracefull Fair, who loves to know,
 Nor dreads the North's inclement Snow;
Who bids her polish'd accent wear
The British diction's harsher air;
Shall read her praise in ev'ry clime,
Where Types can speak, or Poets rhyme.

For Madame DUSSON.

FEIGN not an ignorance of what I speak;
 You cou'd not miss it's meaning, were it Greek;
'Tis the same language Belgium utter'd first,
The same which from admiring Gallia burst.
True Sentiment a like expression pours;
Each country says the same to Eyes like Yours.

12.

Dusson, 9 lines.' Both Martin and Lowndes follow Baker in listing these French versions as SH pieces (Lowndes 90 and 91).

But no copy has been seen. Neither J. W. K. Eyton nor George Smith, nineteenth-century collectors who possessed two of the largest collections of SH Detached Pieces, had copies, and the French versions are not with HW's letter to Montagu in the Kimbolton MSS. Dr. Toynbee could not find any for his bibliography in the JPO.

It seems doubtful whether the French versions were ever printed, at SH or elsewhere. HW says of the English version (in the JPO): 'the following lines . . . were taken off'; but of the French version he says merely: 'The next day the Duc de Nivernois translated the verses thus.' (The whole entry in the JPO looks as if it had been written at one time, perhaps during the next week.) In writing to Montagu, on the nineteenth, he says: 'Monsieur de Nivernois, who had been absorbed all day and lagging behind, translating my verses, was delivered of his version, and of some more lines. . . . P. S. I enclose a copy of both the English and the French verses.' Again there is no mention of printing the French version: he had returned from the outing at Esher late the night before, and he went to Arlington Street for dinner on the nineteenth. By the time he returned to SH, on the twenty-second, there would have been little occasion for printing the French translations.

I suggest, albeit with some trepidation, that Nos. 90 and 91 in Lowndes are bibliographical ghosts.

COPIES

Victoria and Albert (Dyce); Huntington (Bull); Duke of Northumberland; Lord Waldegrave; WSL (the Spoor copy—probably the copy sold with Mrs. Damer's books at Hodgson's in 1902).

13. VERSES SENT TO LADY CHARLES SPENCER. 1764.

Lowndes 55; Martin, p. 508.

HW did not record this piece in the JPO, but it was probably printed between 23 April 1764 (when HW finished printing *Poems by Anna Chamber, Countess Temple*, JPO, p. 13) and the end of May, since the verses were printed in the *Gentleman's Magazine* for May 1764 (issued early in June). Inasmuch as Lord Charles Spencer married Mary Beauclerk 2 October 1762, the last line of the poem, 'And Spencer will vouch it, tho' married a year,' seems to date the writing of the verses late in 1763 or early in 1764.

[181]

VERSES

SENT TO

* LADY CHARLES SPENCER

With a painted TAFFETY,

Occasioned by saying she was low in Pocket and could
not buy a new Gown.

SINCE the times are so bad and are still growing worse,
  You may make this your own without sinking your
purse.

The nymphs and the fauns say the pattern is new,

And that Flora's gay pencil design'd it, is true;

It was finish'd and destin'd for Beauty's fair queen;

So to whom it belongs is most easily seen.

Tho' flow'rets soon wither, yet these will not die,

When fading reviv'd by a beam from your eye:

If you only breathe on them they'll fill the whole room

With sweets far surpassing Arabia's perfume.

Refuse not this trifle; your title is clear,

And Spencer will vouch it, tho' married a year.

* Mary Beauclerc, daughter of lord Vere, and wife of lord Charles Spencer.
Niece of Lady Temple.

VERSES

SENT TO

*Lady CHARLES SPENCER

With a painted TAFFETY,

Occafioned by faying fhe was low in pocket and could
not buy a new Gown.

SINCE the times are fo bad and are ftill growing worfe,
   You may make this your own without finking your
  purfe.

The nymphs and the fauns fay the pattern is new,

And that Flora's gay pencil defign'd it, is true ;

It was finifh'd and deftin'd for Beauty's fair queen ;

So to whom it belongs is moft eafily feen.

Tho' flow'rets foon wither, yet thefe will not die,

When fading reviv'd by a beam from your eye :

If you only breathe on them they'll fill the whole room

With fweets far furpaffing Arabia's perfume.

Refufe not this trifle ; your title is clear,

And Spencer will vouch it, tho' married a year.

* Mary Beauclerc, daughter of lord Vere, and wife of lord Charles Spencer.

VERSES TO LADY CHARLES SPENCER

In a bound volume at Chewton entitled 'Poems Strawberry Hill 1757–89,' with Charles Bedford's bookplate, there is a copy of the verses with Kirgate's note at bottom: 'By Anna Chamber, Countess Temple: should be added to her poems.' Another copy at Chewton has the following note by Kirgate: 'By Anna Chamber Countess Temple. This was a supplemental leaf to Lady Temple's poems, which had been printed at Strawberry Hill in 1764.'

The verses are printed on one side of a quarto leaf measuring approximately 25.5 x 20.2 cm. trimmed. They were reprinted by Kirgate, probably after 1787, and again in the nineteenth century.

States and Variants

The existence of two editions of these verses was first noted, as far as we are aware, in the Catalogue of the Hanrott Sale at Evans's, 5 March 1834, lot 2658. Two copies, 'one with a variation,' were sold at Sotheby's in May 1848 (Eyton Sale), lot 1479; perhaps these were from the Hanrott Sale. If one of these copies could be proved to be the nineteenth-century reprint in Wilson type, we could date all those reprints 'before 1834'; but the 'two editions' were probably the original and Kirgate's reprint.

The *three* editions illustrated can be easily differentiated: the last line of the original edition is 10.4 cm., and 'Pocket' in line 5 has a capital 'P'; in Kirgate's reprint, 'Pocket' has a lower-case 'p'; in the nineteenth-century reprint in Wilson type, 'Pocket' has a capital 'P,' but the last line is extended to 11.1 cm.

The original edition is above suspicion: HW's copy, with his MS note, and Cole's copy provide sufficient authentication. The paper, not otherwise seen as early as this (the Garrick Verses on this paper are presumed to be a later reprint by Kirgate), appears to be the same as that used for the quarto edition of the *Works*, begun in 1768.

Kirgate's reprint on wove paper is defined by the evidence presented under Lady Temple's *Poems* (No. 12 in the *Bibliography* above). Copies at Harvard and Princeton, as well as three copies at Farmington, were printed as the last leaf of the *Poems,* although some copies (at Princeton, for example) have since been detached from the *Poems*. Other copies, with the same setting of type, are on paper like that used in 1787 for the last sheet of the *Works* (and leaves O and O$_2$ of the large *Description of SH*): it is obvious that these were printed separately when the *Poems* were reprinted.

VERSES

SENT TO

*Lady CHARLES SPENCER

With a painted TAFFETY,

Occafioned by faying fhe was low in Pocket and could
not buy a new Gown.

SINCE the times are fo bad and are ftill growing worfe,
  You may make this your own without finking your
  purfe.
The nymphs and the fauns fay the pattern is new,
And that Flora's gay pencil defign'd it, is true;
It was finifh'd and deftin'd for Beauty's fair queen;
So to whom it belongs is most eafily feen.
Tho' flow'rets foon wither, yet thefe will not die,
When fading reviv'd by a beam from your eye:
If you only breathe on them they'll fill the whole room
With fweets far furpaffing Arabia's perfume.
Refufe not this trifle; your title is clear,
And Spencer will vouch it, tho' married a year.

* Mary Beauclerc, daughter of lord Vere, and wife of lord Charles Spencer.

13. NINETEENTH-CENTURY REPRINT.

The nineteenth-century reprint (discussed more fully under the Verses to Lady Townshend, No. 2 above) is also on wove paper, but a different paper from that of Kirgate's reprint.

COPIES

Original edition: Huntington (Bull); Mr. Frederick Coykendall (Thomas Barrett's copy); Mr. W. M. Elkins (Pinkerton's copy); WSL (3 copies: one bound in HW's copy of Lady Temple's *Poems,* and one in Cole's copy).

Kirgate's reprint: Harvard (Merritt: 2 copies); Princeton (Morgan); Lord Waldegrave (2 copies; not seen, but undoubtedly of this edition); WSL (7 copies, including three printed as last leaf of Lady Temple's *Poems*).

Nineteenth-century reprint: WSL (2 copies).

Other copies (not seen, and therefore not differentiated as to edition): British Museum (Grenville); Eton College (Storer); Victoria and Albert (Dyce); Lord Derby.

14. A SONG, 'THERE WAS A LITTLE MAN.' 1764.

Lowndes 73; Martin, p. 510.

JPO, p. 13: '31 May 1764. Printed some copies of a ballad by Sir Ch. Sidley, beginning, There was a little man.'

The note in the JPO (p. 46) identifies the author as Sir Charles Sedley (*ca.* 1639–1701), the Restoration wit, but the poem does not appear in *The Works of Sir Charles Sedley* (London 1720), or in *The Poetical and Dramatic Works of Sir Charles Sedley,* ed. V. De Sola Pinto (London 1928).

The author of this song is probably Sir Charles Sedley, Bt. (*ca.* 1721–1778), the contemporary of HW and the great-grandson of the Restoration wit. He and HW as members of White's may have been well acquainted: HW became a member in 1744, and Sir Charles Sedley in 1755 (see *History of White's* by Algernon Bourke, London 1892, ii.77). Mr. Walter N. H. Harding of Chicago writes that, in indexing English songbooks, he has found no record of 'There was a little man' in any collection prior to 1770; it appears first in Scotch songbooks: *The Scots Nightingale* (Edinburgh 1778) and *The Charmer* (Edinburgh 1782), but not in the earlier editions of *The Charmer.*

The authorship of the verses is wrongly attributed to Silvester Harding in *A Catalogue of Books and Tracts printed at . . . Strawberry Hill* (London, J. McCreery, 1813, p. 10), in *Bibliotheca Grenvilliana* (4 vols., London 1842–72, iii.432), and in Hodgson's Catalogue, 30 April 1902 (Damer Sale), lot 181.

The Song is printed on one side of a quarto leaf measuring 24 x 18 cm. trimmed.

STATES AND VARIANTS

That this is the original edition, there is some doubt. The water-

A SONG.

THere was a little Man, and he woo'd a little Maid,
   And he faid my little Maid will you wed?
I have little more to fay, than will you yea or nay?
For little faid is foon mended.

Then this little Maid fhe faid, little Sir you've little faid,
To induce a little Maid for to wed;
You muft fay a little more, and muft add a little dower,
E'er I make a little print in your bed.

Then this little Man reply'd, if you'll be my little bride,
I'll raife my love note a little higher;
Tho' I little love to prate, yet you'll find my heart is great,
With the little God of Love all on fire.

Then the little Maid fhe faid, your fire may warm the bed,
But what fhall we do for to eat?
Will the flames you're only rich in, make a fire in the kitchen,
And the little God of Love turn the fpit?

Then this little Man he figh'd, and fome fay a little cry'd,
And his little heart was big all with forrow;
I'll be your little Slave, and if the little that I have,
Be too little, little Dear I will borrow.

Then this little Man fo fhent, made the little Maid relent,
And fet her little foul a thinking;
Tho' his little was but fmall, yet fhe had his little all,
And could have of a Cat but her fkin.

14. PROBABLY A REPRINT BY KIRGATE.

A SONG.

THere was a little Man, and he woo'd a little Maid,
  And he ſaid my little Maid will you wed?
I have little more to ſay, than will you yea or nay?
For little ſaid is ſoon mended.

  Then this little Maid ſhe ſaid, little Sir you've little ſaid,
To induce a little Maid for to wed;
You muſt ſay a little more, and muſt add a little dower,
E'er I make a little print in your bed.

  Then this little Man reply'd, if you'll be my little bride,
I'll raiſe my love note a little higher;
Tho' I little love to prate, yet you'll find my heart is great,
With the little God of Love all on fire.

  Then the little Maid ſhe ſaid, your fire may warm the bed,
But what ſhall we do for to eat?
Will the flames you're only rich in, make a fire in the kitchen,
And the little God of Love turn the ſpit?

  Then this little Man he ſigh'd, and ſome ſay a little cry'd,
And his little heart was big all with ſorrow;
I'll be your little Slave, and if the little that I have,
Be too little, little Dear I will borrow.

  Then this little Man ſo ſhent, made the little Maid relent,
And ſet her little ſoul a thinking;
Tho' his little was but ſmall, yet ſhe had his little all,
And could have of a Cat but her ſkin.

mark (lily, VDL, with countermark IV) seems to link this edition with the group discussed under the Pentycross Verses, No. 18 below. Five copies at Farmington, one at Huntington, and one at Harvard (the only copies examined) are on this paper. At least four of the copies at Farmington seem to derive from Kirgate, in itself a fact that may cause some questioning.

This edition could quickly be vindicated or condemned if either one of the two undoubtedly authentic copies could be traced: (1) the copy offered with Mrs. Damer's books at Hodgson's, 30 April 1902, lot 181, and bought by Denham for £2.6.0; (2) the copy that was presumably in HW's collection of Detached Pieces, bought at Utterson's Sale by Monckton Milnes. But neither has been found.

The nineteenth-century reprint in Wilson type, known to me only from the two copies at Farmington (one purchased from Quaritch in 1939 and the other in a set of Warburton's *Memoirs of HW*), is discussed under the Verses to Lady Townshend, No. 2 above.

COPIES

British Museum (Grenville); Eton College; Victoria and Albert (Dyce); Harvard (Merritt); Huntington (Bull); Lord Derby; Lord Waldegrave; WSL (5 copies).

Nineteenth-century reprint: WSL (2 copies).

15. AIR, 'TRISTES REGRETS, SORTEZ DE MA PENSÉE.' 1764.

Lowndes 93; Martin, p. 511.

JPO, p. 13: '13 June 1764. [Printed some copies] of a French Song, for Lady Susan Stewart, Tristes regrets.' The date seems to be HW's error, since his letter to Montagu assigns the party to the eighteenth, 'to-day.'

HW to George Montagu, 18 June 1764: '[The guests] went to the printing house, and saw a new fashionable French song printed.'

The author was Pierre Antoine de La Place (1707–1793), writer and translator. The song appears in *Anthologie Françoise, ou Chansons choisies* (3 vols., Paris, 1765), ii.181, where the author is given as M. de La Place, 'author of the *Théâtre Anglois* and editor of the *Mercure de France*.' It is also reprinted in *Nouveau receuil des chansons choisies* (4 vols., Genève, 1785), ii.96, without the last stanza, and there entitled 'L'Amante Délaissé,' to the air, 'Un tendre amant veut-il dire qu'il aime.'

The verses are printed on one side of an octavo leaf measuring approximately 19.6 x 12.3 cm. (Harvard).

A I R.

I.

TRISTES regrets, fortez de ma penfée;
    Tout me l'apprend; j'ai perdu mon Ami;
Colin m'aimoit, Colin m'a delaiffée:
Raifon me dit de l'oublier auffi.
Raifon, je cede à ta voix courroucèe:
Mais qui jamais me plaira comme lui?

II.

Tous nos Bergers, empreffez à me plaire,
S'offrent fans ceffe à calmer mes ennuis:
J'ai pû ravir Lycidas à Clithere,
Le beau Cleon pour moi f'eft attendri.
Contre l'ingrat tout aigrit ma Colere;
Mais qui jamais me plaira comme lui?

III.

Le grave Orgon, oracle du village,
De mes parens a recherchè l'appui;
Le fier Hilas, fi riche & fi volage,
Semble pour moi fe fixer aujourdhui.
L'ingrat Colin n'eft ni riche, ni fage,
Mais qui jamais me plaira comme lui?

IV.

Parmi les pleurs, l'efpoir et les alarmes,
Mon pauvre cœur laffè d'avoir langui,
Pour fe combattre effaya d'autres armes,
Dont en fecret le cœur meme a gemi.
Du changement j'ai confultè les charmes;
Mais nul jamais ne me plaira comme lui.

15.

STATES AND VARIANTS

The extra-illustrated copy of Austin Dobson's *Horace Walpole* (now in the Widener Collection at Harvard) contains a version of this song that seems to be either a very clumsy attempt to set it in French, or more probably, in what is whimsically conceived to be Old French or an old dialectal form. Nothing more is known of this version.

COPIES

British Museum (Grenville); Eton College (Storer: 2 copies); Harvard (Merritt); Huntington (Bull); Lord Waldegrave; WSL.

16. EPITAPH ON LORD WALDEGRAVE. 1764.

Lowndes 38; Martin, p. 507.

JPO, p. 13: '3 October 1764. Printed 100 copies of my brother's Epitaph on Lord Waldegrave.' This reference nullifies Kirgate's note on the WSL copy: 'This was certainly not printed at Strawberry-hill, as it is in English Letter [i.e., English Roman, Caslon Old Style] of which there was none till after I came in 1768. T. Kirgate.' Perhaps before 1768 there was comparatively little 'English.' Baker, whose information doubtless came from Kirgate, questions in his *Catalogue* of 1810 whether the Epitaph was printed at SH, and Martin expresses like doubt. Despite Kirgate's rejection of the piece, however, it must be accepted on the evidence of the JPO. Kirgate's rejection of it, furthermore, proves that he prepared no reprints of it.

HW to the Earl of Hertford, 5 October 1764: 'I enclose an epitaph on Lord Waldegrave, written by my brother. . . .'

The Epitaph, on the two Earls, is printed on one side of a folio leaf measuring approximately 38.5 x 24.5 cm. untrimmed (Harvard).

COPIES

Bodleian; Harvard (Merritt); Huntington (Bull); WSL. Another copy, owned by Messrs. Robinson, was offered at Sotheby's in July 1939.

17. THE MAGPIE AND HER BROOD. 1764.

Lowndes 54; Martin, p. 508.

'Short Notes,' p. xlviii: '15 October 1764. Wrote the fable of *The Magpie and her Brood* for Miss Hotham, then near eleven years old, great-niece of Henrietta Hobart, Countess Dowager of Suffolk. It was taken from *Les Nouvelles Récréations de Bonaventure des Periers*, Valet-de-Chambre to the Queen

Underneath this MONUMENT are the Remains
OF THE
Two firſt EARLS of WALDEGRAVE, Father and Son,
both of the Name of JAMES,
Both Servants of that excellent PRINCE
KING GEORGE the Second,
Both by him created Knights of the moſt noble ORDER of the GARTER.

JAMES the Father was employed in foreign Embaſſies to the Courts
of Vienna and Verſailles by King GEORGE the Firſt, and by King
GEORGE the Second; and he did his Court and Country Honour and
Service, and was reſpected wherever his Negotiations made him known.
In his private Capacity, the Affability and Benevolence of his Diſpo-
ſition, and the Goodneſs of his Underſtanding, made him beloved and
eſteemed throughout his Life.

THE Antiquity of his illuſtrious and noble Family is equal to that
of moſt that may be named in any Country or Time, and needs not to
be here recited.

HE died of the Dropſy and Jaundice on the 3d of April, 1741,
aged 57.

HIS eldeſt Son JAMES before-mentioned, and interred within
this Vault, died of the Small-pox, on the 8th of April 1763, aged 48.

THESE were his Years in Number; what they were in Wiſdom, hardly
belongs to Time. The univerſal Reſpect paid to him while he lived,
and the univerſal Lamentation at his Death, are ample Teſtimonies of
a Character not eaſily to be paralleled. He was for many Years the
choſen Friend and Favourite of a King, who was a Judge of Men, yet
never that King's Miniſter, though a Man of Buſineſs, Knowledge and
Learning, beyond moſt of his Cotemporaries; but Ambition viſited
him not, and Contentment filled his Hours. Appealed to for his Arbi-
tration by various contending Parties in the State, upon the higheſt
Differences, his Judgment always tempered their Diſſentions, while his
own Principles, which were the Freedom of the People and the Main-
tenance of the Laws, remained ſtedfaſt and unſhaken, and his Influence
unimpaired, though exerciſed through a long ſeries of Struggles, that
ſerved as Foils to his diſintereſted Virtue. The Conſtancy and Firmneſs
of his Mind were Proof againſt every Trial but the Diſtreſſes of Mankind, and therein he was as a Rock with many Springs, and his Gene-
roſity was as the Waters that flow from it nouriſhing the Plains beneath. He was wiſe in the firſt Degree of Wiſdom, Maſter of a pow-
erful and delicate Wit, had as ready a Conception and as quick Parts
as any Man that ever lived, and never loſt his Wiſdom in his Wit, nor
his Coolneſs by Provocation. He ſmiled at Things that drive other Men
to Anger. He was a Stranger to Reſentment, not to Injuries; thoſe
feared him moſt that loved him; yet he was revered by all, for he was
as true a Friend as ever bore that Name, and as generous an Enemy as
ever bad Man tried. He was in all Things undiſturbed, modeſt, placid
and humane. To him broad Day-light and the Commerce of the
World were as eaſy as the Night and Solitude. To him the Return of
Night and Solitude muſt have been a Seaſon of ever bleſt Reflection.
To him this now deep Night muſt through the Merits of his Redeemer
Jeſus Chriſt be everlaſting Peace and Joy.

O Death, thy Sting is to the Living! O Grave, thy Victory is over the
unburied, the Wife---the Child---the Friend that is left behind?

THUS ſaith the Widow of this incomparable Man, his once moſt happy Wife, now the faithful Remembrancer of all his Virtues, MARIA
Counteſs Dowager of WALDEGRAVE, who inſcribes this Tablet to his
beloved Memory.

*This was certainly not printed at Strawberry-hill, as it is in Engliſh
Letter, which there was none till after I came in 1768. J. Kirgate*

16. REDUCED. WIDTH OF ORIGINAL 13.4 cm.

THE
MAGPIE and her BROOD,
A FABLE,

From the Tales of Bonaventure des Periers, *Valet de Chambre
to the* Queen *of* Navarre;

ADDRESSED to Miſs HOTHAM.

HOW anxious is the penſive Parent's thought!

How bleſt the fav'rite Fondling's early lot!

Joy ſtrings her hours on pleaſure's golden twine,

And Fancy forms it to an endleſs line.

But ah! the charm muſt ceaſe or ſoon or late,

When Chicks and Miſſes riſe to Woman's 'ſtate.

The little Tyrant grows in turn a ſlave,

And feels the ſoft anxiety ſhe gave.

This truth, my pretty Friend, an ancient Wit,

Who many a jocund Tale and Legend writ,

Couch'd in that Age's unaffected guiſe,

When Fables were the wiſdom of the wiſe.

To careleſs notes I've tun'd his gothic ſtyle;

Content, if you approve, and Suffolk ſmile.

ONCE

*Miſs Hotham was only child of Sir Charles Hotham Thompſon by Lady Dorothy Hobart,
only Daughter of John firſt Earl of Buckinghamſhire, and lived at Marble-hill,
Twickenham, with her great aunt Henrietta Hobart, Counteſs dowager of Suffolk.*

of Navarre.' HW's copy of Bonaventure Despériers is listed in the SH *Catalogue*, iii.105.

JPO, p. 13: '17 October 1764. [Printed 200 copies] of the Fable of the Magpie and her Brood.'

HW included a copy of the verses in his letter to Cole, 30 October 1764.

One half-sheet, quarto; four pages. An untrimmed copy measures approximately 24.3 x 19.5 cm.

STATES AND VARIANTS

The nineteenth-century reprint in Fry type is discussed more fully under the Verses to Lady Townshend, No. 2 above. It is likely that the original was relatively rare when this reprint was prepared, but 45 copies of the original were in the SH Sale, v.200, bought by Thorpe, and three more were sold with Mrs. Damer's books in 1902; in recent years, therefore, the original has been one of the more common Detached Pieces, whereas the reprint seems to be very rare.

COPIES

Original edition: Huntington (2 copies); Princeton; Yale; WSL (9 copies—one with MS note by Kirgate); Mr. Wade White.

Nineteenth-century reprint: Clark Memorial Library (from Robinson, 1921); WSL.

Copies not seen (but probably original edition in most cases): Bodleian; British Museum (Grenville); Eton College (Storer); New York Public Library; Texas; Victoria and Albert Museum (Dyce); Lord Derby; Lord Strachie; Lord Waldegrave (2 copies); Spoor Collection (sold 1939).

18. VERSES BY THOMAS PENTYCROSS. 1758?

Lowndes 68; Martin, p. 510.

Thomas Pentycross (1748–1808) was for many years rector of St. Mary's, Wallingford, in Berkshire. In addition to these verses, he was the author of some verses on General Oglethorpe (see Nichols's *Literary Anecdotes*, ix.782). The story of his acquaintance with HW is told in the letters here quoted. A copy of Spence's *Parallel*, 1758, presented by HW to Mr. Pentycross, is now WSL.

HW to Mary Berry, 16–17 August 1796: '[I have lately had a visit] from a Mr. Pentycross, a clergyman and schoolmaster of Wallingford, of whom I had heard nothing for eight-and-twenty years, and then having only known him as a Blue-coat boy from Kingston: and how that happened, he gave me this account last week. He was born with a poetic impetus, and walked over hither

THE
MAGPIE and her BROOD,
A FABLE,

From the *Tales of* Bonaventure des Periers, *Valet de Chambre*
to the Queen *of* Navarre;

ADDRESSED to Miſs HOTHAM.

HOW anxious is the penſive Parent's thought!

How bleſt the fav'rite Fondling's early lot!

Joy ſtrings her hours on pleaſure's golden twine,

And Fancy forms it to an endleſs line.

But ah! the charm muſt ceaſe or ſoon or late,

When chicks and Miſſes riſe to Woman's 'ſtate,

The little Tyrant grows in turn a ſlave,

And feels the ſoft anxiety ſhe gave.

This truth, my pretty Friend, an ancient Wit,

Who many a jocund Tale and Legend writ,

Couch'd in that Age's unaffected guiſe,

When Fables were the wiſdom of the wiſe.

To careleſs notes I've tun'd his gothic ſtyle;

Content, if you approve, and Suffolk ſmile.

ONCE

I.

THRO' the bosom of yon trees
Dies away the panting breeze!
Thro' the long-drawn cloysters pale,
Trembling to the busy gale,
Silv'ring sweeps the moon along,
And suggests sweet-soothing song.
Nature sleeps, and all is still,
But the lyre that wakes at will.
WALPOLE does the strings inspire,
To WALPOLE wakes and swells the lyre.

II.

Health, thou rosy-dimpled maid,
Roving gay the sylvan glade,
On the hospitable gate
With thy choicest blessings wait.
Peace, with learned Ease, attend
On the Patron and the Friend.
Smiling Candour join the train,
And protect this artless strain.
To generous WALPOLE haste away,
And at his feet subject the Bard's unpolish'd lay.

T. PENTYCROSS.

18.

with a copy of verses by no means despicable, which he begged old Margaret [Margaret Young, HW's housekeeper] to bring up to me. . . . I saw him, and let her show him the house. I think he sent me an ode or two afterwards, and I never heard his name again till this winter. . . .'

HW to William Cole, 24 July 1776: '[Mr. Pentycross] was a blue-coat boy and came hither then to some of my servants, having at that age a poetic turn.'

'Eight-and-twenty years' before 1796 would be 1768, and this furnishes a likely enough date for his juvenile verses. But as a date for the printing of the verses, 1768 is less satisfactory. See STATES AND VARIANTS below.

The Verses are printed on one side of a quarto leaf, measuring approximately 24 x 18.8 cm.

STATES AND VARIANTS

That the copy illustrated was printed in 1768 seems to me very unlikely. The juvenile verses were undoubtedly composed at the time of the visit in 1768 or soon afterwards, and they may have been printed then, although HW makes no mention of the Verses in the JPO.

But copies seem curiously plentiful for such an ephemeral piece; and a good many derive from Kirgate. In the sale of George Smith's library at Sotheby's, July 1867, in Kirgate's collection of Detached Pieces, a copy of the Pentycross Verses was listed, 'with the original in the author's autograph.' (The collection is now at Chewton Priory, but the Pentycross Verses, to judge from Lord Waldegrave's list, seem to have strayed.) One is led to wonder whether Kirgate, finding the MS copy of the Verses, decided to print them on his own responsibility in 1797: in Baker's *Catalogue* of 1810, this piece is marked with an asterisk to indicate that it was not printed for HW. (Kirgate added a note to Bull's MS list of SH imprints to the effect that very few were printed.)

In John Major's *Catalogue* of SH books, 1812, a copy of the Pentycross Verses is offered, and then the next entry reads as follows: 'Another copy, struck off on paper of a smaller size. At the top, in the handwriting of Kirgate the printer, in pencil, "but one good one left." ' Paper of a smaller size suggests (but does not prove) a different setting of type. Perhaps the copy sold with Mrs. Damer's books at Hodgson's in 1902, if it could be traced, would resolve our uncertainty.

[197]

That the copy illustrated was printed in 1797 seems to me, on the evidence of the watermark, almost certain. The watermark itself (lily, VDL, with countermark IV) appears to be possible for 1768, since I have found it in MSS of 1769 and 1770 (and in some copies of the special title-page for the *Description of SH* in 1784, No. 57 below), but it is inescapably linked with other Detached Pieces that are certainly late. The group of six pieces can conveniently be discussed here: I. Tuer le tems (No. 1); II. Portrait of Lord Granville (No. 11); III. 'There was a little man' (No. 14); IV. the Verses by Pentycross (No. 18); V. The Disaster (No. 45); VI. The Printer's Farewell (No. 48). It is hardly conceivable that these pieces could all be on the same paper and yet be variously printed in 1757, 1763, 1764, 1768, and 1797. No. V and No. VI were legitimately printed in 1797, so that their authenticity is not in doubt; since an earlier printing of No. II has been recovered, I have had little hesitation in assigning the reprint (on this paper watermarked 'lily, VDL') to 1797 because of Kirgate's numerous identified reprints. Thus, Nos. I, III, and IV are left as highly suspicious: because so many copies derive from Kirgate, I regard them as his unacknowledged reprints; and because the watermark is like that in Nos. V and VI, I suggest that they were prepared by Kirgate in 1797.

Two copies of the Pentycross Verses can be certainly traced to Kirgate: (1) sold by Kirgate in 1800 to Francis Annesley, then in the collection of Robert Holford, and now WSL; (2) bought at Kirgate's sale in 1810 by E. V. Utterson, and now WSL. The bibliographical evidence suggests that Richard Bull's copy (now Huntington) also came from Kirgate, and at least two other copies probably passed through Kirgate's hands. It is true, of course, that after 1765, when Kirgate first took charge of the Press, extra copies of SH pieces may have been left more or less legitimately in his hands; but in the case of the Pentycross Verses, the watermark combines with the records of provenance to condemn him.

COPIES

British Museum (Grenville); Harvard (Merritt and Widener); Huntington (Bull); Victoria and Albert Museum (Dyce); Dr. R. W. Chapman; Lord Derby; WSL (6 copies).

19. VERSES TO MADAME Du CHATELET, MADAME De DAMAS, MADAME De VILLEGAGNON, AND MADAME De LA VAUPALIERE. 1769.

Lowndes 94–97; Martin, p. 512.

JPO, p. 14: '9 May 1769. I gave a great dinner to the French ambassador and all the French then in England. These were Madame du Châtelet, the ambassadress; Madame de Damas, her sister, Madame de Villegagnon, and Madame de la Vaupalière, granddaughter of Marshal Berwick. When they went into the printing house they found the following verses ready set. . . . The translations were made by Monsr. de Lisle, a French officer then in England.' HW also wrote an account of this party to George Montagu, 11 May 1769, inclosing a copy of the Verses that he had composed.

The Verses were printed together on one side of a half-sheet of post paper, measuring approximately 40 x 25 cm. untrimmed (Lord Waldegrave's copy). In some copies the leaf has been cut in two horizontally, and in other copies it has been quartered to produce the four separate leaves (in octavo) listed by Martin and Lowndes.

OTHER EDITIONS

The Verses were reprinted in the *Gentleman's Magazine* for May 1771, in the *Annual Register* for 1771, and in the first volume of the *New Foundling Hospital for Wit* 1784. The French translation of the verses to Madame du Châtelet was also included in the *Almanach des Muses* 1772.

COPIES

Eton College (Storer—2 copies); Harvard (Merritt: 4 separate octavo leaves); Huntington (Bull: divided horizontally into two leaves); Lord Derby (4 separate octavo leaves); Lord Waldegrave (2 copies, one formerly Thomas Barrett's); WSL (2 copies, divided variously). Mrs. Damer's copy was bought at Hodgson's in 1902 by Tregaskis for £9, cut into four separate octavo leaves, and offered at £4.4.0 for each leaf; these are presumably the leaves now at Harvard.

20. [LIST OF PRINTS DESIRED BY WALPOLE. 1769?]

Not in Martin or Lowndes.

In a letter to William Cole, 15 July 1769, HW asked for help in finding prints of a considerable list of people. Since he wrote out these names in manuscript, it is clear that the printed list was prepared later than 15 July 1769; but

TO

MADAME DU CHATELET.

WHEN beauteous Helen left her native air,
    Greece for ten years in arms reclaim'd
    the Fair.
Th' enamour'd boy withheld his lovely prize,
And ſtaked his Country's ruin 'gainſt her eyes.
Your charms leſs banefull, not leſs ſtrong, appear:
We welcome any Peace that keeps you here.

A

MADAME DU CHATELET.ˣ

LORSQU' Helene eût quittè la Grece,
    Tout y prit feu contre Paris ;
Et les beaux yeux de ſa Maitreſſe
Firent les maux de ſon pays.
Vos charmes auſſi fûrs de plaire
Produiſent de plus doux effets ;
Nous voulons maintenir la Paix
Pour vous garder en Angleterre.

TO

MADAME DE DAMAS,
Learning Engliſh.

THO' Britiſh accents your attention fire,
    You cannot learn ſo faſt as we admire.
Scholars, like you, but ſlowly can improve,
For who wou'd teach you but the verb, *I love?*

A

MADAME DE DAMAS.

QUOIQUE vous donniez à l'Anglais
    Toute l'etude qu'il demande,
Plus vous y faites de progrès,
Et plus notre Surpriſe eſt grande.
Vous devriez ne profiter
Qu'avec une lenteur extreme ;
Quel Maitre peut vous repeter
Un autre mot que le mot, *J'aime?*

Guillotined in France in 1794.

19.

MADAME DE LA VAUPALIERE.

SHALL Britain figh, when fav'ring Zephyr's care
    Wafts to her fhores the bright la Vaupaliere?
Ah! yes; defcended from the Britifh throne
She views a Nymph fhe muft not call her own.
She fees how dear has Stuart's exile coft
By Clermont's charms and Berwick's valour loft.

A

MADAME DE LA VAUPALIERE.

QUAND le fouffle heureux des Zephirs
    Vous amene fur ces rivages,
Faut il meler à nos hommages
    Et des regrets & des foupirs?
Oui, fille de nos Rois, dans nos mûrs etrangere,
Vos graces, votre efprit, vos traits rappelleront,
Que Stuart exilè fit perdre à l'Angleterre
Le courageux Berwick & la belle Clermont.

MADAME DE VILLEGAGNON.

On the Seizure of her Cloaths by the
    Cuftom-houfe Officers.

PARDON, fair Traveller, the Troop
    That barr'd your wardrobe's way;
Nor think your filks, your gown and hoop,
    Were objects of their prey.
Ah! who, when authoriz'd by law
    To ftrip a form like yours,
Wou'd reft content with what he faw,
    And not exert his pow'rs?

A

MADAME DE VILLEGAGNON.*

PARDONNEZ, belle Voyageufe,
    A tous les fermiers d'Albion;
Ce n'etoit robe ni jupon
    Dont leur troupe etoit curieufe.
Mais de depouiller la beautè
Nos loix leur donnaient l'avantage;
Et qui vous voit eft bien tentè
    De mettre ces loix en ufage.

Afterwards married to Thomas Walpole the Banker

19.

The French Translations were by Monsr Jolile.

since a number of these names do not appear in the printed list, it is likely that he had acquired some of the desired portraits before the printed list was prepared.

The first mention of the printed list is in HW's letter to Cole, 21 December 1769: 'I take the liberty of troubling you with a list I have printed (to avoid copying it several times). . . . I need not say I suppose that the names scratched out in my list are of such prints as I have got since I printed it, and therefore what I no longer want.'

The list was therefore printed somewhat before 21 December 1769. It contains 223 names printed on both sides of the leaf. The copy that HW gave to Richard Bull measures 27.4 x 18.2 cm.

COPIES

The only copy found is in Richard Bull's collection of Detached Pieces, now in the Huntington Library.

21. THE PRESS TO THE EARL OF CHESTERFIELD. 1770.

Lowndes 60; Martin, p. 509.
JPO, p. 16: '5 June 1770. Lord Chesterfield coming to Strawberry Hill, in the library found on the table the following verses printed.'

The Verses are printed on one side of a quarto leaf measuring approximately 23.3 x 18.3 cm. (trimmed).

STATES AND VARIANTS

The copy illustrated is the only edition found, and I believe it to be genuine. One copy at Farmington can be traced to Kirgate, and the bibliographical evidence in Bull's collection of Detached Pieces suggests that Bull acquired his copy of this piece (perhaps from Kirgate) later than 1791. But no copy was in Kirgate's collection of Detached Pieces (now Lord Waldegrave) or in Eyton's collection (most of which came from Kirgate), and it seems possible that Kirgate was content to sell the copy or two left from the original printing.

The paper is different from that used for the fourth volume of the *Anecdotes,* begun in the autumn of 1770. But since the countermark (in one copy) appears to be identical with that in the paper used by HW in a letter to David Dalrymple, 23 January 1770, I think the paper need not be questioned. (Another copy, vertical chain-lines

THE

PRINTING-PRESS

AT

STRAWBERRY-HILL

To the EARL of CHESTERFIELD.

FEW Paces hence, beneath yon grotto'd Road,
From dying POPE the laſt ſweet Accents flow'd.
O! *Twit'nam,* wou'd the Friend of POPE but bleſs
With ſome immortal Page thy favour'd Preſs,
The happier Emblem wou'd with Truth depoſe,
That where one Phœnix died, another roſe.

with no watermark visible, seems to be the paper used for the quarto *Works* of 1770.) It is not, at any rate, the paper that Kirgate used for reprinting the Pentycross Verses (No. 18) and other pieces. Complete certainty will be possible only when the copy in HW's set of Detached Pieces has been found, or the copy sold with Mrs. Damer's books at Hodgson's in 1902.

COPIES

Huntington (Bull); Lord Derby; wsl (3 copies); a copy offered by Quaritch in Catalogue 530 (1937).

22. VERSES PRESENTED TO THE KING OF SWEDEN BY THE DUCHESS D'AIGUILLON. 1771.

Lowndes 62; Martin, p. 509.
JPO, p. 16: '8 October 1771. Printed 40 copies of a poem presented by the Duchess dowager d'Aiguillon to the King of Sweden at Ruel—sent 24 copies to her.'
The Verses were presented 9 March [not May] 1771. The occasion is described by Baron de Grimm in a letter to Diderot, 1 April 1771. Mme. du Deffand asked HW to send her the copies for Mme. d'Aiguillon, but HW had already dispatched the packet to the Duchess; see Mme. du Deffand to HW, 23, 27, 30 October and 6, 13 November 1771.

The Verses are printed on both sides of a quarto leaf measuring approximately 24 x 19 cm. uncut. The paper of all copies examined seems to be the same as that used in the fourth volume of the *Anecdotes,* completed in the spring of 1771, and in the first part of *Mémoires du Comte de Grammont.*

COPIES

Bodleian; Eton College (Storer); Victoria and Albert (Dyce); Harvard (Merritt); Huntington (2 copies, including Bull's copy); Lord Derby; Lord Waldegrave (2 copies, including Thomas Barrett's copy); wsl (4 copies).

23. THE MASTER OF OTRANTO TO THE FAIRY BLANDINA. 1772.

Lowndes 98; Martin, p. 512.
Richard Bull (in a note probably supplied by Kirgate and copied by Bull) on his copy: 'Printed at Strawberry Hill in the year 1772, when Lady Blandford

VERS

Presentés à sa Majesté

LE ROI DE SUEDE,

A Ruel le Samedy 9 Mai 1771, par Madame la Duchesse d'Aiguillon douairiere, en lui montrant le Portrait du Cardinal de Richelieu.

DES champs Eliséens quel charme me rappelle?
Et me force à revoir le sejour des humains?
Quel Mortel fait briller d'une beauté nouvelle
Ces bosquets fortunés que planterent mes mains?
Si j'en crois ses discours & ses graces touchantes,
C'est un Prince elevé dans la Cour de Louis.
Mais du bandeau des Rois les traces imposantes
Attachent sur son front mes regards eblouis.
C'est *Gustave*---à ce nom soudain mon cœur s'enflamme!
Heros victorieux, qu'à la fleur de tes ans
Lutzen vit expirer sous tes lauriers sanglans,
Eveille toi! ce jour doit plaire à ta grande ame.
De puissans interets nous unirent tous deux.
Viens contempler assis aupres de mes neveux
Le digne Possesseur de ton vaste heritage,
Et vois la Majesté sourire à leur homage.

Fideles

22.

The Master of *Otranto* being in Durance and not able to receive the Fairy BLANDINA in the Manner he wishes, has nevertheless ordered his Senechal to deliver up the Keys of the Castle to her Hautesse; and all his Vassals will with pleasure obey her sovereign Commands.

23. ORIGINAL EDITION.

The Mafter of *Otranto* being in Durance and not able to receive the Fairy BLANDINA[*] in the Manner he wifhes, has neverthelefs ordered his Senechal to deliver up the Keys of the Caftle to her Hauteffe; and all his Vaffals will with pleafure obey her fovereign Commands.

[*] *Lady Blandford, who came to fee Strawberry-hill, when Lord Orford was confined to his bed with the Gout.*

'Twas on this lofty Vafe's Side,
Where CHINA's gayeft Art has dy'd
  The azure Flowers, that blow;
Demureft of the tabby Kind,
The penfive SELIMA reclin'd,
  Gaz'd on the Lake below. *&c.*   GRAY.

Label for the Tub in which Mr Walpole's Cat was drown'd, and on which Mr Gray wrote an Ode.

23. KIRGATE'S REPRINT.

came to visit Mr. Walpole at that time confin'd to his bed with the gout; it was printed with so large a type, because her Ladyship was almost blind with age.'

George Baker says in his *Catalogue* of 1810 that the piece was printed when Lady Blandford was 78 years of age and Walpole (born 1717) 55. HW was confined to his bed with a severe attack of gout in the autumn of 1772; see his letter to William Cole, 7 November 1772: 'I have not been out of my bedchamber these five weeks to-day'; and his letter to Cole, 8 January 1773: 'I am quite free from pain, and . . . have been four times to take the air in the park. Indeed, after fourteen weeks, this is not saying much.'

Although HW makes no mention of the greeting for Lady Blandford, it seems safe to assume that it was printed in the autumn of 1772.

The Master of Otranto is printed on one side of a small slip measuring approximately 11.8 x 19.2 cm. It was reprinted by Kirgate, probably after 1781, with the label for the China tub (No. 24) on one side of a quarto leaf measuring 24 x 19.5 cm. (The two pieces have of course been separated in some copies.)

STATES AND VARIANTS

The two settings can be differentiated by the position of the word 'ordered' (line 4) under the word 'Manner.' In the original, it is slightly to the right, but in the reprint, slightly to the left. The paper of the first setting has the crown and post horn watermark, with J Whatman as countermark, entirely appropriate for 1772. Furthermore, one copy of this setting is almost certainly the copy sold with Mrs. Damer's books at Hodgson's in 1902; it was bought in a collection by WSL at the Parke-Bernet Galleries, 4 May 1939 (Spoor Sale), lot 888.

The paper of the reprint has the watermark: crown, lily, scroll W. Since this paper first appears in SH Press books in the Appendix to the *Description of SH* prepared about 1781, the reprint must be not earlier than 1781; bibliographically, no more accurate date can be established. But since the copies of the reprint derive from Kirgate, they are likely to have been prepared later, perhaps as late as 1797.

COPIES

Original edition: WSL (3 copies).

Kirgate's reprint: Harvard (Merritt); Huntington (Bull); WSL (3 copies).

Other copies (not seen and therefore not differentiated as to edition): British Museum (Grenville); Eton College (Storer—2 copies); Victoria and Albert (Dyce); Lord Derby; Lord Waldegrave.

24. LABEL FOR THE PEDESTAL OF THE CHINA TUB. 1773?

Lowndes 100; Martin, p. 512.

Gray's *Ode on the Death of a Favourite Cat* was written in March 1747. In a letter to William Mason, 29 July 1773, HW wrote: 'I have a pedestal making for the tub in which my cat was drowned; the first stanza of the Ode is to be written on it.' Probably the pedestal was completed before 4 June 1774, when HW paid £50 'for the Mason's work about the Shrine and two pedestals.' (*SH Accounts*, ed. Dr. Paget Toynbee, Oxford 1927, p. 15.)

In *The Poems of Mr. Gray*, York 1775, p. 76, Mason's note reads: 'Mr. Walpole, since the death of Mr. Gray, has placed the China vase in question on a pedestal at Strawberry Hill, with the four [Mason's error for six] lines of the Ode for its inscription.' The two changes in Gray's text, in the first two lines, make the stanza more appropriate as a label.

The date for the printing of the label can therefore be fixed within these limits: after July 1773 and before 1775. Whether any copy of this label has survived, I do not know; the copies described below are undoubtedly a reprint by Kirgate.

The blue and white china tub in which Selima was drowned stood on the pedestal in the Small Cloister, on the north side of the house. At the SH Sale, xix.32, the tub was bought by Lord Derby; it is now at Knowsley Hall.

The stanza was reprinted by Kirgate, on one side of a quarto leaf, with The Master of Otranto, No. 23, probably after 1781. (The two pieces have of course been separated in some copies.)

STATES AND VARIANTS

This piece is classed as a reprint and not as the original for the following reasons. All four copies examined are printed from the same setting of type. Two copies are printed with The Master of Otranto on a single leaf, and this edition of The Master of Otranto is certainly a reprint; see No. 23 above. (It is, I think, impossible to believe that HW in 1773 or 1774 would have asked Kirgate to print on the same leaf with the label a few more copies of the greeting he had prepared the year before for Lady Blandford.) Three copies have MS notes by Kirgate and are therefore under suspicion; two others probably derive from Kirgate; the sixth, in Richard Bull's copy of the *Description of SH*, 1784, might have come from HW, but the volume was grangerized probably after 1790, and the stanza for the pedestal looks as if it were a still later insertion.

Since therefore the evidence of the paper shows this edition to be not earlier than 1781 (see No. 23) and the evidence of provenance casts suspicion on all known copies, I think it was probably printed much later, with Kirgate's other reprints.

COPIES

Victoria and Albert Museum (Dyce); Lord Waldegrave; WSL (4 copies). There was no copy in the collection of Mrs. Damer's books sold at Hodgson's in 1902.

25. THE TICKET TO VIEW STRAWBERRY HILL. 1774.

Lowndes 103; Martin, p. 512.
Visitors were admitted to SH only on presentation of a ticket, at least during all the later years. On 30 July 1764, HW wrote to Grosvenor Bedford: 'I enclose the warrant, and a ticket for Strawberry.' On 27 June 1771, he wrote to Lady Ossory: 'I enclose the ticket your Ladyship ordered, and . . . I have made the order for five instead of four.' On 11 June 1780, he wrote to Mrs. Abington: 'My common custom is to give a ticket for only four persons at a time. . . .' *The World* for 23 July 1789 has the following note: 'Strawberry Hill, as usual, cannot be seen without tickets, from Mr. Walpole. These, however, he distributes with gentlemanlike ease to all the neighbourhood.'
It is likely that most tickets of this sort would be thrown away, by the visitor or by the housekeeper. But it is unlikely that all copies would be destroyed except for the year 1774, when at least seven were preserved. I believe, therefore, that printed cards were prepared in 1774 only, and that all the other tickets were in the form of written notes to his housekeeper: it was such a note that he sent to William Cole, 4 May 1773.

The ticket is printed on one side of a small slip measuring approximately 7 x 9 cm. All copies are trimmed, and the dimensions vary.

STATES AND VARIANTS

One copy examined is on a card, and the date has not been filled in; but HW's signature is a proof of authenticity. The other copies examined are on paper. The dated copies range from 4 August to 13 September.

COPIES

Harvard (Merritt); WSL (4 copies). Three copies were sold with Mrs. Damer's books at Hodgson's in 1902; one of these is the Harvard copy. Another ticket (the eighth) was preserved in a copy of the *Description of SH*, 1774, red mo-

This Ticket, on being delivered to the Houſekeeper, will admit Four Perſons, and no more, on Monday Auguſt 29 1774, *between Twelve and Three, to ſee Strawberry-Hill, and will only ſerve for the Day ſpecified.*

N. B. The Houſe and Garden are never ſhown in an Evening; and Perſons are deſired not to bring Children with them.

Hor Walpole

rocco, offered in a clipping from an unidentified book catalogue. The Eyton Collection (sold 1848) contained two tickets, one of which (perhaps) was owned by Maggs Brothers in 1914.

26. THOMAS GRAY, THE CANDIDATE. 1774?

Not in Lowndes or Martin.

Mr. Leonard Whibley's arguments for including *The Candidate* among the SH imprints are generally sound, I think, and this poem seems to belong among the Detached Pieces. We have nothing to add to Mr. Whibley's statement of the case, but a brief summary of it is included.

The verses were undoubtedly written in 1764 when the Earl of Sandwich (Jemmy Twitcher) was a candidate for the office of High Steward of the University of Cambridge. But that Gray published them at that time or at any time is extremely unlikely; he gave HW a MS copy, and other copies in MS were perhaps circulated. They were contributed to the *London Evening Post* in February 1777 by a correspondent who signed himself Anti-Twitcher; they were contributed to the *Gentleman's Magazine* in January 1782 by a correspondent who signed himself Adurfi; and they were printed in the fourth volume of the *New Foundling Hospital for Wit* in 1784. The verses are attributed to Gray in all three instances, and the title reads: Jemmy Twitcher, or The Cambridge Courtship. The last two lines are omitted, and there are a few changes in the text. These appearances serve well enough for published versions of the poem, but they have little to do with the SH edition.

HW's first reference to the poem appears to be in a letter to William Mason, 16 September 1774: 'What should I have found, but the thing in the world that was most worth finding? . . . I tell you it is what I have searched for a thousand times. . . . I thought I never lost anything in my life. I was sure I had them, and so I had; and now am I not a good soul, to sit down and send you a copy incontinently? . . . I am in a panic till there are more copies than mine. . . . Well, here it is! I think your decorum will not hold it proper to be printed in the *Life* [of Gray], nor would I have it. We will preserve copies, and the devil is in it, if some time or other it don't find its way to the press. My copy is in his own handwriting [a MS copy in HW's hand is now in the Morgan Library]; but who could doubt it: I know but one man upon earth who could have written it but Gray.' HW suggested changes in the last couplet in order to make the poem printable.

A date soon after this letter seems the most likely for the SH edition; one bit of conflicting evidence is a MS note on a copy in the Forster Collection at South Kensington: 'Published anno 1787, dedicated to the Rt. Hon. Earl of Sandwich 1788.' The Press was in operation both in 1774 and in 1787, and there seems to be no way of establishing the preference, unless copies of *The Candidate* are found to have a significant watermark.

Mr. Whibley's chief reason for assigning the poem to the SH Press is the

THE CANDIDATE:

BY

Mr. GRAY.

WHEN fly Jemmy Twitcher had fmugg'd up his face
  With a lick of court white-wafh, and pious grimace,
A wooing he went, where three Sifters of old
In harmlefs fociety guttle and fcold.
  Lord! Sifter, fays Phyfic to Law, I declare
Such a fheep-biting look, fuch a pick-pocket air,
Not I, for the Indies! you know I'm no prude;
But his nofe is a fhame, and his eyes are fo lewd!
Then he fhambles and ftraddles fo oddly, I fear—
No; at our time of life, 'twould be filly, my dear.
  I don't know, fays Law, now methinks, for his look,
'Tis juft like the picture in Rochefter's book.
But his character, Phyzzy, his morals, his life;
When fhe died, I can't tell, but he once had a wife.

presence of a copy in Anthony Storer's collection of SH pieces (now Eton College); this collection has a special title-page, printed in 1791, which reads: 'A Collection of the Separate Poems and other Detached Pieces Printed at the Press of the Honourable Horace Walpole at Strawberry Hill.' All the other pieces in the volume are closely associated with SH, and at least twenty-four were printed at SH. There is thus a strong presumption that *The Candidate*, in Caslon type, was also printed there. (Mr. Whibley's detailed discussion may be found in a letter to the *Times Literary Supplement*, 21 August 1930, and in his edition of the *Correspondence of Thomas Gray*, Oxford 1935, iii.1236–1242.

The poem is printed on the inside pages of a quarto half-sheet; the trimmed copy in the Storer Collection measures approximately 25 x 19.3 cm. The second page of the poem is numbered 2, but there is no imprint or date. Mrs. Lewis reports that no watermark is visible in Storer's copy, and I do not know whether other copies are on watermarked paper. The only copy in the United States, apparently, was offered at the Spoor Sale in 1939; since it was bought, for $1400, by Lord Rothschild and returned to England, I have been unable to examine a copy.

COPIES

Bodleian; British Museum (Wise); Eton College (2 copies); Pembroke College, Cambridge; Victoria and Albert (Forster); Lord Rothschild. A copy found by Mr. Charles Whibley in 1889 in the Cambridge University Library is no longer to be found.

The absence of this piece from the usual SH collections (Barrett, Bull, Cole, and especially Kirgate) can only be explained, perhaps, by assuming that HW decided, after printing it, that it was inappropriate even for limited circulation. The only alternative, I think, is to believe that it was not printed by Kirgate but by some other printer.

27. VERSES TO LADY CRAVEN, 'GENIUS HOWE'ER SUBLIME, PATHETIC, FREE.' 1775.

Lowndes 84; Martin, p. 511.

JPO, p. 17: '10 June 1775. Lady Elizabeth Berkeley wife of Lord Craven dining at Strawberry Hill with some company, desired to see the Printing house; Mr. Walpole said, if she would give him something to print (for she was a Poetess) he would let her see it. They went into it, and she found these lines ready set.'

T. Kirgate (on a copy of the Verses now at Chewton): 'Written and printed in June, 1775, when Lady Craven dined at Strawberry Hill.'

The Verses are printed on one side of a small leaf, approximately 12 x 19 cm. They were reprinted, about 1783 or later, with 'Tonton to Madam la Vicomtesse de Cambis,' on a quarto leaf, approximately 22.5 x 19 cm.

STATES AND VARIANTS

The Verses were printed at least twice by Kirgate, perhaps three times. At Texas, bound in Utterson's copy of *Cornélie* (and presumably bought with *Cornélie* at the Kirgate Sale in 1810) is a slip containing a copy of the Verses in HW's hand; on the other side is a printed copy of the Verses with one proof correction. The type seems to be Caslon small pica. It is likely that HW (or Kirgate) thought the type too small and therefore discarded this setting without printing any copies. (Should an authentic copy of this setting be discovered, however, it would take precedence over the settings described in the following paragraphs.)

The putative first edition, 1775, is printed in Caslon English. In the two copies at Farmington, part of the countermark 'HR' is visible: although this mark appears in no other SH work (a slightly larger 'HR' is in the Verses to Chesterfield, No. 21 above), it is present in writing-paper used by HW a few years earlier and can therefore be accepted as satisfactory. Among these copies a slight variant can be recorded: the copy illustrated has no space between 'Her' and the colon in line 4; the second WSL copy and the copy of this setting at Harvard both have a spaced colon. The copy illustrated was sold at Hodgson's in 1902, with Mrs. Damer's books, to Tregaskis; WSL bought it in a collection at the Parke-Bernet Galleries, 4 May 1939 (Spoor Sale), lot 888.

The Verses were reprinted on a single leaf with 'Tonton'; since the latter piece was originally printed in 1783 (No. 32 below), one can assume that the two were not printed together by Kirgate before 1783, and probably not until considerably later with Kirgate's other reprints. (Some copies, of course, have been separated from 'Tonton,' but the type shows that they were printed at the same time.) One WSL copy, with 'Tonton,' shows a watermark that is characteristic of 1780–81 (and of no earlier SH printing). The copy illustrated here, which has been separated from 'Tonton,' has the countermark of the same

GENIUS, howe'er fublime, pathetic, free,
Trufts to the Prefs for Immortality.
To Types would CRAVEN her fweet Lays transfer,
The Prefs would owe immortal Fame to Her:
While She, too carelefs of fo fair a Face,
Would breathe eternal Youth on ev'ry Grace,
Ages unborn computing with furprife
From her own Wit the brightnefs of her Eyes.

GENIUS, howe'er fublime, pathetic, free,
Trufts to the Prefs for Immortality.
To Types would CRAVEN her fweet Lays transfer,
The Prefs would owe immortal Fame to Her:
While She, too carelefs of fo fair a Face,
Would breathe eternal Youth on ev'ry Grace,
Ages unborn computing with furprife
From her own Wit the brightnefs of her Eyes.

27. VERSES TO LADY CRAVEN.
Original edition above; reprint below.

paper. Both these copies can be traced to Kirgate: the former, with a MS note in his hand, is apparently the copy sold to Annesley in 1800 (see next paragraph); the latter is in a collection of pieces purchased at the sale of Kirgate's library, 1810, by E. V. Utterson.

In an itemized bill (now WSL) of the sale of a number of detached pieces to Francis Annesley, 25 March 1800, Kirgate lists the two pieces together, 'Verses on Tonton. Ditto on Lady Craven,' for four shillings.

COPIES

MS and proof: Texas.
Original edition: Harvard (Merritt); WSL (2 copies).
Kirgate's reprint: WSL (2 copies).
Other copies (not seen and therefore not differentiated as to edition); Eton College (Storer); Victoria and Albert (Dyce); Lord Derby; Lord Waldegrave.

28. CHARLES JAMES FOX, TO MRS. CREWE. 1775.

Lowndes 70; Martin, p. 510.

JPO, p. 18: 'June 1775. In this month printed 300 copies of Dorinda, a Town Eclogue, by the Honorable Richard Fitzpatrick, only brother of John Earl of Ossory; and the next week, a loose sheet, added to it, of Charles Fox's verses to Mrs. Crewe.'

Bull's MS list (now Huntington) and Baker's *Catalogue*, 1810, both say that 300 copies of the Verses were printed. Since they were printed to accompany *Dorinda* (*Bibliography* above, No. 25), this is doubtless correct.

According to G. O. Trevelyan's *Early History of Charles James Fox* (Second ed. 1880, p. 326), both pieces were written in May, in compliment to Mrs. Crewe. On 27 May 1775, HW sent a MS copy of the Verses to Mason. Mme. du Deffand had the Verses translated into French prose by two of her friends; see her letter to HW, 1 July 1775.

The Verses are printed on both sides of a quarto leaf measuring approximately 24 x 19 cm. untrimmed. For the nineteenth-century reprint, see the discussion under the Verses to Lady Townshend, No. 2 above.

OTHER EDITIONS

The Verses were reprinted in the *Annual Register* for 1775 and in the first volume of the *New Foundling Hospital for Wit*, 1784.

T O

Mrs. CREWE.

WHERE the lovelieſt Expreſſion to Feature is join'd,
By Nature's moſt delicate Pencil deſign'd;
Where Bluſhes unbidden and Smiles without Art
Speak the Sweetneſs and Feeling that dwell in the Heart;
Where in Manners enchanting no Blemiſh we trace,
But the Soul keeps the Promiſe we had from the Face:
Sure Philoſophy, Reaſon, and Coldneſs muſt prove
Defences unequal to ſhield us from Love.
Then tell me, myſterious Enchanter, O! tell,
By what wonderful Art, or by what magic Spell,
My Heart is ſo fenced, that for once I am wiſe,
And gaze without Madneſs on Amoret's Eyes:
That my Wiſhes, which never were bounded before,
Are here bounded by Friendſhip, and aſk for no more.
Is it Reaſon?---no, That my whole Life will belye,
For who ſo at variance as Reaſon and I?
Is't Ambition that fills up each Chink of my Heart,
Nor allows to one ſofter Senſation a Part?
Ah! no, for in this all the World muſt agree
That one Folly was never ſufficient for me.

Is

T O
Mrs. C R E W E.

WHERE the lovelieſt Expreſſion to Feature is join'd,
    By Nature's moſt delicate Pencil deſign'd ;
Where Bluſhes unbidden and Smiles without Art
Speak the Sweetneſs and Feeling that dwell in the Heart ;
Where in Manners enchanting no Blemiſh we trace,
But the Soul keeps the Promiſe we had from the Face :
Sure Philoſophy, Reaſon, and Coldneſs muſt prove
Defences unequal to ſhield us from Love.
Then tell me, myſterious Enchanter, O ! tell,
By what wonderful Art, or by what magic Spell,
My Heart is ſo fenced, that for once I am wiſe,
And gaze without madneſs on Amoret's Eyes :
That my Wiſhes, which never were bounded before,
Are here bounded by Friendſhip, and aſk for no more.
Is it Reaſon ?---no, That my whole Life will belye,
For who ſo at variance as Reaſon and I ?
Is't Ambition that fills up each Chink of my Heart,
Nor allows to one ſofter Senſation a Part ?
Ah! no, for in this all the World muſt agree
That one Folly was never ſufficient for me.

                                                   Is

28. NINETEENTH-CENTURY REPRINT.
The tight binding of the volume is responsible for the
distortion of the left margin.

COPIES

Bodleian; British Museum (Grenville); Eton College (Storer); Victoria and Albert (Dyce); Harvard (Merritt); Huntington (2 copies); Princeton; Lord Derby; Lord Strachie; Lord Waldegrave (2 copies); Mr. G. H. Nettleton; WSL (7 copies); Spoor Collection (sold 1939).

No copy of the nineteenth-century reprint has been found, except the one at Farmington. Copies listed above as in England have not been examined, but they are almost certainly genuine.

29. PROPOSALS FOR A PONY RACE ON TWICKENHAM COMMON. 1776.

Lowndes 66; Martin, p. 509.

In Baker's *Catalogue* of 1810, this piece is marked with an asterisk, to indicate that it was not printed for HW. The note in the Catalogue of the Eyton Sale, Sotheby's, 22 May 1848, lot 1479, reads: 'Printed unknown to H.W. see note.' Lowndes says merely: 'Printed unknown to Horace Walpole.' Since there is no indication in the JPO or elsewhere, that the Press was active in 1776, the notes seem entirely correct: this piece was one of the items printed by Kirgate on his own responsibility for his friends in the village.

The Proposals are printed on one side of a quarto leaf (vertical chain-lines without watermark), measuring approximately 24.2 x 17.5 cm.

COPIES

WSL (Kirgate has written on the back: 'very scarce, but one more. Mr. B.' This copy may have been intended for Richard Bull or for George Baker; the latter is more likely since no copy is now known in Bull's collections); Eyton Collection (sold 1848).

30. CHARLES MILLER'S VERSES TO LADY HORATIA WALDEGRAVE. 1780.

Lowndes 75; Martin, p. 510.

JPO, p. 19: '1780. At the end of January printed 150 copies of Mr. Charles Miller's Verses to Lady Horatia Waldegrave on the death of the Duke of Ancaster to whom she was to have been married.'

HW to William Mason, 22 January 1780: 'Kirgate . . . is gone to Strawberry to print some verses of Mr. Miller . . . and very pretty they are. I shall send them to you.'

HW to Lady Ossory, 29 January 1780: 'I enclose a copy of verses, which I have just printed at Strawberry, only a few copies, and which I hope you will think pretty. They were written three months ago [they are dated 'A. D. 1779' at the end] by Mr. Charles Miller.'

To be RUN for,

On TWICKENHAM-COMMON,

On *Tuesday* the 17th of September, 1776,

A Subscription Purse of Five Pounds;

BY PONIES, not to exceed Thirteen Hands high, to carry Catch Weights, that never won a Prize valued or published at Five Pounds, at any one Time, Matches excepted. To Run the best of Three Heats; Twice round the Course to a Heat: after which, the losing Ponies to Run one Heat for one Guinea. To Enter at the *Post-Boy* in *Twickenham*, the Day before Running, and to pay 5s. Entrance, or 7s. at the Post.

On *Wednesday* the 18th, will be RUN for, on the said Common, a SADDLE, BRIDLE, WHIP, and a pair of plated SPURS, by PONIES, not to exceed Twelve Hands One Inch high, that never won a Prize valued or published at Three Pounds, at any one Time, Matches excepted, to carry Catch Weights. To Run the best of Three Heats; Twice round the Course to a Heat; the Pony that wins the first Two Heats to have the *Saddle* and *Bridle*: after which, the losing Ponies to Run one Heat for the *Whip* and *Spurs*; the Winner to have the *Whip*, the Second the *Spurs*. To Enter at the *Post-Boy*, aforesaid, the Day before Running, and to pay 3s. Entrance, or 5s. at the Post.

The same Day, One Guinea will be given to be Run for, by JACK ASSES, between the Heats; the best of Three Heats, once round the Course to a Heat: no Entrance Money required.

To start each Day at Three o'Clock. No less than Three reputed Racers to start each Day. Disputes to be decided by the Clerk of the Course.

T O

Lady HORATIA WALDEGRAVE,

O N   T H E

DEATH of the DUKE of ANCASTER.

YES, beauteous Virgin, yes, thy Tears are juſt;
    They pay the laſt ſad Tribute to the Duſt;
The ſacred Duſt, the cold unfeeling Earth,
That once was Virtue, Valour, Spirit, Worth:
That once could charm with Youth and Beauty's Glow,
Ah! why?---but 'twas Heav'n's Will; 'tis ours to bow
Without repining to its high Beheſt,
And to believe, Whatever is, is beſt.
Yet hard the Taſk to teach unpractis'd Youth
This ſerious Leſſon, this important Truth.
Nature, imperious Queen, ſpeaks in thy Eyes
With forceful Eloquence; thy heart-felt Sighs

Proclaim

One half-sheet, quarto; pp. [1]–3 text, with p. [4] blank. An untrimmed copy measures approximately 24.8 x 19 cm.

COPIES

British Museum (Grenville); Eton College (Storer); Victoria and Albert (Dyce); Clark Memorial Library; Harvard (Merritt); Huntington (2 copies); New York Public Library; Princeton; Lord Derby; Lord Waldegrave (2 copies); WSL (6 copies); Spoor Collection (sold 1939). Eighteen copies were sold in 1842, SH Sale, v.210.

31. SMALL LABEL, 'THE FOUR PICTURES NEAR THE SHRINE.' 1780?

Lowndes 41; Martin, p. 507.

HW to William Cole, 20 February 1777: 'I have bought at Mr. Ives's sale (immensely dear) the shutters of the altar at St. Edmundsbury. . . . They have suffered in several places, though not considerably. Bonus is to repair them.'

HW to Dr. Lort, 4 June 1779: '[The panels] are at Mr. Bonus's in Oxford Road. . . . He has kept them these two years, and not finished them yet. I design them for the four void spaces in my chapel, on the sides of the shrine.'

HW to William Cole, 30 May 1780: 'At last I have got from Bonus my altar doors. . . . I intend to place them in my chapel, as they will aptly accompany the shrine.'

Presumably the pictures were put in place soon afterwards, and the printing of the label is therefore assigned to the year 1780. In any case, the pictures were in place when HW printed the Appendix to the *Description of SH* in 1781, although the small label is not specifically mentioned.

Kirgate's note (concerning the two labels in the Chapel) to Richard Bull reads: 'The inclosed was printed by me at Strawberry-hill; but the large label, describing the shrine, was not; *that* was done at Brentford, there not being enough of such large letter at Strawberry.' For the large label, Lowndes 42, see Appendix below, No. 86.

The label is printed on a narrow strip of gray cartridge paper, measuring approximately 3.8 x 41.5 cm.

COPIES

Huntington (Bull); Eyton Collection (sold 1848).

32. TONTON TO MADAME LA VICOMTESSE DE CAMBIS. 1783.

Lowndes 86; Martin, p. 511.

On a copy at Harvard is Kirgate's note: 'Intended as a Compliment to the

TONTON

TO

Madame la Vicomteſſe de CAMBIS.

FRIEND of my dear departed Miſtreſs, hail!
Here all Du DEFFAND's Merits ſtill prevail.
Whoe'er partook her Love, or ſooth'd her Pains
Supreme in WALPOLE's grateful Memory reigns
And when his Fondneſs on her *Dog* is pour'd,
If I am happy, You muſt be ador'd.

32.

Lady who dined there July 29, 1783, but was not presented, nor but this and one more printed.' It is not clear why the verses were not presented to Madame de Cambis. Tonton was the dog bequeathed to HW by Mme. du Deffand.

The Verses are printed, with the Verses to Lady Craven, on one side of a quarto leaf, approximately 22.5 x 19 cm. (Some copies have been separated, but the type shows that they were printed at the same time.)

STATES AND VARIANTS

It is impossible to accept this edition as a genuine original, although the watermark in the paper seems to fit 1783 well enough. But its appearance on a single leaf with the Verses to Lady Craven (No. 27 above) is a damaging fact. At least five of the six copies recorded derive from Kirgate. The most convincing proof is Kirgate's note quoted above on the Harvard copy: '. . . nor but this and one more printed.' Yet the *two* copies at Farmington are certainly printed from the same setting of type, and the copies in England may well be; in this case more clearly than in any other, Kirgate reveals himself as a forger and a liar.

Martin describes the piece as six lines and eight lines, on one leaf: this is clearly a copy printed with the Verses to Lady Craven, probably the Cruden-Eyton copy.

COPIES

Harvard (Merritt); Lord Derby; Lord Waldegrave; wsl (2 copies); Eyton Collection (sold 1848). There was no copy in Mrs. Damer's Collection sold at Hodgson's in 1902.

33. RULES FOR OBTAINING A TICKET TO SEE STRAWBERRY HILL. 1784.

Lowndes 64; Martin, p. 509.
JPO, p. 19: '1784. Printed a page of rules for admission to see my House.'
According to Bull's MS list (now Huntington), '2 or 300' copies were printed, and this is a likely enough figure for a leaflet that HW intended to use over a series of years. Bull himself preserved three copies.
After he succeeded to the title of Earl of Orford in 1791, HW had the Rules reprinted in roman type, beginning 'Lord Orford is very ready to oblige.' But this edition was printed in London; see the Appendix below, No. 90.

Mr. Walpole is very ready to oblige any curious Persons with the Sight of his House and Collection; but as it is situated so near to London and in so populous a Neighbourhood, and as he refuses a Ticket to nobody that sends for one, it is but reasonable that such Persons as send, should comply with the Rules he has been obliged to lay down for showing it.

Any Person, sending a Day or two before, may have a Ticket for Four Persons for a Day certain.

No Ticket will serve but on the Day for which it is given. If more than Four Persons come with a Ticket, the Housekeeper has positive Orders to admit none of them.

Every Ticket will admit the Company only between the Hours of Twelve and Three before Dinner, and only one Company will be admitted on the same Day.

The House will never be shown after Dinner; nor at all but from the First of May to the First of October.

As Mr. Walpole has given Offence by sometimes enlarging the Number of Four, and refusing that Latitude to others, he flatters himself that for the future nobody will take it ill that he strictly confines the Number; as whoever desires him to break his Rule, does in effect expect him to disoblige others, which is what nobody has a right to desire of him.

Persons desiring a Ticket, may apply either to Strawberry-Hill, or to Mr. Walpole's in Berkeley-Square, London. If any Person does not make use of the Ticket, Mr. Walpole hopes he shall have Notice; otherwise he is prevented from obliging others on that Day, and thence is put to great Inconvenience.

They who have Tickets are desired not to bring Children.

Mr. Walpole is very ready to oblige any curious Perſons with the Sight of his Houſe and Collection; but as it is ſituated ſo near to London and in ſo populous a Neighbourhood, and as he refuſes a Ticket to nobody that ſends for one, it is but reaſonable that ſuch Perſons as ſend, ſhould comply with the Rules he has been obliged to lay down for ſhowing it.

Any Perſon, ſending a Day or two before, may have a Ticket for Four Perſons for a Day certain.

No Ticket will ſerve but on the Day for which it is given. If more than Four Perſons come with a Ticket, the Houſekeeper has poſitive Orders to admit none of them.

Every Ticket will admit the Company only between the Hours of Twelve and Three before Dinner, and only one Company will be admitted on the ſame Day.

The Houſe will never be ſhown after Dinner; nor at all but from the Firſt of May to the Firſt of October.

As Mr. Walpole has given Offence by ſometimes enlarging the Number of Four, and refuſing that Latitude to others, he flatters himſelf that for the future nobody will take it ill that he ſtrictly confines the Number; as whoever deſires him to break his Rule, does in effect expect him to diſoblige others, which is what nobody has a right to deſire of him.

Perſons deſiring a Ticket, may apply either to Strawberry-Hill, or to Mr. Walpole's in Berkeley-Square, London. If any Perſon does not make uſe of the Ticket, Mr. Walpole hopes he ſhall have Notice; otherwiſe he is prevented from obliging others on that Day, and thence is put to great Inconvenience.

They who have Tickets are deſired not to bring Children.

33. KIRGATE'S REPRINT.

The Rules are printed on the first page of a quarto half-sheet, measuring approximately 20 x 15.5 cm. trimmed. In a good many copies, the blank leaf is missing, and some copies may have been printed on a single leaf. The Rules were reprinted by Kirgate after 1790.

STATES AND VARIANTS

In the collection of Mrs. Damer's books, sold at Hodgson's in 1902, there was a copy of the Rules on pink paper; this is undoubtedly the copy now at Harvard, and its provenance is a guarantee of its authenticity. The type shows a few minor readjustments, but it is the same setting as the first edition illustrated here; I therefore regard it as exactly what it seems to be, a proof.

The first edition seems to have been printed on two different lots of paper: some copies have the 'crown, post horn, scroll W' watermark that was used in the *Muse Recalled,* but other copies have the Dutch lion (or its countermark). This edition's genuineness is proved by a copy (now owned by Mrs. Augustus Loring) on which HW has written a note to Edmond Malone.

The reprint might at first glance be considered authentic, ordered by HW at some time before 1791. But the three copies of this that can be traced to early owners all derive from Kirgate, and they are printed on paper made by the firm of Edmeads and Pine. My records are incomplete, but I have examined thousands of specimens of paper of this period, from literally hundreds of sources, and although I have found examples of Edmeads and Pine paper in 1790 and in later years, I have found no paper from that mill before 1790. It is certain, therefore, that this reprint was prepared not earlier than 1790; and it seems probable that Kirgate reprinted the Rules in 1797, when he found that he had no more originals to sell. (But the copy, now WSL, that he sold to Annesley in 1800 is of the first edition.)

COPIES

Original edition: Harvard (Merritt: proof on pink paper); Huntington (3 copies); Mrs. Augustus Loring; WSL (3 copies).

Kirgate's reprint: Harvard (Merritt); Yale; WSL (3 copies).

Other copies (not seen and therefore not differentiated as to edition); British Museum; Eton College (Storer); Victoria and Albert (Dyce); Lord Waldegrave.

Quaritch's Catalogue 530 (1937), lots 1081 and 1114, offered two copies with differing type: presumably one was the original edition and one the reprint by Kirgate, unless there was an unrecorded nineteenth-century reprint.

34. LABEL FOR A SCREEN OF OLD TAPESTRY. 1784.

Lowndes 101; Martin, p. 512.

The Label was intended for the folding mahogany screen listed by HW in the *Description of SH* (edition of 1784, p. 84; *Works* of 1798, ii.404): 'A two-leafed screen, containing part of a map of Surry and Middlesex. It is a piece of the first tapestry woven in England, and came from Weston in Warwickshire, the seat of the Sheldons, who introduced the manufacture. The complete suite of hangings were purchased by Mr. Walpole, and presented by him to the Earl of Harcourt. This specimen had never been hung up.' Since this item was added to the *Description* at the last moment, in the summer of 1784, it is perhaps safe to assume that the Label was printed at about the same time.

The screen itself was sold in 1842 (SH Sale, xvii.59) to Strong of Bristol, for £12.12.0; offered in Strong's Catalogue of 1843, p. 184; Sotheby's, 26 March 1926 (Birkhesh Sale), lot 183, to Harris, £1010. The hangings that HW gave to Lord Harcourt were given in 1827 by Edward Vernon Harcourt, Archbishop of York, to the York Philosophical Society; they are now on permanent loan at the Victoria and Albert Museum.

The Label is printed on a small slip of paper; Lord Waldegrave's copy measures 15.7 x 10.3 cm. The WSL copies have been considerably trimmed, so that they are smaller.

STATES AND VARIANTS

This edition seems to me very suspicious. All copies known are in collections that came from Kirgate. (For these later pieces, of course, the possession of extra copies by Kirgate is not unnatural.) There was no copy in Mrs. Damer's collection, or in Richard Bull's. The typographical error in 'Oxfordshire' seems unlikely to have escaped HW's eye when the label was put in place, although the arrangement of the type case makes it an understandable error. (In the second copy at Farmington, this error has been corrected, perhaps by hand.) In a reprint by Kirgate, probably in 1797, the error seems more likely to have escaped notice.

COPIES

Lord Waldegrave (in Kirgate's collection); Eyton Collection (sold 1848); WSL (Annesley and Utterson copies).

This Screen was made of part of the firſt Tapeſtry that was wrought in England, and came from Weſton in Warwickſhire, the Seat of Ralph Sheldon, Eſq; whoſe Anceſtor brought the Art into England.   The reſt of the firſt Suit of Tapeſtry is now at the Earl of Harcourt's, at Nuneham in Oxfordſhi:e, 1784.

34. LABEL FOR A SCREEN OF OLD TAPESTRY.

35. LABEL FOR THE FISHING EAGLE MODELLED BY MRS. DAMER. 1787.

Lowndes 102; Martin, p. 512.

Mrs. Damer modelled the Eagle and wrote her name in Greek at the base. HW then had the label printed and placed beneath the name. The compliment was suggested by Marcus Agrati's inscription for his statue of St. Bartholomew in Milan Cathedral: 'Non me Praxiteles sed Marcus finxit Agrati.' (See HW to Lady Ossory, 14 June 1787.)

The Eagle was taken in Lord Melbourne's park in 1786, and the model was completed the next year. It is listed in the *Description of SH* (edition of 1784, p. 94, added in 1789; *Works* of 1798, p. 445) with the note: 'Mr. W. added this line, *Non me Praxiteles finxit*, at Anna Damer, 1787.'

The model was placed in the library. It was sold in 1842 (SH Sale, xix.1) to Sir Alexander Johnston, whose wife had inherited Mrs. Damer's collection, for £7.7.0.

The Label is printed on a narrow slip of paper measuring 1.8 x 11.5 cm. (Bull's trimmed copy).

STATES AND VARIANTS

Possibly this piece should be classed with No. 34 as 'suspicious,' but there is less evidence. Richard Bull's copy appears to have been inserted as an afterthought in his extra-illustrated *Description*, but it is not thereby proved a reprint. There was no copy in Mrs. Damer's collection.

COPIES

Eyton Collection (sold 1848); WSL (Bull's copy).

36. THE PRESS TO MISS MARY AND MISS AGNES BERRY. 1788.

Lowndes 61; Martin, p. 509.

Kirgate's note on a copy now at Chewton Priory: 'This was written extempore immediately after a visit from the ladies, Oct. 11th, 1788, and was presented to them two days after when they came to see the Printing House.'

JPO, p. 20: '1788. Miss Mary and Miss Agnes Berry . . . living at Twickenham in 1788, Mr. Walpole inviting them Oct. 13 to see his Printing House, they found there the following Stanzas ready set; (Mr. Walpole's age, 71).'

HW to Lady Ossory, 19 October 1788: 'The Berrys were to come and see my printing-press. I recollected my gallantry of former days, and they found these stanzas ready set.'

THE PRESS

AT

STRAWBERRY-HILL

TO

Miſs MARY and Miſs AGNES BERRY.

TO MARY's Lips has ancient Rome
    Her pureſt Language taught;
And from the modern City home
    AGNES its pencil brought.

Rome's ancient Horace ſweetly chants
    Such Maids with lyric Fire;
Albion's old Horace ſings nor paints----
    He only can admire.

Still wou'd his Preſs their Fame record,
    So amiable the Pair is!
But ah! how vain to think *his* Word
    Can add a Straw to BERRYS!

36. ORIGINAL EDITION.

THE PRESS

AT

STRAWBERRY-HILL

TO

Miſs MARY and Miſs AGNES BERRY.

TO MARY's Lips has ancient Rome
    Her pureſt Language taught;
And from the modern City home
    AGNES its pencil brought.

Rome's ancient Horace ſweetly chants
    Such Maids with lyric Fire;
Albion's old Horace ſings nor paints----
    He only can admire.

Still wou'd his Preſs their Fame record,
    So amiable the Pair is!
But ah! how vain to think *his* Word
    Can add a Straw to BERRYS!

36. NINETEENTH-CENTURY REPRINT.

The Verses are printed on one side of a quarto leaf measuring approximately 23.8 x 19.2 cm. untrimmed. There can be no doubt, I think, that this edition is genuine: two copies were sold with Mrs. Damer's collection at Hodgson's in 1902 (one of them is probably the Spoor-wsL copy), and the bibliographical evidence suggests that Bull's copy (now Huntington) was acquired before 1791. That copies are relatively common indicates merely that HW was sufficiently pleased to have a number of copies printed and that by 1788 collectors were interested in saving SH pieces.

For a discussion of the nineteenth-century reprint in Wilson type, see the Verses to Lady Townshend, No. 2 above.

COPIES

Bodleian; British Museum (Grenville); Victoria and Albert (Dyce: 2 copies); Huntington (Bull); Princeton (Morgan); Lord Derby; Lord Waldegrave (Barrett and Kirgate copies); Mr. W. M. Elkins; wsL (6 copies).
Nineteenth-century reprint: Harvard (Merritt); wsL (2 copies).

37. THE PRESS TO THE DUKE OF CLARENCE. 1790.

Lowndes 59; Martin, p. 509.
Kirgate's note (on a copy at Chewton Priory): 'His Royal Highness doing Mr. Walpole the Honour to make him a Visit at Strawberry-hill, when he had the Gout, Decr. 22d, 1790, Mr. W. the next day sent him these Verses.'
This piece, like No. 36, is relatively common, and its history is perhaps about the same, except that this was not reprinted, so far as we know, in the nineteenth century.

The Verses are printed on one side of a quarto leaf measuring approximately 24 x 19.5 cm. untrimmed. Copies seem to have been printed on three different lots of paper, but I have observed no variants in the text. There were two copies in Mrs. Damer's collection.

COPIES

British Museum (Grenville); Eton College (Storer); Victoria and Albert (Dyce); Clark Memorial Library; Harvard (Merritt); Huntington (Bull); Princeton (Morgan: 2 copies); Lord Derby; Lord Strachie; Lord Waldegrave (Barrett and Kirgate copies); wsL (8 copies).

38. VERSES BY MRS. RACHEL HOLMES. 1790.

Lowndes 74; Martin, p. 510.
Martin says that these Verses were printed in 1790; his information may

The Press at Strawberry-Hill
T O
HIS ROYAL HIGHNESS
T H E
DUKE of CLARENCE.

SIR,

When you condefcend to grace
  An ancient Printer's Dwelling,
He fuch a Moment muft embrace
  Your Virtues to be fpelling:

Your Naval Talents, Spirit, Zeal,
  Shall other Types record;
He but one Sentiment can feel,
  ---And Gratitude's the Word.

Condemn not, Sir, the Truths he fpeaks,
  Tho' homely his Addrefs;
A Prince of Brunswic never checks
  The Freedom of the Prefs.

37.

By Mrs. RACHEL HOLMES,

DAUGHTER of ROBERT and SARAH SPURLING,

Of ROMFORD in ESSEX.

SEVEN Children had my Parents, and no more,
 The Lord took three, and left them only four;
I, the Authoress of these Lines wrote here,
Am seventh Daughter of those Parents dear.
The first, the third, the fifth, was call'd from hence,
The other four were left to recompence
Our Parents meek, who taught us in our youth
To shun all Vice, and seek Virtue and Truth;
To worship God with all Humility,
And treat Mankind with Love and Charity.
Not to uplifted be, or low cast down,
At either fickle Fortune's Smile or Frown;
Nor envy or despise another's State,
But humbly be contented with our Fate;
Return God Thanks for ev'ry Thing he's giv'n,
And hope by Faith, and Deeds, to merit Heav'n.
O let us strive these Precepts to observe!
Nor ever from the Paths of Virtue swerve;
But daily pray that They, who taught us this,
And We, may know eternal heav'nly Bliss.

38.

have come from a note on the Cruden-Eyton copy. In Baker's *Catalogue* of 1810, this piece is marked with an asterisk, to indicate that it was not printed for HW. Since Mrs. Holmes, like Kirgate's relative Mrs. Cloak (see No. 41 below), was from Romford (Kirgate spells it Rumford in No. 41) in Essex, it is likely that she knew Kirgate and that he printed her Verses for her. There was no copy of the Verses in Mrs. Damer's collection.

The Verses are printed on one side of a quarto leaf measuring 24.6 x 20 cm. untrimmed (Lord Waldegrave's copy). The copy at Harvard is on writing paper, but the other copies examined are on a cheaper paper with vertical chain-lines. Kirgate's pencilled correction in line 5 ('was' to 'were,' not shown in the facsimile) seems to be made in all copies.

COPIES

Harvard (Merritt); Lord Waldegrave; WSL (2 copies). A fifth copy was offered in Quaritch's Catalogue 530 (1937), lot 1089.

39. VERSES ON MRS. CLIVE, 'YE SMILES AND JESTS.' 1791.

Lowndes 85; Martin, p. 511.

The Verses were written, 'as a sportive and innocent amusement . . . by way of epitaph, and on a supposition that Mrs. Clive was dead,' in October 1774. See William Cole's account of his visit to SH, 29–31 October 1774, in Yale edition of HW's *Correspondence with Cole,* 1937, ii.374.

At some time after Mrs. Clive's death in 1785, an urn was erected in her garden at Cliveden, and the Verses cut on the pedestal. HW's note, in his *Description of SH,* 1784 (now WSL), says that the urn was 'erected in the garden at Cliveden near Twickenham, 1792.' But HW's account book may be more accurate than his later notes, and in 1791 he records a payment of £3.6.0 for 'pedestal for urn at Cliveden.' (*SH Accounts,* ed. by Dr. Paget Toynbee, Oxford 1927, p. 19.) Furthermore, Kirgate, in an addition to Bull's MS list (now Huntington) dates the printing of the Verses in 1791.

The Verses were printed in the *Public Advertiser* for 1791, the *European Magazine* for 1791, the *Annual Register* for 1791, and in D. Lysons, *The Environs of London,* 1795.

It is not known when the urn was removed to SH, but the pedestal, with enough of the inscription legible to identify it, now stands in the garden at SH. A note on it by Mr. P. J. Crean appeared in *Notes and Queries,* 16 April 1932.

The Verses are printed on one side of a small slip (some copies are on very heavy paper) measuring approximately 10.5 x 14.5 cm. There seems to be no particular reason to believe that HW ordered the

Ye Smiles and Jefts, ftill hover round;
This is Mirth's confecrated ground:
Here liv'd the laughter-loving Dame,
A matchlefs Actrefs, CLIVE her Name.
The Comic Mufe with Her retir'd,
And fhed a tear when She expir'd.

H. W.

39. VERSES ON MRS. CLIVE.

An EPITAPH on a Woman who fold Earthenware.

Bene	VI.
AT. HT. HISST.	Seab AT Eyo
O NELI ESKA	URG.
T. Harin, e. g. Rayc,	RIE FANDD
Hang'd.	Ryy. ov Rey.
F. R.	Esf. or Wha.
O Mabv Syli Fet	TA
O. L.	Vai. . . . Lfa Flo
J. FELESSC.	O Doft Ear Swho.
Lay bye Art	K. Now Sbu
HAND.	T. Ina Ru.
C. LAYSHEG.	NOFY e ARSI
O Th. Erpel	N. S. O.
FAND.	METALL PIT
No W. S. H. E'ft. Urn	CHERO RBRO
'D. Toe Art	A. D.
H. H. Erfelfy Ewe	Panfhe Inhe
EPI N. G. FRI	R. S. H.
END.	OPMA. yb EAGA.
SLET MEAD	I. N.

40. EPITAPH.

Verses printed, since all copies found can be traced to Kirgate, but the piece is undoubtedly genuine in its way: possibly Kirgate, knowing that the lines would be of interest, printed a few copies either when the urn was erected or in 1797. When he added this piece to Bull's MS list, Kirgate wrote that there were 'very few.' There was no copy in Mrs. Damer's collection.

COPIES

Victoria and Albert (Dyce); Harvard (Merritt); Huntington (Bull); WSL (3 copies).

40. EPITAPH ON A WOMAN WHO SOLD EARTHENWARE.

Lowndes 104; Martin, p. 512.

There seems to be no way of dating this piece very precisely. It was printed by Kirgate on his own responsibility (Martin calls it 'a whim of Kirgate's,' and on one WSL copy Kirgate himself has written, 'A whim of T. Kirgate's'), and most of the pieces of this sort appear to have been printed in 1790 or later. The bibliographical evidence of Bull's copy suggests that he acquired it, from Kirgate, after 1791.

This epitaph (with a few differences in the division of words) was published in the *London Chronicle*, 4 October 1764, with the title: 'An Epitaph, found in a Country Churchyard.' But since it is the kind of piece that is passed from hand to hand (and doubtless reprinted), we need not believe that Kirgate found it in the files of the *London Chronicle*. Kirgate did not print the explanation, 'Beneath this stone lies Katharine Gray,' etc.

The Epitaph is printed on a card measuring approximately 12.5 x 9.8 cm. Other copies are printed on a somewhat larger slip of paper measuring approximately 17.3 x 11.3 cm.

COPIES

Victoria and Albert (Dyce); Harvard (2 copies); Huntington (Bull); Lord Derby; Lord Strachie; Lord Waldegrave; WSL (5 copies). The copy sold in Mrs. Damer's collection at Hodgson's in 1902 was probably the Spoor copy, now WSL.

41. VERSES BY MRS. CLOAK OF RUMFORD, IN ESSEX.

Lowndes 71; Martin, p. 510.

Like a number of other pieces, this one is marked with an asterisk in Baker's *Catalogue* of 1810, to indicate that it was not printed for HW. A note by Kirgate, preserved in Richard Bull's collection (a similar note is at Chewton), tells

By Mrs. ☐

Of RUMFORD, in ESSEX.

TO see a Lass, with so much Grace,
   With so much Wit, and such a Face,
So slatternly, is shocking:
If you would with *Venus* vie,
Your Pen and Poetry lay by,
   And learn to mend your Stocking.

SEE, Sister, in this shatter'd Glass,
   The Fate of many a pretty Lass.
Women, like Glass, are frail and weak,
Apt to slip and apt to break:
Therefore guide ev'ry step with caution,
For frail as Glass is Reputation;
Both break together in once falling,
When once 'tis gone its past recalling.

41. VERSES BY MRS. CLOAK.

the occasion of the piece: 'This was printed at Strawberry-hill, by T. Kirgate, for his Cousin Mrs. Cloak, as a Rebuke to her Niece, who was much inclined to reading and scribbling; but as Mrs. Cloak took the above verses from Magazines, she would not pass for the Author, and therefore cut out her Name.' Mrs. Cloak's name has been cut out of the title in the Huntington, Chewton Priory, and WSL copies.

Like No. 40, this piece can be dated only approximately. Most of Kirgate's pieces of this kind were printed in the later years; the Verses by Mrs. Holmes (No. 38: since both women lived in Romford, the two pieces may have been printed at about the same time) are said by Martin to have been printed in 1790; the paper (of one copy examined) seems to be the same as that used for the Verses to the Berry sisters; the copy at Harvard is printed on the back of a small handbill that must be dated, for various reasons, later than 1787.

The Verses are printed on one side of a quarto leaf measuring approximately 24.6 x 20 cm. uncut (Lord Waldegrave's copy).

COPIES

Harvard (Merritt); Huntington (Bull); Lord Waldegrave; WSL.

42. VERSES BY MISS ANN PRIOR.

Lowndes 69; Martin, p. 510.

Baker, in his *Catalogue* of 1810, marks this piece with an asterisk, to indicate that it was not printed for HW. Like No. 38 and No. 41, it was probably printed by Kirgate to please one of his friends. Like the others, it can be dated only as a late piece, probably after 1790; the watermark also suggests a late date.

On the copy at Chewton Priory is a note by Kirgate: 'The above was certainly taken from some Magazine by Miss Prior, who wished to pass for the Author of them.' But no source for the verses has been found, and they hardly seem to be beyond the capacity of the unknown Miss Prior.

The Verses are printed on one side of a quarto leaf measuring approximately 20.3 x 16.4 cm. (WSL copy, trimmed).

COPIES

Harvard (Merritt); Lord Waldegrave; WSL.

43. COCKEY'S NEW YEAR'S ADDRESS.

Lowndes 67; Martin, p. 509.

On most copies, Kirgate wrote a note similar to the following explanation by

VERSES,

BY MISS ANN PRIOR,

OF

HORN-CHURCH, ESSEX.

Ye lovely Birds, that muſt endure
  The keeneſt cold of piercing froſt,
With me your food ſhall be ſecure,
  Till winter is in ſun-beams loſt.

Expos'd to the ſevereſt cold,
  Yet ſtill you tune your vocal ſtrain;
Your chearing notes will not withhold,
  While other birds ſilent remain.

Sweet beguilers of each hour,
  Fear not my bounty to partake;
You ſtill may exerciſe that pow'r,
  Thy privilege of fate.

Secure from danger may you feed;
  Why flutter at my approach,
Or quit the place with winged ſpeed?
  I mean not to encroach.

I ſeek you not for to enſnare,
  That liberty you fondly prize;
Your freedom it ſhall be my care,
  At real alarms you can ariſe.

Till winter's dreary reign is o'er,
  Receive this token from my hand;
Till nature hath reveal'd her ſtore,
  Nor in need of my relief you ſtand.

Then mingle with your feather'd throng,
  And welcome the return of ſpring;
With your renew'd, united ſongs,
  Make the groves and valleys ring.

There with pleaſure I'll attend,
  To hear the fav'rite Birds of mine;
Others their warbling notes will lend,
  In melody rejoin'd.

COCKEY's NEW YEAR's ADDRESS.

TO you, my worthy Masters, whom each Day
   I early call, to Labour, or to Play,
Your faithful Watchman COCKEY wishes Health,
Each new Year happy, Peace, Content, and Wealth;
And all the Comforts that this World can give,
'Till Life's last Stage I hope you will receive.

  'Tis common with us Watchmen, at this Time,
To compliment our Friends in humble Rhyme;
To remind you that we watch your Houses,
While you're safely sleeping with your Spouses;
To tell the Hardships that we undergo,
In long, bleak Winter Nights, Hail, Rain, and Snow:
And then, our drooping Spirits to revive,
Submissively we hope you'll something give.
But I, whose Strength and Courage seldom fail,
Ask not to taste your Cake, cold Chine, or Ale;
Nor am I yet a Beggar grown so bold,
Or covetous, to wish or expect Gold;
But some small Gift, beneath a Dollar,
I humbly crave, towards a COLLAR:
Which if your Bounty will on me bestow,
Grateful I'll wag my Tail, and *Bow-wow-wow*.

43.

Richard Bull on his copy: 'Cockey was the Name of a Dog belonging to Mr. Matthews, a Publican on Twickenham Common, and was remarkable for barking round the Neighbourhood every Morning at Five o'clock, which roused the labouring Men to work, who from that practice called him their Watchman. A Copy of the above Verses was stuck up in his Master's House, over a tin Christmas Box, into which was put by the Neighbours Money enough to buy him a handsome Collar.'

Bull added at the bottom of his copy: 'Printed at Strawberry-hill after Lord Orford's death.' (But see STATES AND VARIANTS below.)

The *Catalogue of Books and Tracts printed at . . . Strawberry Hill*, London, M'Creery, 1813, lists *Cockey's New Year's Address* 'by Mr. Harding,' and says that six copies only were printed in October 1797.

The Address is printed on one side of a quarto leaf (in reality a foolscap folio, but most copies have been trimmed to quarto size) measuring approximately 32 x 20.2 cm. (Lord Waldegrave's copy).

STATES AND VARIANTS

The Catalogue of the Eyton Sale (Sotheby's, 22 May 1848, lot 1479) lists 'Two copies, in different type, one with the author's autograph.' On Lord Waldegrave's copy is a note by Kirgate: 'But three copies of the preceding being printed, and several Friends requesting a copy, Kirgate printed this in small type to give away.' These two notes agree well enough, and prove that the copy illustrated is Kirgate's reprint. The original could hardly have been printed later than December of 1796, and it may have been prepared for an earlier year.

But Kirgate must have told Bull that his copy (of the new edition in smaller type) was printed after HW's death, and the watermark (L Munn 1796) supports Bull's note.

COPIES

Original edition: Eyton Collection (sold 1848).

Kirgate's reprint: Harvard (Merritt); Huntington (Bull); Lord Waldegrave; WSL (2 copies); Eyton Collection.

44. EPITAPH ON A CANARY BIRD. 1797.

Lowndes 105; Martin, p. 513.

On several copies, Kirgate indicated that these lines were written by Silvester Harding (1745–1809), and on the copy now at Chewton Priory he added the date, 1790.

EPITAPH ON A CANARY BIRD.

HERE lies interr'd the Muſe's Friend,
The ſweeteſt Warbler on the Spray;
Ye ſacred Yew-Trees o'er him bend,
And ſhade his Turf from ſcorching Day.

Nor ſhall the horned Bird of Night,
Or flittering Bat, be ever ſeen;
But ſome kind Fay or Fairy Spright
Shall guard this Sod and keep it green.

Nor dare, proud Man, to view with Scorn,
The little graſſy Tomb we raiſe;
But learn, like him, at Eve and Morn,
To ſing thy heav'nly Maker's Praiſe.

Richard Bull's copy (now Huntington) has the following note, probably from information supplied with the piece by Kirgate, in Bull's hand: 'Written by Mr. Silvester Harding, Miniature Painter. Printed at Strawberry-hill after Lord Orford's death.' There seems to be no reason to doubt this information, especially since the piece is marked (in Baker's *Catalogue* of 1810) with an asterisk, to indicate that it was not printed for HW.

The Epitaph is printed on one side of a small slip (with horizontal chain-lines) measuring approximately 15 x 16.3 cm. One copy (Utterson-WSL) is on a considerably larger slip (with vertical chain-lines), 17 x 21 cm.

COPIES

Victoria and Albert (Dyce); Harvard (Merritt); Huntington (Bull); Lord Waldegrave; WSL (7 copies). Mrs. Damer's copy, sold at Hodgson's in 1902, may be the copy at Harvard or one of those at Farmington.

45. THE DISASTER. 1797.

Lowndes 72; Martin, p. 510.

Richard Bull's note on his copy (now Huntington): 'Written extempore in August, 1794, by Silvester Harding, Miniature Painter, on William Bawtree, Senior, Engraver, fond of Physic and Physical Books; from whence called Dr. Printed at Strawberry-hill after Lord Orford's death.' There is no doubt, I think, that Bull's information was derived from Kirgate.

A MS account (now WSL) by Bawtree's grandson, written in 1871, says merely that the episode occurred 'One fine July day somewhere about the year 1790.'

The Verses are printed on one side of a quarto leaf measuring approximately 24.2 x 18.8 cm. trimmed.

STATES AND VARIANTS

One WSL copy, marked 'First Proof' by Kirgate, is marked for correction in two places; the other copies show that the corrections were duly made.

Two copies (Huntington and WSL) are printed in blue ink. See the title-page for the *Description of SH,* No. 58 below, for more of Kirgate's experiments with colored inks.

COPIES

Huntington (Bull); WSL (3 copies, including proof); Eyton Collection (sold 1848).

THE DISASTER.

THE morning fair, the fky ferene,
 The DOCTOR drefs'd quite fmug and clean,
Taking his leave of fhop and wife,
" I think, my dear, upon my life,
" The weather looks fo clear and fair,
" I'll breathe a little *Twick'n'am* air,
" KIRGATE, you know, expects me there."
Then, fortifying well his nofe,
With brandifh'd cane away he goes;
To *Piccadilly*, now, with fpeed,
The DOCTOR fwings with graceful tread;
The coach furveys with eager care,
To fee what paffengers are there:
When, oh! moft difmal to relate,
The fickle hand of cruel fate
Had plac'd three bouncing damfels there,
Like *Rubens'* graces fat and fair.
Struck with furprife the DOCTOR ftands,
His cane and fnuff-box in his hands;
Turns from the coach with great difguft,
And to himfelf the cafe difcufs'd.
" Shall I, in my beft feafting cloaths,
" Ride with fuch porpoifes as thofe?
" Shall I, who fcarce can fetch my breath
" In *Goldfmith's-hall*, be prefs'd to death
" By three fuch greafy frows as thefe,
" Melting like butter in hot peas?
" No, no, let KIRGATE rail and fwear,
" And call me blockhead, I don't care;
" By *Jove*, to *Heav'n* I would not ride,
" With fo much blubber by my fide."
Then fhuts his box and fwings his cane,
And homeward frets and fweats again.
There, with a carelefs, languid air,
He throws himfelf into his chair;
While the kind Genii gently fhed
The duft of poppy o'er his head,
Then foftly to his brain they creep,
And lock up all his cares in fleep.

46. ADVERTISEMENT. STOLEN OR STRAYED, A SMALL BROWN SHOCK WATER DOG.

Lowndes 106; Martin, p. 513.

In Baker's *Catalogue* of 1810, this piece is marked with an asterisk, to indicate that it was not printed for HW. A note adds: 'A joke on a waterman who had absented himself from his Club. Printed by B. Nobody, at Brentford.'

No copy has been found (but one was in the Eyton Collection, sold 1848); if it is a genuine SH piece, it was doubtless printed by Kirgate at some time during the later years of the Press.

47. MRS. DAMER'S RULES FOR THE LIBRARY. 1797.

Lowndes 65; Martin, p. 509.

Martin says that this piece was the last thing printed at SH, but he says the same of No. 48, *The Printer's Farewell;* both pieces were doubtless printed in October 1797. No copy is listed in the collection of Mrs. Damer's books sold at Hodgson's in 1902.

The Rules are printed on one side of a quarto leaf measuring approximately 23 x 19 cm. trimmed. The two parts have been divided in Bull's copy of the *Description of SH* (now WSL) and trimmed to fit beneath the view of the library.

COPIES

Eton College (Storer); WSL (2 copies).

48. THE PRINTER'S FAREWELL TO STRAWBERRY HILL. 1797.

Lowndes 77; Martin, p. 510.

Kirgate's note (on one WSL copy): 'Written by Mr. Silvester Harding, Friend of T. Kirgate, Printer.' Another WSL copy has the following note by Kirgate: 'The last Thing Printed at Strawberry hill.' That Kirgate placed his own initials at the end is understandable, since Harding makes Kirgate the speaker in the poem; the date at the end is certainly correct.

The Verses are printed on one side of a quarto leaf: a copy on wove paper (Utterson-WSL, trimmed) measures approximately 27.3 x 21.5 cm. The Verses were reprinted in the nineteenth century.

STATES AND VARIANTS

Copies of the original printing exist on two lots of paper: a heavy

If any Perſon ſhould take a Book out of the Library, they are particularly requeſted to ſet down their Name on this Slate, and the Title of the Book.

A. S. D.

Rule for replacing a Book.

Each Volume is lettered on the inſide; the firſt Numeral refers to the Diviſion, and the ſecond to the Shelf: alſo, on many, the Number of the Book as placed on the Shelf is noted.

THE PRINTER's FAREWELL

TO STRAWBERRY-HILL.

ADIEU! ye Groves and Gothic Tow'rs,
  Where I have spent my youthful Hours,
    Alas! I find in vain:
Since he who could my Age protect,
By some mysterious, sad neglect,
  Has left me to complain!

For thirty Years of Labour past,
To meet such slight Reward at last,
  Has added to my Cares:
To quit the quiet Scenes of Life,
T'encounter Bus'ness, Bustle, Strife,
  Hangs heavy on my Years.

Farewell! my PRINTING-HOUSE, farewell!
Where I no more shall calmly dwell,
  Within thy peaceful Door:
No more in Conversation free,
Enjoy my Friend and sip my Tea;
  Ah! no; those Days are o'er.

On thee, my Fellow-Lab'rour, dear,
My PRESS, I drop the silent Tear
  Of Pity, for thy Lot;
For thou, like me, by Time art worn,
Like me, too, thou art left forlorn,
  Neglected and forgot!

October, 1797.   T. K.

48. ORIGINAL EDITION.

THE PRINTER's FAREWELL

TO STRAWBERRY-HILL.

ADIEU! ye Groves and Gothic Tow'rs,
  Where I have fpent my youthful Hours,
    Alas! I find in vain:
Since he who could my Age protect,
By fome myfterious, fad neglect,
    Has left me to complain!

For thirty Years of Labour paft,
To meet fuch flight Reward at laft,
    Has added to my Cares:
To quit the quiet Scenes of Life,
T'encounter Bus'nefs, Buftle, Strife,
    Hangs heavy on my Years.

Farewell! my PRINTING-HOUSE, farewell!
Where I no more fhall calmly dwell,
    Within thy peaceful Door:
No more in Converfation free,
Enjoy my Friend and fip my Tea;
    Ah! no; thofe Days are o'er.

On thee, my Fellow-Lab'rour, dear,
My PRESS, I drop the filent Tear
    Of Pity, for thy Lot;
For thou, like me, by Time art worn,
Like me, too, thou art left forlorn,
    Neglected and forgot!

October, 1797.   T. K.

48. NINETEENTH-CENTURY REPRINT.

wove paper with the watermark 'J Whatman 1794'; and a laid paper with the watermark 'lily, VDL' that helps to date some of Kirgate's reprints (see No. 18 above).

For a discussion of the nineteenth-century reprint in Wilson type, see the Verses to Lady Townshend, No. 2 above.

COPIES

Huntington (Bull); WSL (4 copies).

Nineteenth-century reprint: Harvard (Merritt); WSL (2 copies).

Other copies (not seen, and therefore not differentiated as to edition): British Museum (Grenville); Victoria and Albert (Dyce); Lord Derby; Quaritch, Catalogue 530 (1937); Dulau, Catalogue 276 (1939).

BIBLIOGRAPHY OF THE STRAWBERRY HILL PRESS

TITLE-PAGES
LABELS FOR BOOKS
AND CARDS OF ADDRESS

49. DRAWINGS AND DESIGNS BY RICHARD BENTLEY.

Not in Lowndes.

HW printed this special title-page for his collection of Bentley's drawings. The seventy-five drawings and sketches are pasted upon the blank leaves of a folio volume bound in contemporary russia. Thirty-four of these drawings were done for the early rooms at SH: several are signed by Bentley and have notes in his hand and in HW's. The title-page is pasted on the first leaf of the volume.

The printing of the title-page is probably to be dated *ca.* 1760, because Bentley's sketches and designs for the Gothic 'improvements' of SH were done during a period of years from 1751 to 1761. (See W. S. Lewis, 'The Genesis of Strawberry Hill,' in *Metropolitan Museum Studies,* Vol. V, part one, June 1934, p. 57.)

The paper appears to be the same as that used in the books printed at the Press from 1758 to 1760.

COPIES

WSL: in SH Sale (London Sale, 23 June 1842), x.1255, to William Knight, £4.2.0; Spencer, May 1926, to WSL, £210.

50. A COLLECTION OF THE MOST REMARKABLE TRACTS PUBLISHED IN THE REIGN OF KING GEORGE THE THIRD. OCTAVO. 1763–1768.

Lowndes 80; Martin, p. 510.

Lowndes specifies Volume IX, possibly because a copy of that leaf was in Eyton's Collection. But the whole collection of tracts, bound in 54 volumes octavo and 5 volumes quarto, is now WSL. It can be traced as follows: SH Sale, iii.110, to Thorpe, £36.15.0; owned by Henry Labouchere, Baron Taunton; Sotheby's, 2 December 1920 (Stanley Sale), lots 454–5, to Quaritch, £248; Quaritch to Sir Leicester Harmsworth, Bt.; sold by the Harmsworth Trustees, June 1938, to WSL, £1000 (with 88 volumes of pamphlets). For the *Tracts* in quarto, see No. 53 below.

Only the first 19 volumes of the *Tracts* in octavo have special title-pages. (In Lord Waldegrave's collection is a single leaf numbered Vol. XX, with no vignette.)

The title-pages are printed on trimmed leaves measuring approximately 20 x 12 cm. The vignette on the title-page (in black ink) is the smaller fleuron first used in the *Catalogue of Royal and Noble Authors,* 1758.

STATES AND VARIANTS

Differences of paper and type make it clear that the title-pages were set up in at least three groups. (1) Volumes I–VI, containing tracts from 1760 to November 1763, on paper with crown, post horn watermark; printed probably at the end of 1763. (2) Volumes VII–VIII, containing tracts from January 1764 to September 1764, on similar paper; printed probably in the autumn of 1764. (3) Volumes IX–XIX, containing tracts from January 1765 to December 1767, on paper with crown, lily, L V G watermark (the paper used for *Cornélie* and the *Mysterious Mother* in 1768); printed probably in 1768, after the reopening of the Press in April.

The vignette in the copy of Volume X in Lord Waldegrave's collection is printed in red ink.

COPIES

WSL (Vols. I–XIX); Lord Waldegrave (Vols. X, XX).

51. A COLLECTION OF THE MOST REMARKABLE POEMS PUBLISHED IN THE REIGN OF KING GEORGE THE THIRD. QUARTO. 1768.

Lowndes 51; Martin, p. 508.

Lowndes specifies Volumes VI and VII, but the whole collection of poems, bound in 22 volumes, is now at Harvard. It can be traced as follows: SH Sale, v.57, to Thorpe, £8.18.6; owned by Henry Labouchere, Baron Taunton; Sotheby's, 2 December 1920 (Stanley Sale), lot 453, to Pickering, £230; given to Harvard by Mr. Augustine H. Parker.

Only the first eight volumes of the *Poems* have special title-pages. Since the last poem in Volume VIII was published in December 1767, and since these title-pages are printed on the same paper as that used for the title-pages of Volumes IX–XIX of *Tracts* (No. 50 above), these title-pages were probably printed in 1768, after the reopening of the Press in April.

The title-pages are printed on quarto leaves measuring approximately 22.4 x 19.6 cm. (untrimmed copy at Chewton Priory). The vignette on the title-page (in black ink) is the smaller fleuron first used in the *Catalogue of Royal and Noble Authors,* 1758.

States and Variants

Martin lists a copy of Volume VII without the vignette.

Copies

Harvard (Vols. I–VIII); Huntington (Bull: Vol. VIII); Lord Waldegrave (Vol. VI); wsl (Vol. VIII).

52. A COLLECTION OF ALL THE DRAMATIC PIECES PUBLISHED IN THE REIGN OF KING GEORGE THE THIRD. Octavo. 1768.

Lowndes 79; Martin, p. 510.

The whole collection, called by HW's binder 'Theatre of George 3,' can be traced as follows: SH Sale, iii.170 (a collection of 59 volumes), to Thorpe, £22.1.0; Sotheby's, 10 June 1914 (Miscellaneous Sale), lot 551, to Maggs, 58 volumes for £210. The collection was broken up by Maggs Brothers, who disposed of a few plays separately, and then sold the rest of the collection to Pickering and Chatto; Pickering and Chatto sold ten of the title-pages to Mr. Merritt in 1922. Over 300 of the plays are now wsl, and 43 of the covers.

Title-pages were prepared for eleven volumes of the plays only, so far as we can tell: Messrs. Pickering and Chatto wrote Mr. Merritt in 1922 that there were eleven in the collection. Since eleven volumes would be needed for the plays from 1760 to 1768, approximately, and since these title-pages are printed on the same paper as that used for the title-pages of the *Tracts* and *Poems* (No. 50 and No. 51), these were also probably printed in 1768, after the reopening of the Press in April.

The title-pages are octavo leaves measuring approximately 19.3 x 12.5 cm. untrimmed. The vignette on the title-page is the smaller fleuron first used in the *Catalogue of Royal and Noble Authors*. 1758.

States and Variants

The vignette is printed in red ink on some copies, but the ten at Harvard are all printed in black; copies also exist without the vignette. Some of the copies at Harvard are printed on paper watermarked with crown, post horn, L V G, the paper used for the second edition of the *Anecdotes of Painting*.

Copies

Harvard (Vols. I–X); Huntington (Vol. X); Lord Waldegrave (Vol. IX); wsl (Vols. VI, VII, VIII, X, and 2 copies of Vol. XI).

53. A COLLECTION OF THE MOST REMARKABLE TRACTS PUBLISHED IN THE REIGN OF KING GEORGE III. QUARTO. 1771.

Lowndes 50; Martin, p. 508.

The history of this collection (five volumes, with title-pages for the first four) is recorded under the *Tracts* in octavo, No. 50. In the Huntington Library, there is a single leaf numbered Vol. VI.

The title-pages are printed on trimmed quarto leaves measuring approximately 23.5 x 18 cm. The vignette on the title-page (in black ink) is the large view of SH first used on the title-page of the *Life of Lord Herbert,* completed in January 1764.

STATES AND VARIANTS

Differences of paper and type make it clear that the title-pages were set up in two groups. (1) Volumes I and II, containing tracts from 1761 to May 1764, on paper with crown, post horn watermark; printed probably in the autumn of 1764. (2) Volumes III and IV, containing tracts from November 1764 to March 1771, on paper with crown, post horn, G R watermark and J Whatman countermark (paper first used in fourth volume of *Anecdotes of Painting,* 1771); printed probably in 1771. Volume VI, perhaps set up in error at that time, seems to be the same setting as Volumes III and IV.

Martin lists the title-page of Volume III 'with view of Ghent,' an amusing error for 'vignette.'

COPIES

Huntington (Vol. VI); Lord Waldegrave (Vol. IV); WSL (Vols. I–IV).

54. PORTRAITS OF PAINTERS, ENGRAVERS, SCULPTORS, &c. FROM WALPOLE'S ANECDOTES OF PAINTING IN ENGLAND.

Lowndes 40; Martin, p. 507.

These title-pages must have been printed between 1771 and 1773. They were probably printed for the volumes which Robins described in 1842 (London Sale, x.1270) as 'A Collection of 470 Drawings and Prints of Portraits of English Painters and Engravers, collected by Mr. Vertue and Mr. Walpole, and arranged according to their Anecdotes of Painting in England, in two portfolios, with leaves.'

[258]

HW bought the drawings from Vertue's widow in 1758, and made extensive use of them as illustrations for the *Anecdotes*. By 1773 they were probably bound with their special title-pages, since the *Description of SH*, 1774, p. 49, lists 'Drawings and prints of heads of English painters and artists, in 2 volumes, folio.' (This part of the *Description* was printed in the summer of 1773.) The other limit is established by the countermark, J Whatman, in the paper; this paper was first used at the Press for the fourth volume of *Anecdotes*, printed in the winter of 1770–71.

The title-page is printed on one side of a trimmed quarto leaf (the volumes were folios) measuring approximately 33 x 25.5 cm.

COPIES

Lord Waldegrave. A second copy was probably in the Eyton Collection (sold 1848). The two portfolios with their title-pages have not been traced since 1842.

55. PORTRAITS IN THE REIGN OF KING GEORGE THE THIRD.

Lowndes 39; Martin, p. 507.

This title-page was probably printed at some time between 1774 and 1784, but there appears to be no way of dating it more precisely. In the *Description of SH*, 1784, p. 37, there is the following entry: 'Five larger [folios of English heads] of the reign of George 3d. and an additional volume of heads of different reigns collected since.' These volumes were listed in Robins's Catalogue, SH Sale, viii.111, but the collection was broken up and the portraits sold separately at the London Sale in June.

Since only 'a large volume of the reign of George 3d. not ranged' is listed in the *Description of SH*, 1774, one can assume that the five folios were arranged afterwards. But William Cole wrote to HW, 9 April 1775, sending a 'drawing by Mr. Gooch . . . which I have an ambition to have placed in your last volume of modern and unknown heads.' [HW put it in his copy of *Description of SH*, 1774, now in the New York Public Library.] Cole's letter suggests that HW was preparing these volumes in 1775, but the title-pages to the five volumes and to the 'additional volume of heads of different reigns collected since' may have been printed then or later.

Since the copies of this title-page have been folded and are somewhat battered [now repaired and rebacked], and since Lord Waldegrave describes his copy of No. 56 as folded and very tattered, it seems possible that these are the title-pages which were originally on the volumes before they were broken up in 1842.

One would expect title-pages for HW's collections of earlier portraits, but we have found no record of any.

The title-page is printed on one side of a trimmed folio leaf measuring approximately 46 x 29.2 cm. The paper is the same as that used for the quarto *Works,* printed 1768–87. The vignette on the title-page (in black ink) is the large view of SH first used on the title-page of the *Life of Lord Herbert,* completed in January 1764.

COPIES

WSL (Vol. II with vignette, and Vol. III without vignette).

56. ADDITIONS TO THE COLLECTION OF ENGLISH POR-TRAITS.

Lowndes 47; not in Martin.

Like No. 55, this title-page was probably printed at some time between 1774 and 1784. The evidence for the date is the same as for No. 55, since this title-page was presumably prepared for the additional volume of heads of different reigns. But HW's phrase, 'collected since,' may mean that this title-page was printed somewhat later than No. 55.

The title-page is printed on one side of an untrimmed folio leaf, without watermark, measuring approximately 48.8 x 31 cm. The vignette on the title-page is the large view of SH first used on the title-page of the *Life of Lord Herbert,* completed in January 1764.

COPIES

Lord Waldegrave.

57. THE CRAFTSMAN, VOLUME V.

Lowndes 83; Martin, p. 511.

This title-page is recorded by Lowndes among the Detached Pieces 'in octavo et infra,' and it is said to have been printed for a copy belonging to Kirgate which wanted the title. No doubt it was included in Kirgate's set of the reprint of the *Craftsman,* in 14 volumes duodecimo, although I do not find the set separately listed in the sale catalogue of Kirgate's library in 1810.

In one of his annotated copies of the *Description of SH,* 1784, p. 2, opposite HW's note about the printer of the *Craftsman,* Kirgate has written his own name, possibly to indicate that he had printed a title-page. Just below Kirgate has written: 'The Printer's apprentice first printed this work in 1784,' referring apparently to the title-page. [Kirgate's note is directly opposite HW's printed note about Pulteney's ballad, *Strawberry-Hill,* but inasmuch as the ballad had been printed long before 1784, the MS note seems more likely to be intended as a reference to the *Craftsman*. I have seen only a transcript, made in 1821, of the notes in Kirgate's copy; but a similar note by Kirgate is said to be preserved in a copy of the *Description* now owned by Lord Walpole of Wolterton Park.]

No collation is possible, since no copy has been found. A copy was sold at Sotheby's in 1875, 'with note by Kirgate certifying that he printed only two copies'; probably this copy came from the Eyton Collection (sold 1848).

58. A DESCRIPTION OF THE VILLA OF MR. HORACE WAL-POLE. 1784.

Martin, p. 503; not separately listed in Lowndes.
A good many copies of this title-page exist, sometimes bound as an additional title-page preceding the regular title, in colors. They appear to have been printed somewhat experimentally as a decorative addition, probably after the 200 titles in black ink had been printed.

The title-pages are printed in colored ink on one side of a quarto leaf measuring approximately 30.3 x 24.5 cm. uncut. The paper of most copies is the same as that used for the *Description*.

STATES AND VARIANTS

The colors used differ, as if Kirgate had tried out different combinations; I have seen copies printed in black and red, in blue and red, in green and red, and in black, blue, and red. The copies in bound volumes of the *Description* are likely to be decorated extensively by hand.

The tenth line ('with an inventory of the'; see *Bibliography*, No. 30) is usually set in capitals, whereas in the ordinary copies printed in black a combination of capitals and small capitals is used.

The spacing between lines is likely to vary from copy to copy, but the copies printed in colors have more room (to be filled by hand-drawn designs) above the imprint.

In one copy (now Huntington Library), the two lines of the imprint have been reversed.

In the set of proof-sheets of the *Description* (now WSL), a title in black and red has the same spacing and capitalization as the ordinary titles in black; this is the principal reason for calling the other copies in colors later than the copies in black.

COPIES

No census is possible, because copies are so often bound with copies of the *Description*. At Farmington, there are three separate copies, and three bound with copies of the *Description*.

59. JOHN CARTER'S DRAWINGS AND SKETCHES, OF THE GOTHIC MANSION AT STRAWBERRY-HILL. 1788.

Lowndes 43; Martin, p. 508.

John Carter made drawings of various rooms and objects at SH, for HW and also for Richard Bull. This title-page was apparently printed by Kirgate at Carter's request; Baker in his *Catalogue* of 1810 marks this title-page with an asterisk, to indicate that it was not printed for HW.

The volume for which the title-page was prepared is now in the Huntington Library; it is a folio, with a copy of the *Description of SH*, 1784, inlaid; preceding the printed title-page is a MS draft (by Carter?) of the title-page.

The title-page is printed on one side of a quarto leaf measuring 29.6 x 23.4 cm. trimmed.

COPIES

Huntington (in Carter's volume); WSL.

60. COLLECTANEA: OR, A COLLECTION OF ADVERTISE-MENTS AND PARAGRAPHS FROM THE NEWSPAPERS, RELATING TO VARIOUS SUBJECTS. PRINTED AT STRAWBERRY-HILL, BY THOMAS KIRGATE, FOR THE COLLECTOR, DANIEL LYSONS.

Lowndes 44; Martin, p. 508.

Kirgate appears to have printed, probably after about 1790 when Lysons came to Putney, a considerable number of these title-pages for the folio scrapbooks kept by the Reverend Daniel Lysons.

The various collections, all in folio, can be partially traced as follows:

1. Collectanea Dramatica, a collection of playbills, advertisements, and theatrical anecdotes; five volumes, with materials from 1711 to 1823. Evans, 17 March 1828 (Lysons Sale), lot 666; not found since 1828.

2. Collectanea Historica, a collection of cuttings concerning interesting events; eight volumes (title-pages for first six only), arranged chronologically from 1746. Evans, 17 March 1828 (Lysons Sale), lot 667; six of the eight volumes were sold by Evans, 17 June 1846 (Upcott Sale), lots 834–5; Volumes III–VI were owned in 1907 by J. Eliot Hodgkin (see *Notes and Queries*, 26 October 1907), and sold with his library at Sotheby's in 1914.

3. Collectanea, a collection of cuttings concerning Publick Exhibitions and Places of Amusement; five volumes, with materials from 1661 to 1840 (continued by a later owner). Evans, 17 March 1828 (Lysons Sale), lot 668, to Philip Hurd, £105; Evans, 17 June 1846 (Upcott Sale), lot 836, to Pocock, £17.17.0; J. Lilly, December 1867, to British Museum, £52.10.0.

4. Collectanea, a collection of cuttings concerning Trades and Professions; two volumes. Evans, 17 March 1828 (Lysons Sale), lot 669, to Philip Hurd, £31.10.0; Evans, 30 July 1845 (Hurd Sale), lot 584, to Dawson Turner, £10; Puttick and Simpson, 19 May 1859 (Turner Sale), lot 1120; T. and W. Boone, November 1863, to British Museum, £14.12.6.

5. Collectanea, a collection of cuttings concerning Law Reports; one volume. Evans, 17 March 1828 (Lysons Sale), lot 670; not found since 1828.

6. Collectanea, a collection of cuttings concerning Orator Henley; one volume. Evans, 17 March 1828 (Lysons Sale), lot 671, to Thorpe, £19.19.0; bought by British Museum, September 1860.

Of these twenty-two volumes in folio, at least eighteen are reported to contain Kirgate's title-page: two of the historical volumes, prepared in the nineteenth century, were without it; the fifth volume of Publick Exhibitions is without it; and nothing is said about a title-page for the Law Reports. Eight of the volumes, containing seven of the title-pages, are now in the British Museum. The other fourteen volumes have not been found.

The title-page is printed on one side of a folio leaf, on rather coarse, unwatermarked paper, measuring approximately 43.5 x 26 cm. trimmed.

COPIES

British Museum (7 copies described above); Harvard (Merritt); Huntington (Bull); Lord Waldegrave; WSL.

61. PUBLICK EXHIBITIONS AND PLACES OF AMUSEMENT. VOLUME I [–V].

Lowndes 45; Martin, p. 508.

These title-pages, five in number, were prepared for the third series of Lysons's *Collectanea* (No. 60 above). Like the general title-pages, these specific titles were presumably printed by Kirgate at Strawberry Hill.

The title-page is printed on one side of a folio leaf measuring approximately 42 x 25 cm. trimmed.

COPIES

British Museum (Vols. I–V). No other copies have been found.

62. THEATRICAL. VOLUME I [–V].

Lowndes 46; Martin, p. 508.

This title-page has not been found, but presumably five were prepared for the first series of Lysons's *Collectanea* (No. 60 above). Like the general title-pages, these specific titles were presumably printed by Kirgate at Strawberry Hill.

63. A COLLECTION OF THE LOOSE PIECES PRINTED AT STRAWBERRY-HILL.

Lowndes 52; Martin, p. 508.

This title-page, by its very nature, must have been printed near the end of the period in which the SH Press was in operation, when such collections were being made up. It seems safe to place it later than 1790, and although Baker's *Catalogue* of 1810 fails to mark this title with an asterisk, to indicate that it was not printed for HW, it is not unlikely that it was printed after HW's death in 1797.

HW's own collection of Detached Pieces does not seem (from its description in the SH and Utterson catalogues) to have contained this title-page, but it does appear in most of the Kirgate collections. Furthermore, Richard Bull printed a special title in 1791 for his collection, and then (apparently) added Kirgate's title-page later.

The title-page is printed on one side of a quarto leaf measuring approximately 30.5 x 24.7 cm. uncut (Lord Waldegrave's copy). The paper is the same as that used for the *Description of SH*, 1784; this is the paper that Kirgate used for several of his late reprints.

STATES AND VARIANTS

On at least two copies, Kirgate printed, in black ink, the large SH fleuron (used on the title-pages of Gray's *Odes* and Hentzner's *Journey* in 1757).

In Lord Waldegrave's collection is a title printed in larger type, with the same wording except for the insertion of the word 'all': 'A collection of all the loose pieces. . . .' On this copy is a note signed by Kirgate: 'Only this proof was printed, and rejected on account of the types being too large.'

COPIES

Huntington (Bull); Lord Waldegrave (one copy, and also the proof described above); WSL (4 copies).

64. LABEL: BUNBURY'S ETCHINGS.

Lowndes 109; Martin, p. 513.

These labels were apparently prepared for the shelf-back of the collection of etchings, prints, and original drawings by Henry William Bunbury, arranged by HW in two large folio volumes. These volumes were sold in 1842 (London Sale in June, v.733) to H. G. Bohn for £7.7.0.

The volumes have not been recovered, and we have found no copy of the label.

65. LABEL: SEVIGNIANA.

Lowndes 110; Martin, p. 513.

This label was apparently prepared for the shelf-back of HW's collection of 144 portraits of Madame de Sévigné and her friends, arranged in a large folio. This volume was sold in 1842 (London Sale in June, iv.577) to Smith for £16.16.0.

The volume has not been recovered, and we have found no copy of the label.

66. THREE LABELS FOR CROKER'S DICTIONARY.

Lowndes 113; Martin, p. 513.

The book in question is Henry Temple Croker's compilation, *The Complete Dictionary of Arts and Sciences,* three volumes, 1766. According to Baker's note, the labels were prepared for Kirgate's copy of the book.

The volumes have not been recovered, and we have found no copy of the label.

67. LABEL: DETACHED PIECES, PRINTED AT STRAW-BERRY HILL.

Lowndes 112; Martin, p. 513.

In Baker's *Catalogue* of 1810, this label is marked with an asterisk, to indicate that it was not printed for HW. No doubt this is correct, for the piece seems to have been prepared by Kirgate as a label for one or more of his collections. Probably 1797 is the correct date.

Kirgate has added a note in pencil above the words 'Strawberry Hill': 'Chiefly by T. Kirgate, at.' The piece is authentically Kirgate's, at least, and there seems no reason to suppose that he did not print it at SH.

The label is printed on a small slip of paper measuring approximately 9.9 x 7.7 cm.

COPIES

WSL.

68. LABEL: LOOSE PIECES PRINTED AT STRAWBERRY HILL.

Lowndes 111; Martin, p. 513.

This label is pasted on Kirgate's portfolio of Detached Pieces now owned by Lord Waldegrave. It is just as likely to be a genuine SH piece as No. 67 above; the same reasoning applies to both labels. Possibly Kirgate discarded one form in favor of the other.

The label is printed on a small slip of paper measuring approximately 8.4 x 3.4 cm.

COPIES

Lord Waldegrave.

CARDS OF ADDRESS

The next nine pieces, Cards of Address, have equal standing. They are all genuine SH pieces, probably, if any one is. They were printed on small slips or cards, measuring usually about 4 x 6 cm., by Kirgate for himself and for his friends; they were probably printed after 1790, when Kirgate began to do more printing on his own responsibility. All are listed in Lowndes, Nos. 114–123.

69. CARD: THOMAS KIRGATE, PRINTER, STRAWBERRY-HILL, TWICKENHAM, MIDDLESEX.

A copy is preserved with Richard Bull's collection in the Huntington Library. A variant, reading 'Thomas Kirgate, No. 127, Pall Mall,' was in the Eyton Collection (sold 1848); this was the address of Silvester Harding's shop, and Kirgate may have prepared this card (before or after he left SH) for the convenience of his London friends and customers.

70. CARD: SILVESTER HARDING, MINIATURE PAINTER AND ENGRAVER, No. 127 PALL MALL.

There is a copy in Kirgate's own collection of Detached Pieces, now owned by Lord Waldegrave.

71. CARD: Coward & Pritchard, Milliners and Haberdashers, King-Street, Richmond.

Three copies are known: Eton College (Storer); Lord Waldegrave; WSL.

72. CARD: Michael Stubbs, Upholsterer & Cabinet-maker, Near the Bull's Head, Twickenham.

There is a copy in Richard Bull's collection, now Huntington Library.

73. CARD: George Smith, Peruke Maker, Near 'The Three Kings' Twickenham.

There is a copy in Kirgate's collection, now owned by Lord Waldegrave.

74. CARD: Beale, Watch & Clock Maker, Twickenham.

There is a copy in Kirgate's collection, now owned by Lord Waldegrave. A variant (not seen) is recorded by Lowndes, with the reading: 'Clock and Watch Maker.'

75. CARD: Mrs. Delane, No. 4, Great Queen Street, Lincoln's Inn Fields.

Listed by Lowndes, No. 117; no copy found.

76. CARD: G. Ewington, Painter, Glazier, and Plumber, Twickenham, Middlesex.

Listed by Lowndes, No. 119; no copy found.

77. CARD: John Ash, Nursery and Seedsman, Twickenham, Middlesex.

Listed by Lowndes, No. 120; no copy found.

APPENDIX B

The following pieces are probably (and some, certainly) not SH productions. They are listed here in approximate chronological order, with whatever significant evidence we have found about each one. Some other pieces have not even attained the dignity of being included in this list of apocryphal works. Among these, one class is composed of Verses about SH; Pulteney's song, *Strawberry Hill,* to which HW contributed some lines, is an example. Bull's special title-page for a collection of Detached Pieces is a sample of another class: this was used not only by Bull but by Storer and other collectors. A third class may be represented by the ballad on Kitty Fisher: the colophon asserts that it was written and printed at Strawberry Hill, but HW himself rejected it (JPO, p. 8).

78. THE NORFOLK GARLAND; OR, THE DEATH OF REYNARD THE FOX.

This ballad, by Sir William Yonge, is not in Lowndes, but it tends to creep into SH collections because of its Walpolian interest. Nos. 78, 79, and 80 were all written, apparently, and printed at about the same time, on the same paper, in a non-Caslon type. From internal evidence, all three can be dated after March 1724 and before May 1733; they are dated 1728, somewhat hesitantly, in the British Museum *Catalogue.*

HW's copy, with his MS notes, is now WSL.

79. PROSPERITY TO HOUGHTON.

This ballad was written by Philip Floyd. It is listed in Lowndes,

No. 48, but it was printed long before 1757; see No. 78 above. But perhaps because about 50 copies of this and *Houghton Hare-Hunting* were sold with the books printed at SH (SH Sale, v.200), both items were listed by Lowndes.

HW's copy, with his MS notes, is now WSL.

80. HOUGHTON HARE-HUNTING.

This ballad was written as a reply to Nos. 78 and 79. It is listed in Lowndes, No. 48, but it was printed long before 1757; see No. 78 above.

81. COAT OF ARMS OF WHITE'S CLUB ('GAMESTER'S COAT OF ARMS').

HW to George Montagu, 20 April 1756: 'I shall send you soon the fruits of my last party to Strawberry; Dick Edgcumbe, George Selwyn, and Williams were with me; we composed a coat of arms for the two clubs at White's, which is actually engraving, from a very pretty painting of Edgcumbe. . . . Here is the blazon. . . .'

There is no doubt, I think, that copies of the engraving were printed at once, a year before the establishment of the SH Press, and the piece has accordingly been relegated to the Appendix. But at some later date it is likely that additional copies were printed, quite possibly in the SH printing-office, from the same plate. Copies exist on the same pink paper (for proofs of engravings) used for a proof of the Rules for seeing the House, No. 33 above; and HW wrote to Anthony Storer, in an undated letter (1789?): 'Voici two arms of White's.'

Perhaps it is safe to say that some copies were printed much later than 1756. Most of the copies in SH collections are undoubtedly of this new impression. The watermark (visible in some copies) also suggests a date after 1780.

COPIES

British Museum (Grenville); Eton College (Storer: 4 copies, including one on pink paper and one printed with green ink); Harvard (Merritt: 2 copies, including Mrs. Damer's copy on pink paper); Huntington (on pink paper); WSL (4 copies, including a copy colored by hand in HW's extra-illustrated *Description of SH*, 1784); Spoor Collection (sold 1939).

82. FRAGMENT OF A NORTH BRITON. 1763.

In the *Times Literary Supplement*, 27 November 1930, Mr. Francis Needham announced the discovery of this four-page folio with a Strawberry Hill colophon; Mr. Needham wrote that he and Dr. Paget Toynbee believed that HW wrote and printed the piece.

That HW either saw the piece or wrote it is clear from his letter to Conway, 1–2 May 1763:

The bitterness of the weather makes me wonder how you can find the country tolerable now. . . . Such hard words have passed between me and the north wind to-day, that, according to the language of the times, I was very near abusing it for coming from Scotland, and to imputing it to Lord Bute. I don't know whether I should not have written a *North Briton* against it, if the printers were not all sent to Newgate, and Mr. Wilkes to the Tower. . . . They found among Wilkes's papers an unpublished *North Briton,* designed for last Saturday. It contained advice to the King not to go to St. Paul's. . . .

But that HW knew what was in the fragment does not prove that he wrote, or printed, it. Perhaps he would hardly be suspected were it not for his joke about the cold wind from the north.

In the first place, one can see no particular reason for HW to print (or reprint) the piece. But other points also argue against it. (1) Since the paper, foolscap folio, is different from that used for Nos. 1–45, this number was obviously not printed at the same press as the earlier numbers; but it is not a paper that was in use at any time at SH. (2) The appearance of the page seems rather beyond the capacity of the inexperienced Pratt. (Pratt was busied just then in finishing the *Catalogue of Engravers.*) (3) The colophon 'Printed at STRAWBERRY HILL' is unusual, since most books from the Press used capitals and hyphen, 'STRAWBERRY-HILL.' (4) If HW had been interested in helping the case against Wilkes by printing the piece, he would scarcely have put the SH colophon at the end, whereas a London printer, knowing that it could not harm Walpole, might very easily have decided to use that colophon as a protection. (5) Copies are in the British Museum, at the University of Chicago (in a bound volume of the *North Briton*), and in the library at Welbeck Abbey (where it was found 'among a pile of loose numbers of the *North Briton*'), but no copies are known in any Walpolian collection. (6) HW's joking reference to a *North Briton* against the weather (in his letter to Conway) seems to me perhaps the strongest evidence that he did not write or print No. 46. Furthermore, I see no explanation for his complete silence if he had printed it.

No single argument is conclusive, of course, and it is fair to add that Professor Kirby is inclined to accept it as genuine.

83. A SKETCH FOR A. D. 1769.

This poem of thirty lines, apparently by Sir Edward Walpole, was published in the *Gentleman's Magazine* for April 1769. A copy of the poem, printed in Caslon type on a single leaf, is inserted in an extra-illustrated copy of Austin Dobson's *Horace Walpole,* now in the Widener Collection at Harvard. The paper on which it is printed is unlike any in use at the Press; there seems to be no evidence that this was printed at SH.

84. FOR THE MONUMENT OF ROSE, A FAVOURITE SPAN- IEL. [1772.]

This piece and No. 85 are carelessly attributed to the SH Press in Henry Lemoine's *Typographical Antiquities,* 1797. p. 93, probably because both were so listed in the Catalogue of Dr. Lort's library in 1791. They were collected by the Earl of Carlisle in his *Poems,* 1773, and the best evidence that they are not SH pieces is contained in HW's letter to William Mason, 25 May 1772: 'Lord Carlisle has written and printed . . . two epitaphs on Lady Carlisle's dog, not bad, and a translation from Dante of the story of Count Ugolino, which I like the best. . . .' (Thomas Gray also translated this episode from Dante.)

A copy of the separate printing (spring of 1772?) now at Farmington is on paper that was never in use at the SH Press; the typography matches that of the published edition of 1773.

This piece was perhaps considered to be from the SH Press because of some remembrance of Edward Burnaby Greene's *Ode* on the death of HW's favorite black spaniel.

85. TRANSLATION FROM DANTE, CANTO XXXIII. [1772.]

This translation is also by the Earl of Carlisle. The evidence concerning it is included under No. 84 above.

86. LARGE LABEL: 'THE SHRINE IN FRONT WAS BROUGHT IN THE YEAR 1768.'

Lowndes 42; Martin, p. 507.

Kirgate's explanation that this large label was not printed at SH has already been quoted under No. 31 above. Like that label, this larger one is printed on gray cartridge paper. But the large label was printed earlier, since the chapel was erected in 1771, and the label is quoted in the *Description of SH* of 1774, pp. 113–14.

87. TITLE-PAGE: ETCHINGS BY LADY LOUISA AUGUSTA GREVILLE, ELDEST DAUGHTER OF FRANCIS EARL OF BROOKE AND WARWICK.

Lowndes 49; Martin, p. 508.

In HW's library was 'a folio, splendidly bound in red morocco,' containing etchings by Lady Carlisle, Lady Louisa Augusta Greville, Lady Cunningham, Viscount Nuneham, and numerous others, with titles to the various collections. Since this book is not listed in the *Description of SH*, 1774, but does appear in the Appendix to that volume, it must have been prepared between 1774 and 1781.

The book was sold in 1842 (London Sale in June, viii.1126) to Pickering, but it was offered in 1843 by Strong of Bristol; Strong's description is in part as follows: 'containing 142 most beautiful etchings from private plates, engraved by various persons of quality, and presented to Horace Walpole, with titles to the various collections printed at Strawberry Hill. . . . It appears to have been prized by Horace Walpole, if we may judge from the splendid binding bestowed upon it, the printed titles, &c. &c.' Resold at Sotheby's, 1851.

One would like to see all the printed title-pages, but the history of the volume since 1851 is not known. Only the title-page for Lady

Louisa's etchings is listed by Lowndes, possibly because only that one was preserved in Kirgate's collection (now Lord Waldegrave). Lord Waldegrave writes that this title is printed on one side of a trimmed quarto leaf measuring 28 x 22.5 cm., and adds that the watermark is not recognizable. But from his partial tracing, it is clear that one word in the watermark is 'Auvergne,' and the paper is therefore certainly of French origin. Since no French paper was used in any SH book during this period, it seems unlikely that this title-page was printed at SH.

Some support for the rejection of Lady Louisa's *Etchings* may be obtained from the fact that none of the other title-pages can be found in any of Kirgate's collections.

88. PLAYBILL FOR HIGH LIFE BELOW STAIRS. 1786.

Henry Lemoine, in his *Typographical Antiquities,* 1797, p. 93, records this as a product of the SH Press. He says the play was performed at the revived (private) theatre at Hinchingbrook. Although I have never seen the playbill, I think it was not printed at SH. HW seems to have watched the performance, however, for he wrote to Lady Ossory, 15 January 1788, of 'the young actress who played Kitty so admirably in *High Life below Stairs.*'

A copy was offered in the sale of Dr. Lort's library, Sotheby's, 20 April 1791, described as 'Folio, Strawberry Hill, 1786'; this catalogue was apparently the source of Lemoine's entry.

89. PROLOGUE AND EPILOGUE TO THE PLAY OF THE WAY TO KEEP HIM, PERFORMED AT RICHMOND HOUSE, IN APRIL, 1787, IN A PRIVATE SOCIETY.

The Way to Keep Him was performed 20 April 1787, at Richmond House; Mrs. Damer played the part of Mrs. Lovemore, and she spoke the Epilogue.

The paper is not unlike that used at SH, being a good grade of post paper from Whatman's mill. But it is not the same, and the type is certainly not Kirgate's Caslon. The piece can therefore be rejected without question.

Another edition is offered in the Catalogue of Dr. Lort's library, 'Folio, Strawberry Hill, 1787,' and listed in Lemoine (see No. 88 above). The title begins in the same way, but the last part reads: 'Performed at Richmond House, on the 17th of May, 1787, before their Majesties and Princesses.' A copy of this edition was included in the sale of Mrs. Damer's books at Hodgson's in 1902, but with no indication that it was from the SH Press. I think that this piece and No. 88 were listed as SH pieces in Dr. Lort's Catalogue under some misapprehension, and although I have seen neither piece, I think they were not printed at SH.

90. RULES FOR OBTAINING A TICKET, 'Lord Orford is very ready to oblige.'

For the edition printed at SH, see No. 33 above.

Kirgate's note (on a copy of the SH edition offered by Quaritch in 1937): 'The Rules in Roman Letter were not printed at Strawberry-hill.' Kirgate inserted a similar note in Richard Bull's MS list (now Huntington): 'Those in Italics were printed at Strawberry; those in Roman, at London.'

HW inherited the title of Earl of Orford upon the death of his nephew, 5 December 1791. Sir Wathen A. Waller, Bt., has a copy of the Rules in roman type with a note by HW dated 2 May 1792. This piece was therefore printed in London between December 1791 and May 1792.

The Rules are printed on the first page of a quarto half-sheet, and the blank leaf has usually survived. They were reprinted, an amusing forgery of a non-SH piece, in the nineteenth century; see the discussion under the Verses to Lady Townshend, No. 2 above.

Copies

Victoria and Albert (Dyce); Clark Memorial Library; Harvard (Merritt: 2 copies); Huntington; Lord Waldegrave; Mr. Wade White; wsl (5 copies).

There are two copies of the nineteenth-century reprint at Farmington.

91. SEAL: Sigillum Horatii Comitis De Orford.

Lowndes 108; not in Martin.

HW's seal as Earl of Orford was doubtless prepared soon after he inherited the title in December 1791. It is likely that some, if not all, copies were printed by Kirgate.

In the original seal, the design and lettering are on a white background. Of this form I have seen six copies on white paper, three on pink proof paper, and one on red paper.*

At some later time the seal was copied, with some differences in the design, on a shaded background. Mr. H. B. Wheatley considered this copy to be the original seal, but I think it was probably prepared in the nineteenth century for one of the Earls of the new creation.

92. VIGNETTES AND FLEURONS, FROM BOOKS, PRINTED AT STRAWBERRY HILL.

This piece is a small label, printed within an ornamental border that is unlike any SH printing. Copies are at Harvard and in the volume of views prepared to accompany Charles Bedford's extra-illustrated *Description of SH* now at Chewton Priory. It seems to have been printed by Kirgate as a heading for a collection of SH ornaments, but since it does not appear in his own collections of Detached Pieces, we assume that it was printed in London after 1797. (HW's set of fleurons, in his extra-illustrated copy of the *Description of SH*, has only a MS title in his hand: 'Fleurons & Vignettes to the Strawberry Editions.')

Among the various pieces are of course the three vignettes first used on the title-pages of Gray's *Odes, Catalogue of Royal and Noble Authors,* and *Life of Lord Herbert,* respectively.

93. ILLUSTRATIONS BY DRAWINGS AND PRINTS OF THE DESCRIPTION OF STRAWBERRY HILL, THE SEAT OF HORACE WALPOLE.

This title-page was printed for a collection of views prepared to

---

* In Bull's copy of *Hieroglyphic Tales,* a smaller but otherwise very similar seal is stamped in gold on black leather; this was probably added as a bookplate by Horatio William, Earl of Orford (1813–1894), who acquired the book about 1880.

accompany Charles Bedford's extra-illustrated *Description of SH* now at Chewton Priory. Since drawings in the volume are dated 1800, 1801, and 1803, respectively, and since the title-page is printed on wove paper, we assume that the title-page was printed in London when the volume was bound.

94. PROLOGUE (BY THE EARL OF MOUNT EDGCUMBE) AND EPI-LOGUE (BY JOANNA BAILLIE), WRITTEN FOR THE THEATRE AT STRAWBERRY HILL, NOVEMBER 1800.

Lowndes 78.

These two pieces are genuine enough (Mrs. Damer, one of the leaders in this continuance of private theatricals, spoke the Epilogue, and several copies were included with her books at Hodgson's in 1902), but they were certainly not printed at SH. Mrs. Damer sent Richard Bull's copies to him, 1 January 1801, but not with any thought of their being mistaken for pieces from the SH Press.

95. EPILOGUE TO THE COMEDY OF THE FASHIONABLE FRIENDS, PERFORMED AT STRAWBERRY-HILL, 1801.

As in the case of No. 94, copies of this piece were appropriately preserved among Mrs. Damer's books, inasmuch as she spoke the Epilogue. An interesting proof, with corrections by Kirgate, is now at Farmington, but the printer was J. Barfield. It was not printed, according to the watermark, until 1804.

OWNERS OF COPIES

Not all association copies are included in this list. It is compiled as an index of the copies specifically recorded or referred to in the text. References are to the page, not to the number of the piece.

ABDY, Sir ROBERT:
Lucan's *Pharsalia* 49.

ACHESON, ARCHIBALD, Earl of Gosford (1806–1864):
Fugitive Pieces 41.

ADAM, ROBERT BORTHWICK (*d.* 1940):
Fugitive Pieces 42.

ALEXANDER, WILLIAM:
Description of the Villa (1784) 126.

ANCASTER, Sir GILBERT HEATHCOTE-DRUM-MOND-WILLOUGHBY, Earl of:
Mémoires du comte de Grammont 98.

ANDREINI, JOSEPH MANUEL (*d.* 1932):
The Mysterious Mother 84.

ANNESLEY, FRANCIS (*d.* 1812):
Letter from Thomas Walpole 121, 123; *Bishop Bonner's Ghost* 140; Tuer le tems 151; Collection of Detached Pieces 157; Court of Exchequer 172; Verses by Pentycross 198; Verses to Lady Craven 217; Rules for showing SH 228; Label for screen 229.

ANNESLEY, GEORGE ARTHUR, Viscount Valentia (1793–1841):
Odes by Mr. Gray 29; Countess Temple, *Poems* 76; *Miscellaneous Antiquities* 104.

ANTROBUS, Sir EDMUND (1818–1899):
Spence, *Parallel* 46.

ARBURY LIBRARY. *See* Newdigate.

ASTLEY, EDWARD:
Miscellaneous Antiquities 105.

ASTLEY, Sir EDWARD (1729–1802):
Plate from *The Humours of Oxford* inserted in *Fugitive Pieces* 41.

AUCKLAND, Lord. *See* Eden.

AVERY, SAMUEL PUTNAM (1822–1904):
Fugitive Pieces 42; Spence, *Parallel* 46; *Description of the Villa* (1774) 109.

BAKER, GEORGE (1747–1811):
Odes by Mr. Gray 28, 30; Advertisement to *Anecdotes* 65; Countess Temple, *Poems* 75; *Works* (1770) 94; *Reply to Dean Milles* 96; *Description of the Villa* 105; *The Muse Recalled* 121; *Letter from Thomas Walpole* 121; *Hieroglyphic Tales* 134; Laws, Rules, and Orders 142; Collection of Detached Pieces 16, 17, 48.

BAKER-WILBRAHAM, G. B. (*library sold* 1903):
Lucan, *Pharsalia* 49.

BAKER, WILLIAM:
Odes by Mr. Gray 29.

BARNSLEY. *See* Musgrave.

BARRETT, THOMAS (1744–1803):
Anecdotes 68; Countess Temple, *Poems* 76; *The Mysterious Mother* 79, 84; *Description of the Villa* (1774) 110; *Essay on Modern Gardening* 132; *Hieroglyphic Tales* 134; Bentley's Verses 162; Garrick's Verses 170; Verses to Lady Spencer 186; Verses to Mme. du Châtelet 199; Verses to King of Sweden 204;

COLE, WILLIAM (1714–1782):
Odes by Mr. Gray 27, 29; Hentzner, Journey 33; Royal and Noble Authors 37; Fugitive Pieces 39, 41; Spence, Parallel 46; Lucan, Pharsalia 49; Catalogue of Engravers 68; Life of Lord Herbert 72; Countess Temple, Poems 74, 75; Cornélie 77; Mysterious Mother 81; Miscellaneous Antiquities 104; Description of the Villa (1774) 109, 110; The Sleep-Walker 116; Letter on Chatterton 119; Verses to Lady Spencer 186.

CONYERS FAMILY:
Mémoires du comte de Grammont 99.

COOKE, JOSEPH JESSE (1813–1881):
Countess Temple, Poems 76.

CORNELL UNIVERSITY LIBRARY:
Lucan, Pharsalia 50.

COURTAULD, SAMUEL:
The Mysterious Mother 84; Description of the Villa (1784) 126.

COWPER, GEORGE NASSAU, 3d Earl Cowper (1738–1789):
Life of Lord Herbert 72.

COYKENDALL, FREDERICK:
Countess Temple, Poems 76; Bentley's Verses 162; Garrick's Verses 167, 170; Verses to Lady Spencer 186.

CRACHERODE, REV. CLAYTON M. (1730–1799):
Holbein Catalogue 50; Devonshire Catalogue 52.

CRAMPON, ALFRED (library sold 1896):
The Mysterious Mother, 84.

CROCKER, TEMPLETON:
Countess Temple, Poems 76.

CROCKETT, S. R.:
Mémoires du comte de Grammont 98.

CROWNINSHIELD, E. A.:
The Impenetrable Secret 146.

CRUDEN, ROBERT PEIRCE (1775?–1847):
Works (1770) 94; Reply to Dean Milles 95; Description of the Villa 105; Hieroglyphic Tales 134; Laws, Rules, and Orders 142; Tonton 225; Verses by Mrs. Holmes 237.

CUMBERLAND, RICHARD (1732–1811):
Lucan, Pharsalia 50.

CUNNINGHAM, PETER (1816–1869):
Fugitive Pieces 40; Mémoires du comte de Grammont 98; Description of the Villa (1784) 128.

CURRIE, BERTRAM WODEHOUSE (1827–1896):
Description of the Villa (1774) 109.

CURRIE, LAURENCE:
Description of the Villa (1774) 109.

CURTIS, Mrs., of Langford Hall:
Fugitive Pieces 41; Description of the Villa (1784) 129.

DACRE, Lord. See Barrett-Lennard.

DAGHLIAN, PHILIP BEWER:
Anecdotes 60.

DALRYMPLE, DAVID, Lord Hailes (1726–1792):
Hentzner, Journey 33; Royal and Noble Authors 37; Whitworth's Russia 44.

DAMER, Mrs. ANNE SEYMOUR (CONWAY) (1749–1828):
Odes by Mr. Gray 29; Holbein Catalogue 50; Anecdotes 65, 67; Life of Lord Herbert 71; Countess Temple, Poems 75, 76; Works (1770) 94; Reply to Dean Milles 95; Mémoires du comte de Grammont 98; Miscellaneous Antiquities 104; Description of the Villa 105; Description of the Villa (1774) 109, 110; Cabinet of Enamels 110, 111; Curiosities in the Glass Closet 112; The Sleep-Walker 116; Description of the Villa (1784) 126, 127; Postscript to Royal and Noble Authors 137; Verses to Lady Townshend 154, 158; Verses to Lady Rochford 160; Bentley's Verses 162; Epitaph on King of Corsica 164; Questions to the Society of Antiquaries 172; Mme. de Boufflers and Mme. Dusson 181; 'There was a little man' 189; Magpie 194; Verses by Pentycross 197; Verses to Mme. du Châtelet 199; Verses to Chesterfield 204; Master of Otranto 208; Ticket to view SH 210; Verses to Lady Craven 215; Rules for showing SH 228; To the Misses Berry 234; To the Duke of Clarence 234; Epitaph 239;

Epitaph on a Canary Bird 246; Arms of White's Club 270; *The Way to Keep Him* 275; Prologue and Epilogue 277; Epilogue to *The Fashionable Friends* 277.

DANIEL, GEORGE (1789–1864):
Odes by Mr. Gray 30; *Fugitive Pieces* 41; *The Mysterious Mother* 85.

DAVENPORT, Mrs. IRA H.:
Odes by Mr. Gray 30.

DERBY, Countess of. *See* Eliza Farren.

DERBY, Sir EDWARD GEORGE VILLIERS STANLEY, Earl of:
Odes by Mr. Gray 30; *Fugitive Pieces* 41; *Anecdotes* 66; Garrick's Verses 170; Questions to the Society of Antiquaries 175; Portrait of Lord Granville 179; Verses to Lady Spencer 186; 'There was a little man' 189; Magpie 194; Verses by Pentycross 198; Verses to Mme. du Châtelet 199; Verses to Chesterfield 204; Verses to King of Sweden 204; Master of Otranto 208; Verses to Lady Craven 217; Verses to Mrs. Crewe 220; Verses to Lady Waldegrave 223; Tonton 225; To the Misses Berry 234; To the Duke of Clarence 234; Epitaph 239; *Printer's Farewell* 252.

DICKENSON, MARY:
Description of the Villa (1784) 127.

DOUGLAS, SYLVESTER, Lord Glenbervie (1743–1823):
The Mysterious Mother 85.

DOUGLAS, WILLIAM:
Royal and Noble Authors 36.

DRUMMOND, ANDREW CECIL (1865–1913):
Letter on Chatterton 118.

DUER, WILLIAM:
Lucan, *Pharsalia* 50.

DYCE, ALEXANDER (1798–1869); Dyce Collection at Victoria and Albert Museum:
Hieroglyphic Tales 134; *Alcidalis and Zelida* 144; Verses to Lady Townshend 158; Verses to Lady Rochford 160; Garrick's Verses 170; Portrait of Lord Granville 178, 179; Mme. de Boufflers and Mme. Dusson 181; Verses to Lady

Spencer 186; 'There was a little man' 189; Magpie 194; Verses by Pentycross 198; Verses to King of Sweden 204; Master of Otranto 208; Label for the China Tub 210; Verses to Lady Craven 217; Verses to Mrs. Crewe 220; Verses to Lady Waldegrave 223; Rules for showing SH 228; To the Misses Berry 234; To the Duke of Clarence 234; Verses on Mrs. Clive 239; Epitaph 239; *Epitaph on a Canary Bird* 246; *Printer's Farewell* 252; Rules for showing SH 275.

EDEN, WILLIAM, Baron Auckland (1744–1814):
Life of Lord Herbert 72.

EDWARDES, Sir HENRY HOPE (1829–1900):
Works (1770) 94.

ELDERTON, Rev. J. W.:
Letters of Edward VI 101.

ELKINS, WILLIAM MCINTIRE:
Garrick's Verses 170; Verses to Lady Spencer 186; To the Misses Berry 234.

ERSKINE, Mrs., grand-niece of Grosvenor Charles Bedford:
Miscellaneous Antiquities 104.

ETON COLLEGE, Storer Collection. *See* Storer.

EYTON, J. WALTER KING (1820?–1872):
Rare pieces from his collection 15; Hentzner, *Journey* 33; Devonshire Catalogue 52; Preface to *Anecdotes* 55; Advertisement to *Anecdotes* 65; *The Mysterious Mother* 84; Hoyland, *Poems* 87; *Works* (1770) 94; *Reply to Dean Milles* 95; *Mémoires du comte de Grammont* 98; *Description of the Villa* 105; *Description of the Villa* (1784) 128; *Hieroglyphic Tales* 134; *Bishop Bonner's Ghost* 139; Laws, Rules, and Orders 142; *Alcidalis and Zelida* 144; Verses to Lady Townshend 158; Verses to Lady Rochford 160; Portrait of Lord Granville 178; Verses to Lady Spencer 184; Ticket to view SH 212; Proposals for Pony Race 220; Label for Shrine 223; Tonton 225; Label for Screen 229;

[EYTON, J. WALTER KING, *continued*]
Label for Fishing Eagle 231; Verses by Mrs. Holmes 237; *Cockey's New Year's Address* 244; *The Disaster* 246; A small brown Shock Water Dog 248; Tracts of George the Third 255; Portraits of Painters 259; *The Craftsman* 261; 'Thomas Kirgate, No. 127, Pall Mall' 266.

FARREN, ELIZA, later Countess of Derby (1759?–1829):
Fugitive Pieces 41.

FENN, Sir JOHN (1739–1794):
Anecdotes 67; *Life of Lord Herbert* (1770) 71.

FITZ-GIBBON, RICHARD HOBART, 3d Earl of Clare (1793–1864):
Anecdotes 66; *The Mysterious Mother* 84.

FITZPATRICK, JOHN, 2d Earl of Upper Ossory (1745–1818):
Hentzner, *Journey* 33; *Letters of Edward VI* 101.

FITZWILLIAM, General JOHN (d. 1789):
Miscellaneous Antiquities 104.

FITZWILLIAM MUSEUM, Cambridge:
Fugitive Pieces 41.

FORD, JOHN WALKER (1838–1921):
Royal and Noble Authors 36; *The Mysterious Mother* 84; *Mémoires du comte de Grammont* 99; *Description of the Villa* 105; *Description of the Villa* (1784) 129.

FORSTER, JOHN (1812–1876); Forster Collection at Victoria and Albert Museum:
Fugitive Pieces 41; *The Candidate* 214.

FOX, HENRY, 1st Baron Holland (1705–1774):
Miscellaneous Antiquities 105.

FRASER, Sir WILLIAM AUGUSTUS (1826–1898):
Odes by Mr. Gray 30; *Description of the Villa* (1784) 129.

FRERE, ARTHUR HOWARD:
Anecdotes 67.

FRERE, WILLIAM (1775–1836):
Anecdotes 67.

GABLE, WILLIAM F. (*library sold* 1923–1925):
Bishop Bonner's Ghost 140.

GAISFORD, THOMAS (1779–1855):
Postscript to Royal and Noble Authors 137.

GALTON, ARTHUR:
Mémoires du comte de Grammont 98.

GARRICK, DAVID (1717–1779):
Hentzner, *Journey* 33; *Royal and Noble Authors* 37; *Anecdotes* 67.

GASKELL, CHARLES GEORGE MILNES (1842–1919):
Anecdotes 67; *The Mysterious Mother* 84.

GASKILL, FRANCIS A. (1846–1909):
Odes by Mr. Gray 29; Hentzner, *Journey* 33; *Royal and Noble Authors* 37; *Fugitive Pieces* 41; Countess Temple, *Poems* 76; *Works* (1770) 94; *Letters of Edward VI* 101; *Miscellaneous Antiquities* 104; *Cabinet of Enamels* 111; *Curiosities in the Glass Closet* 112; *Dorinda* 114; *The Sleep-Walker* 116; *Letter from Thomas Walpole* 123; *Bishop Bonner's Ghost* 140; *Alcidalis and Zelida* 144.

GATHORNE-HARDY, R. E.:
Description of the Villa (1784) 126.

GLENBERVIE, Lord. *See* Sylvester Douglas.

GLYNN, Dr. ROBERT (1719–1800):
Royal and Noble Authors 37.

GOLDSMID, JOHN LOUIS (*library sold* 1815):
Alcidalis and Zelida 144.

GOODWIN, HOWARD T. (*library sold* 1903):
Royal and Noble Authors 37.

GOSDEN, THOMAS (1780–1843):
Letter on Chatterton 119.

GOSFORD, Earl of. *See* Acheson.

GOUDY, FREDERIC W.:
Description of the Villa (1784) 128.

GOUGH, RICHARD (1735–1809):
The Mysterious Mother 84.

GRANT, FRANK:
Dorinda 114.

GRAY, THOMAS (1716–1771):
Odes by Mr. Gray 25, 27, 30; *Fugitive Pieces* 41; Garrick's Verses 170.

GRENVILLE, GEORGE, Earl Temple (1753–1813):

LYSONS, SAMUEL (1763–1819):
Anecdotes 60, 67; *The Mysterious Mother* 79, 84.

MADAN, GEOFFREY:
Spence, *Parallel* 46; Lucan, *Pharsalia* 49; Countess Temple, *Poems* 76; Hoyland, *Poems* 87; *Miscellaneous Antiquities* 104; *Essay on Modern Gardening* 132.

MALONE, EDMOND (1741–1812):
Hentzner, *Journey* 33; Rules for showing SH 228.

MAUDE, JOHN, of Moor House:
Anecdotes 68.

MERRIAM, OLIN L. (*library sold* 1920):
Anecdotes 66, 67; *Works* (1770) 94; *Letter from Thomas Walpole* 123; *Postscript to Royal and Noble Authors* 137.

MERRITT, PERCIVAL; Merritt Collection at Harvard (*see also* Harvard College Library):
Fugitive Pieces 41; Lucan, *Pharsalia* 50; *Holbein Catalogue* 50; *Anecdotes* 67; *Life of Lord Herbert* 71; Countess Temple, *Poems* 76; *Cornélie* 77; *Works* (1770) 94; *Cabinet of Enamels* 111; *Curiosities in the Glass Closet* 112; Epitaph on King of Corsica 164; Garrick's Verses 170; Court of Exchequer 172; Questions to Society of Antiquaries 172, 175; Verses to Lady Spencer 186; 'There was a little man' 189; 'Tristes regrets' 191; Epitaph on Lord Waldegrave 191; Verses by Pentycross 198; Verses to Mme. du Châtelet 199; Verses to King of Sweden 204; Master of Otranto 208; Ticket to view SH 210; Verses to Lady Craven 217; Verses to Mrs. Crewe 220; Verses to Lady Waldegrave 223; Tonton 225; Rules for showing SH 228; To the Misses Berry 234; To the Duke of Clarence 234; Verses by Mrs. Holmes 237; Verses on Mrs. Clive 239; Verses by Mrs. Cloak 241; Verses by Miss Prior 241; *Cockey's New Year's Address* 244; *Epitaph on a Canary Bird* 246; *Printer's Farewell* 252; Theatre of George the Third 257; *Collectanea* 263; Arms

of White's Club 270; Rules for showing SH 275.

MILNES-GASKELL, C. G. *See* Gaskell.

MILNES, RICHARD MONCKTON, later Lord Houghton (1809–1885):
Collection of Detached Pieces 15, 189.

MONTAGU, GEORGE (1713?–1780):
Lucan, *Pharsalia* 50; *Anecdotes* 60; *Encaustic* 143; Bentley's Verses 160.

MONTFORT, Lord. *See* Bromley.

MORE, HANNAH (1745–1833):
Bishop Bonner's Ghost 139.

MORGAN, JUNIUS SPENCER; Morgan Collection at Princeton:
Odes by Mr. Gray 27, 30; Whitworth's *Russia* 44; Lucan, *Pharsalia* 50; *Holbein Catalogue* 50; *The Mysterious Mother* 84; *Reply to Dean Milles* 95; *Mémoires du comte de Grammont* 98; *Letter from Thomas Walpole* 123; *Description of the Villa* (1784) 127; *Essay on Modern Gardening* 132; *Hieroglyphic Tales* 134; *Postscript to Royal and Noble Authors* 137; Bentley's Verses 162; Garrick's Verses 170; Court of Exchequer 172; Verses to Lady Spencer 186; Magpie 194; Verses to Mrs. Crewe 220; Verses to Lady Waldegrave 223; To the Misses Berry 234; To the Duke of Clarence 234.

MORGAN LIBRARY:
Odes by Mr. Gray 27, 30; *Anecdotes* 66; *The Mysterious Mother* 84; *Dorinda* 114.

MORRIS, PERCY (*d.* 1927):
Works (1770) 95; *Dorinda* 112.

MOUNT-STEPHEN, GEORGINA MARY, Lady (1863?–1933):
Odes by Mr. Gray 30; *Fugitive Pieces* 41; Countess Temple, *Poems* 76; *Letters of Edward VI* 101; *Cabinet of Enamels* 111; *Dorinda* 114; *The Muse Recalled* 121.

MURDOCK, HAROLD (1862–1934):
Royal and Noble Authors 37.

MURRAY, Sir JOHN:
MS of Countess Temple's *Poems* 74.

MUSGRAVE, Sir WILLIAM (1735–1800):
Description of the Villa (1784) 127.

OWNERS OF COPIES

MYNDERSE, WILHELMUS (1849–1909):
Royal and Noble Authors 37.

NETTLETON, GEORGE HENRY:
Verses to Mrs. Crewe 220.
NEW YORK PUBLIC LIBRARY:
Description of the Villa (1774) 110;
Magpie 194; Verses to Lady Waldegrave
223.
NEWDIGATE FAMILY, of Arbury Hall:
Countess Temple, *Poems* 76; *Description of the Villa* (1784) 128; Garrick's
Verses 170.
NEWHAILES. *See* Dalrymple.
NIVERNOIS, LOUIS JULES BARBON MANCINI
MAZARINI, duc de (1716–1798):
Essay on Modern Gardening 132.
NOEL-HILL, WILLIAM, Baron Berwick
(1772?–1842):
The Mysterious Mother 84; *Alcidalis
and Zelida* 144.
NORTHAMPTON, Central Public Library:
The Muse Recalled 121.
NORTHUMBERLAND, Lady ELIZABETH SEY-
MOUR, Countess of (1716–1776):
Royal and Noble Authors 36.
NORTHUMBERLAND, Sir HENRY GEORGE
ALAN PERCY, Duke of:
Mme. de Boufflers and Mme. Dusson
181.
NUNEHAM PARK. *See* Harcourt.

ORFORD, HORATIO WILLIAM, Earl of (1813–
1894):
Lucan, *Pharsalia* 50; *Hieroglyphic Tales*
134.
ORMEROD, GEORGE (1785–1873):
Life of Lord Herbert 72.
OSSORY, Lady. *See* Liddell.
OSSORY, Lord. *See* Fitzpatrick.
OWEN FAMILY:
Royal and Noble Authors 37.

PARSONS, WILLIAM (*fl.* 1785–1807):
Essay on Modern Gardening 131.
PEMBROKE COLLEGE, Cambridge:
The Candidate 214.

PENN, GRANVILLE, of Stoke Park (1761–
1844):
Odes by Mr. Gray 30; *Fugitive Pieces*
41.
PENNANT, THOMAS (1726–1798):
Fugitive Pieces 39, 41.
PENTYCROSS, THOMAS (1749–1808):
Spence, *Parallel* 46.
PHILLIPPS, Sir THOMAS (1792–1872):
Mémoires du comte de Grammont 99.
PINKERTON, JOHN (1758–1826):
Description of the Villa (1784) 127;
Garrick's Verses 170; Verses to Lady
Spencer 186.
POOR, HENRY WILLIAM (1844–1915):
Cornélie 77; *The Mysterious Mother*
85.
PORTLAND, Lady MARGARET CAVENDISH
HARLEY, Duchess of (1715–1785):
Letter on Chatterton 119.
POTTS, ARTHUR (1814–1888):
Verses to Lady Townshend, Verses to
Lady Rochford, Garrick's Verses, Verses
to Lady Spencer, 'There was a little
man,' Magpie, Rules for showing SH,
and *Printer's Farewell* 154.
PRINCETON UNIVERSITY LIBRARY. *See* Mor-
gan, Junius Spencer.
PROBASCO, HENRY (1820–1902):
Description of the Villa (1784) 127.
PRUYN, Mrs. JOHN V. L.:
Fugitive Pieces 41.
PURDY, J. HARSEN (d. 1916):
Mémoires du comte de Grammont 98.

RAFTOR, CATHERINE. *See* Mrs. Clive.
REYNOLDS, Sir JOSHUA (1723–1792):
Anecdotes 68.
DE RICCI, SEYMOUR:
Cabinet of Enamels 111.
ROSENBACH, ABRAHAM S. W.:
Odes by Mr. Gray 27.
ROTHSCHILD, VICTOR, Lord Rothschild:
Odes by Mr. Gray 27, 29, 30; *Description of the Villa* (1784) 127; Garrick's
Verses 170; *The Candidate* 214.

SADA, CORNELIA KENNEDY:
Cornélie 77.

[289]

INDEX

This index is chiefly intended as an alphabetical list of the various pieces, which are dispersed through the book in chronological sequence. The alphabetical list of collectors immediately precedes this index. References are to the page, not to the number of the piece.